HOME GROUND

A Gardener's Miscellany

by Allen Lacy

Houghton Mifflin Company

BOSTON NEW YORK LONDON

Library of Congress Cataloging-in-Publication Data

Lacy, Allen, date.
Home ground : a gardener's miscellany / by Allen Lacy.
p.   cm.
Includes index.
ISBN 0-395-60730-2
1. Gardening.   I. Title.
SB455.3.L33   1992   91-34797
635.9 — dc20   CIP

Printed in the United States of America

BP   10   9   8   7   6   5   4   3   2   1

Acknowledgments are made to *The Green Scene,
Horticulture, The Philadelphia Inquirer,* and
The Wall Street Journal, where parts of this
book originally appeared.

HOME GROUND

For Hella, Paul, & Michael

Preface

This book is about some of the plants I have lived with and loved (and a few that I have disliked or that did not return my affection) over a lifetime of gardening that got underway in Irving, Texas, during World War II, after I bit a teacher on the leg and was sentenced to do penance for this gross misdeed by working in an iris patch. It is also about places where I have lived and gardened in the intervening years —the places that have been home ground for me. And it is about people. To garden is inescapably to be involved with other people, to be indebted. In this collection of essays I have tried to pay a few debts. I have a cast of characters, including my family and some friends and neighbors.

One word of warning, for those who may glance at this preface to decide whether to read the book it introduces. This is not, for the most part, a practical book on horticulture. I offer little advice, except in the most incidental way, about how deep to plant the daffodils, or when to prune the privet, or what measures to take when some dread malady threatens the aspidistra. If I offered such advice, it would be almost entirely secondhand—information gleaned from the standard assortment of gardening books on my library shelves, slightly tempered by my own experience, when the reference books disagree. An objective and impersonal approach to gardening is certainly desirable for people seeking only instruction. But gardening is also a highly subjective matter, and I have chosen to write about it quite personally, displaying many a preference and prejudice along the way.

Many of the essays that follow are new, never having been published elsewhere. Others are revised versions of pieces written for

Preface

various magazines and newspapers since 1979. To several fine editors I owe debts I would like to acknowledge. Ted Weidlein and Margie Weeks of *The Chronicle of Higher Education* and its short-lived offspring, *Books and Arts*, have my thanks for agreeing to let me review books on gardening, as well as those more particularly suited to their journals. After *Books and Arts* folded, Rebecca Sinkler of the *Philadelphia Inquirer* gave me the same dispensation. My debt to Roger Swain, the science editor of *Horticulture*, is enormous; it was he who pulled one of my first garden essays out of the slush pile, published it, and encouraged me to keep writing about gardening. I owe an equal debt to Manuela Hoelterhoff, the arts editor of *The Wall Street Journal*, for deciding that I should initiate a garden column for her pages, and to Raymond Sokolov, who succeeded her as my immediate editor, for the help he has given in his turn. I should also like to thank Jean Byrne, editor of *Green Scene*, and Judy Powell and Barbara Ellis of the American Horticultural Society, who have given me their consideration and help on several matters. My debt to my editor at Farrar, Straus and Giroux, Pat Strachan, is incalculable, and I will not attempt to reckon it here.

Finally, I must offer both thanks and apologies to my wife, Hella, who weeded while I wrote about weeding. In this household, I must now confess, she is the truest gardener of us all.

New Jersey
August 1983

Contents

Contents

II. PETS, PEEVES & CONFESSIONS

Contents

HOME GROUND

Roots of a Passion

I am at this moment sitting in my cramped and sublimely messy study on a rainy Sunday in mid-June, looking at one of the bleakest and most desolate sights I have ever seen, short of the barren plains of La Mancha in early January. My back is turned to the window and its view of the luxuriant June greens of my own and several neighboring gardens. In front of me is a photograph which I know on sight to have been taken by my Grandfather Surles in the 1920s, with the 180-degree panoramic camera he owned in that decade, when he was traveling through the West and Southwest on business for the U.S. government. This rather faded sepia photograph, four by eleven inches, just turned up by chance this morning when I was rummaging for something else in a steamer trunk of tribal memorabilia, the artifacts of five generations on both sides of my family.

The identification on the back of the photograph, written in my mother's hand, reads *Baird, Texas—Mother's birthplace,* so what it pictures is indisputably an ancestral home dating back at least to 1890, when my grandmother Mollie Adeline McAdoo Surles was born in Baird. At that time Baird was a small but growing town on the Texas and Pacific railroad line in West Texas, a little east of Abilene. Its citizens treasured the misbegotten belief that it would in time eclipse Dallas in population, and they were proud that it was the county seat of Callahan County. (The 1975 population of Baird stood at 1,552 souls, with only 9,238 in the whole county.)

As an ancestral home, the house where my Grandmother

Surles was born is hardly Blenheim or Chatsworth. The photograph shows a simple frame structure only one story tall, with five rooms at most. Brick chimneys mark two stoves or fireplaces, probably in the kitchen and in a seldom-used front parlor reserved for visiting Baptist preachers and funerals. A horsehair sofa is probable in that parlor, a reed organ possible. The house has a porch out front and another in the back. It is in decent repair but unpainted.

I've never been to Baird, except for passing through on a Pullman car when I was three years old and my mother and I were en route to visit an aunt in Lordsburg, New Mexico, in the aftermath of a nasty squabble between my parents. Although my mother and her sisters as well as my grandmother were born in Baird, and although I'm told that near the courthouse there's still an office bearing the name of the Russell-Surles Title Company my grandfather co-founded, I've never felt inclined to visit it on a sentimental pilgrimage, for reasons the photograph makes obvious. Taken in the harsh glare of midwinter West Texas sunlight, it shows a barren and inhospitable landscape. The wide dirt road curving in front of my grandmother's birthplace merges imperceptibly with the front yard, which comes nowhere close to being a lawn. Perhaps today the citizens of Baird have sprinkling systems and green grass and dense shrubbery, but the evidence of that photograph shows that for its first thirty-odd years at least, the house where my grandmother was born sat forlornly on empty land, with not a single shrub in sight. Behind the house, near a chicken coop and a privy, several gaunt and tortured mesquite trees provide the only vegetation except for a few scattered patches of tall grass.

Almost a century after that house was built and my grandmother was born, from half a continent away, my back turned to the lush and verdant northeastern gardens beyond the windowpane, I think not about my Grandmother Surles but about my Great-grandmother McAdoo, for whom I say a belated prayer: I hope that she did not possess a passion for gardening, for if she did, Baird was barren ground for her indeed.

I know very little about Mrs. McAdoo, only a few facts, probably mixed with rumors, that one of my aunts jotted down some years ago when she was in a genealogical frame of mind. Her father was named James Bar Armstrong. He is believed to have owned a large plantation somewhere east of Texas. When she was born in 1859, her parents christened her Dama Adeline. When she was nine, her family moved to Somervell County or what in 1875 became Somervell County—pleasant, green, hilly country where the Paluxy River flows into the Brazos, where the rainfall is sufficient annually to support farm crops and many wildflowers, and where the limestone outcroppings along the two rivers have fossilized dinosaur tracks large enough for a man to sit in. Two of Dama Adeline Armstrong's brothers fought in the Civil War, one of them dying in battle. I don't know when she married Joseph McAdoo, a tall and slender man whose teetotaling extended even unto root beer and who thought radio was a tool of the devil. And I don't know when she moved from the pleasant landscape of Somervell County to the bleakness of Baird. I do know that she had seven children—that house in Baird must have been a very crowded place when they were growing up. Perhaps Dama McAdoo had no time for a garden, even if she had wanted one and the earth she lived on had been more hospitable.

But I suspect she did want one and that she did what she could with what she had, as all gardeners must. The evidence, again, is in that photograph, where a second, closer look reveals something beyond barrenness and bleakness. Someone has taken hundreds of small stones, about the size of tennis balls, and used them to outline pathways leading from the road to the front porch, from the front porch along one side of the house to the back porch, and from the back porch to the privy. The pathways are made of dirt, as is the yard, but within the boundaries of the stones, which are set at regular intervals and carefully placed, the pathway has been swept clean of sticks, mesquite twigs and leaves, and other rubble. Someone here—and who if not Dama McAdoo?—has been overwhelmed by the urge to tidy up the natural world, to give it an order it does not itself possess, and to stamp a human signature on it. It is this urge—capable of expression in Baird as well as at Versailles—that separates people who garden from those who don't.

I am enough of a Freudian to understand that if I make the effort to unravel the ultimate sources of the passions and the antipathies of my life, I shall probably get everything wrong. So it must be with my love of gardening. But it seems to me that I know the time, the place, and the person who influenced me toward an abiding interest in plants, rather than in jogging and other perversions. The time was 1943. The place was Irving, Texas, and the person was named Mrs. Harkey.

My father was raised in a city, so like many city boys he was infected by the desire to live on a farm, tending cows and chickens, mending barbed-wire fences, and slopping hogs. My mother was raised in the aforementioned Baird, Texas. The houses all had chicken coops out back, and there was precious little going on after the sun went down at night, and not much more before that. She was happy that her parents moved to Dallas when she was in high school. She liked having department stores and picture shows close at hand. And she would have preferred to stay in Dallas, with no rustic interludes, the rest of her days.

Pearl Harbor, however, gave my father just the excuse he was looking for to overcome her objections and move to the country. He started talking about "the land" and "one's own piece of earth," as if he were Scarlett O'Hara fleeing Atlanta for the red dirt of Tara. Despite the fact that the Trinity River wasn't at all navigable, he worried aloud about the Germans sailing right up it and invading the Dallas suburb of University Park, where Mother was quite content to remain. So in the fall of 1942 we moved to the farm he bought—eleven acres of sticker-burr-infested sandy loam on Kit Loan Star Road Continuation, a dusty gravel lane four miles west of Irving, a sleepy village halfway between Dallas and Fort Worth. Today our farm has been gobbled up by what the citizens of Dallas and Tarrant Counties call their "Metroplex." But in 1943 it was country—and my mother despised it. She hated the copperheads and the black widow spiders. She loathed the well that frequently went dry and pumped up gray mud into the sink or the bathtub without warning. She had no love for the chickens, and she wasn't particularly sorry when our cow died. She especially disliked the truck farmer next door, who kept a flock of noisy guinea hens and occasionally hitched up his wife and her sister to a plow.

I had my problems, too. I had left a good elementary school in Dallas for a quite primitive one in Irving, where reading and writing were taught to the proverbial tune of the hickory stick. I was sent to the principal's office at least once a week by Mrs. Leghorn, my third-grade teacher. My love affair with horticulture began in the early spring of 1943, on the day I bit Mrs. Leghorn on the ankle.

To this day I am convinced that the deed was condign, that Mrs. Leghorn deserved what she got. In punishment for some peccadillo of mine that apparently wasn't serious enough to merit the principal's rod, she ordered me under her desk, and continued quizzing the rest of the class about our spelling lesson. An hour later I was still there, as she drilled my classmates on their multiplication tables. The afternoon was hot, the air under her desk close and stuffy, I had to go to the bathroom, and I finally mumbled a protest against my continued confinement. She kicked me in answer—a sharp tap from the toe to my chin. I seized my chance and her leg and bit her as hard as I could.

There was an awful ruckus. I was locked up in a back room. My parents were called. Some hours later I was brought before the principal, my mother and father, and Mrs. Harkey, who taught the fourth grade. A punishment had been worked out: every Saturday for the remainder of the term I would be placed in Mrs. Harkey's custody, paying for my grave misdeed by hard labor in her greenhouse and iris fields. In exchange, she would tutor me two afternoons a week in the subjects I would miss out on in class, since I was expelled for the remainder of the year, freeing me and Mrs. Leghorn from the burden of each other's company.

Never has crime had so sweet a reward. Mrs. Harkey was a beautiful lady in every way worth mentioning. I thought she was very old, but she must have been only in her early fifties. She taught me things I never would have learned from Mrs. Leghorn, introducing me to the Oz books and to Mark Twain. She lent me the wonderful collections of Texas lore by J. Frank Dobie. She eased my problems with multiplication involving nines by tipping me off that the digits in any multiple of nine always eventually added up to nine. And I lived for those required Saturdays at her nursery, so much so that I volunteered every weekday afternoon as well. She simply assumed that I had a love for plants, and I believe that it was this assumption, this faith, that brought such love into being. I believe that she may have been lonely and that teaching me about the care of plants gave her something she needed. She was a widow, and her only son was fighting in the Pacific. In any case, she showed me how to divide a clump of iris and set the divided plants out in neatly labeled rows in the field. She instructed me about the mysteries of repotting orchid plants and taught me which plants loved shade and which sun. She initiated me into the wonders of the art and science of hybridization, showing me how to take the anther of an iris or a daylily, apply it to the stigma of another, tie a tag to the blossom with a number referring to the stud book where the cross and the date were recorded, and then await the swelling of the seed pod that meant the cross had taken. She showed me what to look for in the seedling patch when the crosses made two or three years ago first bloomed—which seedlings to discard and why, which ones had sufficient merit to keep for further observation.

She told me about Gregor Mendel and the things he had learned about genetics by paying close attention to garden peas and by experiment. From her I first heard the name of Luther Burbank, one of her heroes—"especially," she said, "for breeding the Shasta daisy." She let me in on some of her deepest dreams, of one day breeding a pink iris that would be really pink or a red daylily genuinely worth the name. "There's nothing a person can do," she said, "which is nicer than breeding a pretty flower, bringing into being something lovely that never existed before. I believe that it amounts to giving God a helping hand in His work of creation." In time, my father's hankering for country life subsided, we moved back to the city, and with the typical ingratitude of the young for the gifts that they are given unasked, I forgot about Mrs. Harkey almost entirely—but not about gardening. I don't know if she ever achieved her dream of a pink iris, or a red daylily worth the name. I never went back to see her, and I'm sorry for that. Once, I tried my hand at a little hybridizing myself, the result being a homely bunch of daylilies out back that I can't bear to throw away, even if they hardly represent much help at all to God in His work of creation. I wish there were something utterly lovely among them. I would like to pay my debts and name it Mrs. Harkey.

I. GARDENS,
WILD & TAME

American Narcissism I

In 1981, Americans imported more than 34 million daffodil bulbs from Holland. My son Paul, an engineer, tells me that that's enough to girdle the earth with bulbs spaced four feet apart along the equator. The idea of circling the earth with daffodils appeals to me. I confess I am obsessed with these bright spring flowers.

It all began harmlessly enough over a decade ago, when my family and I exchanged monthly rental payments for monthly mortgage payments. The old house we bought was surrounded by a large yard that couldn't really be called a garden. We moved in in July. I sent for a catalog from a mail-order firm specializing in Dutch bulbs. When it arrived, I made a list of everything I wanted: crocuses, grape hyacinths, tulips, and lots of daffodils. I knew that King Alfred, which has been around for more than eighty years, had been superseded, but I included a dozen anyway, in deference to memories of my mother's Texas garden, where hundreds of them gleamed a rich golden yellow every March. But most of the daffodils I wanted were those touted by the catalog as "new and modern": Carlton, Cheerfulness, Dutch Master, Golden Harvest, and especially Unsurpassable, whose mere name promised it to be the daffodil equivalent of a Rolls-Royce Silver Cloud.

My list came to $985.67, plus shipping. I pruned it drastically, ordering 100 daffodils instead of 750. Next spring when they bloomed it was appallingly clear that I'd been too stingy with daffodils, so that fall I ordered 200 more and another 200 the fall after that. Thus, one April morning when our postman,

Serge, came up the walk and handed me a catalog from Oregon, I was feeling pretty smug about the 500 daffodils blooming in my front garden.

"Nice flowers," Serge said.

I nodded agreement, but privately I thought that Serge was being a bit grudging with his praise. Nice flowers? To my eye, they were easily the finest daffodils in town. Finally, there were almost enough of them. We could cut as many as we needed for house and for friends without making an appreciable dent in the garden display. I suspected that I was probably growing about half the named daffodils in existence: Beersheba and Binkie, Dick Wellband and Duke of Windsor, Flower Record and Fortune, on and on through a litany of daffodil names.

I was proud of my daffodils. I considered myself to be not just an aficionado but an expert. I knew they came from Holland, along with tulips, Gouda cheese, and strong, undrinkable green gin. English poets from Shakespeare to Wordsworth to Masefield have extolled them. Daffodils may not be "forever," but they're much more dependable than tulips, which tend to steal away home to Jesus after the first season. A daffodil bulb will increase year after year until eventually there's a thick clump that must be divided to ensure continued bloom.

I also knew that I had been mistaken in my childhood, when, like everyone else in my tribe, I had called daffodils "jonquils." Jonquils are one section of the genus *Narcissus*, so that all jonquils are narcissuses, but not the other way round. Daffodil is the common English name, perfectly interchangeable with narcissus, which is both a common name and the botanical name for the genus. (Calling daffodils "jonquils"—and sometimes even "buttercups"—is a Southern eccentricity.)

I understood enough about the culture of daffodils to meet their uncomplicated requirements. In my sandy soil I planted the bulbs fairly deep, about eight inches. In the spring I gave them a light dressing of Milorganite, and after they finished blooming I refrained from cutting back the foliage or braiding it; unsightly, sprawling daffodil leaves in May and June are the price paid for next year's bloom.

However, there was that troubling conversation on an airplane, which led to the appearance of a catalog from Oregon. I was seated next to an Anglican priest who matched me martini for martini from Philadelphia to Dallas/Fort Worth. We had in common, it turned out, something besides faith in the power of gin to lessen the terrors of flying: we were both gardeners. The conversation turned eventually to daffodils. My companion asked me what cultivars I raised. He grew quiet as I listed them— February Gold, Mary Copeland, and, of course, Unsurpassable. He mentioned mildly that he was a member of the American Daffodil Society (an organization I'd never heard of) and changed the topic to his considered opinion that no movie star would ever become President, certainly not Ronald Reagan. But as the plane landed, he scribbled an address on a scrap of paper and handed it to me.

"You should try some American daffodils," he said. "Write Grant Mitsch's Daffodil Haven, in Oregon, for their catalog."

American daffodils? The notion sounded as improbable as Turkish jazz or German pizza. But I sent for the catalog anyway. When it came, I glanced at the picture on the cover, a handsome clump of something called Impresario, and flipped through glossy pages filled with color photographs of daffodils with totally unfamiliar names like Dickcissel, Oryx, and Cotinga.

I went into my front garden to brood a bit. The daffodils there hadn't changed. Nice flowers, as Serge had said. But something had happened to me, an alteration of my perception. I had experienced what Paul Tillich called "the shaking of the foundations." It's only human to resist as long as possible any piece of information that doesn't fit comfortably within the system of things we think we know. It really isn't at all surprising that Galileo got into trouble for suggesting that Joshua, Ptolemy, and Aquinas had their celestial mechanics dead wrong. Learning to enjoy being corrected is an acquired taste. My daffodils still looked "nice," but only that. And if the photographs in the Mitsch catalog were even halfway accurate, whoever named Unsurpassable had badly jumped the gun.

I was smitten by Grant Mitsch's daffodils.

I finished brooding and went inside, turning to the catalog description of Impresario, a flower completely unlike anything I had ever grown or seen. The description read:

IMPRESARIO (Mitsch) 1975 EM 2d 16" (W12/1[P5/8 x Lunar Sea] x Salem) F88/2. The quite narrow crown makes this appear to be a trumpet, but measurement indicates otherwise. Perianth opens pale yellow and deepens in color as it ages, reflexing somewhat in maturing. The crown opens lemon, fading out to nearly white, with a little gold rim. One of the best reverses we have raised. $50 each.

The detailed language of the description was a bit baffling: most bulb catalogs say "golden yellow" or "soft, creamy ivory," and leave it at that. But after consulting the key to the symbols in the Mitsch catalog, I was able to decipher it. Impresario, hybridized by Grant Mitsch from the numbered seedlings and named cultivars in parentheses, was a 1975 introduction, blooming in early mid-season and standing 16 inches high. Its crown or cup is not quite long enough for it to be classified as a trumpet daffodil (Division 1 in the classification scheme of the Royal Horticultural Society), so officially it belongs to Division 2—"Large-Cupped Narcissus of Garden Origin," the last three words meaning that it's not a species daffodil or a naturally occurring hybrid collected in the wild.

My immediate inclination was to order 100 bulbs of Impresario. My wife had been saying that we had enough daffodils out front and that we needed some in the back yard, where we could see them from the kitchen windows. But although $5,000 worth of Impresario would no doubt be a fine and splendid sight on an April afternoon, I knew it was not to be, or even $50 worth. Our old station wagon was afflicted with terminal rust, college tuition payments loomed ahead, and a decent respect for the neighbors suggested a new coat of paint for the house.

I put the Mitsch catalog in the drawer next to my side of the bed, for late-night reading. I mulled over the probable merits of Butterflower, Eclat, and Silken Sails. I discovered Lyrebird, at $100 a bulb. I read about crowns that were crinkled and fluted, ruffled and frilled, shaped like bells or saucers or bowls; about such improbable colors for daffodils as brilliant plum-rose, deep salmon-pink suffused with lavender, and soft beige-yellow. The lavish language of the catalog suggested that Mr. Mitsch loved colorful English as well as colorful flowers. He was also extremely precise in describing the transformations the blossoms undergo from their first opening. Thus the perianth of Aircastle "opens milk white but in a few days turns to greenish beige," and Rima has a trumpet "opening creamy yellow but soon developing to a rich salmon pink with a hint of lilac in its composition." (All these metamorphoses were news to me; I'd always thought that daffodils just opened, bloomed, and then wilted, nothing more complicated than that.)

Undeniably Grant Mitsch had a way with words, but did he have daffodils to match? I couldn't work myself into a skeptical frame of mind. I'd heard about the Mitsch catalog from a priest. Mitsch described the shortcomings of some of his bulbs with reassuring candor: the deep orange-red cups of Ardour "will burn if left in the sun." El Capitan is an "inconsistent performer," Daydream "difficult to grow in many areas." Before long I had the catalog nearly memorized. I could shut my eyes and populate the whole back yard with Mitsch daffodils in my imagination. Finally, I broached the subject with my wife.

"I've got this daffodil catalog from Oregon," I said, hoping my tone of voice didn't betray mania, obsession, or grave infatuation. "Did you know that a daffodil called Lyrebird costs $100 for just one bulb? What kind of damned fool would pay that sort of money for one bulb?"

"Be careful now," she said. It was clear that she suspected that I might be precisely the sort of damned fool I referred to.

"What do you mean, 'Be careful'?" I asked.

She had me cold. I once bought the same shirt in eight different colors, and I had just shaken a mania for daylilies. The perennial border out front was mostly a daylily border, and I had imposed a moratorium on buying new ones, vowing not even to look at a daylily catalog, with the same troubled intensity with which St. Anthony had renounced the temptations of the flesh. The love affair with daylilies ended—or its fires at least banked—I was in danger of embarking on another. I had no intention of buying Lyrebird, but by dwelling on its outrageous price I was perfectly capable of convincing myself that at only $50 Impresario was an outright steal.

I decided to be sensible. I carefully went through the Mitsch catalog, making a list of every cultivar selling at $1.25 or less, twenty-four in all. I then cut the list down to ten and ordered a single bulb each of eight cultivars and three each of two reasonably priced cultivars for which the catalog had especially kind words: Accent (a white with a large pink cup) and Festivity (a "magnificent giant flower with very wide spread, broad, flat, smooth perianth of beautiful texture and finish, and a rather long but well-balanced clear yellow crown . . . one of the best flowers we have raised"). I also ordered two dozen bulbs of a seedling mixture—Mitsch hybrids not distinctive enough in his judgment to be named but still a good value in the garden. The thirty-eight bulbs came to $28, or less than 80 cents per bulb.

When the bulbs arrived in September, I was pleased at how beautiful and firm and fat they were and elated to discover the free bulb of Jetfire ($7.50 in the catalog). I prepared a bed by spading it eighteen inches deep and forking in a generous measure of dried cow manure. I set the bulbs at least a foot apart, somewhat irregularly, to avoid the parade-ground effect of straight rows. I underplanted the bed with vinca as a ground cover, and I made a careful map so that next spring I would know which was Jetfire and which Accent.

The daffodil season got underway with February Gold, in March (notwithstanding its name), a perky little yellow trumpet daffodil announcing that spring was about to happen. Soon my front yard was aglow with my older daffodils—the "nice flowers." The Mitsch cultivars, planted in a slightly shadier location, were slower to appear, so that it was early April before I could look at all my daffodils with a sharp, comparative eye. As each new blossom appeared out back, it became clearer and clearer that Grant Mitsch really did have the flowers to match his words. The substance of the blossoms was excellent, and the stems were strong enough to resist wind and rain. The pink-cupped ones really were pink. (With every other "pink daffodil" I had seen, it seemed to me that the pink was mostly in the eye of the beholder—or in the ink of the catalog.) Even the unnamed seedlings were greatly superior to any daffodil I had ever grown.

Mitsch had me. Another order went off to Oregon that summer and another the following summer. When people admire the daffodils out front, I invite them into the back garden, where I now grow more than thirty named Mitsch hybrids, a couple of hundred of his seedlings, and some other daffodils, both species sorts and hybrids by breeders in Great Britain and Tasmania which I bought from the Daffodil Mart in Gloucester, Virginia. The verdict of garden visitors is unanimous: "I never dreamed that there were daffodils like these. Where can I get some?"

The question reveals a problem. The Mitsch farm—now run

by Grant's son-in-law and daughter, R. D. and Elise Havens—is small, under five acres. Although a few Mitsch cultivars are also offered by the Daffodil Mart, these bulbs are simply not available in large enough numbers to meet the potential demand from home gardeners, if they knew more about them. If a hundred thousand people in this country should suddenly decide to grow dozens of Mitsch daffodils, the bulbs would clearly have to come from Holland. But the Dutch aren't growing Accent and Festivity; they're growing Carlton and Unsurpassable and good old King Alfred. Until they mend their ways, most American gardeners will continue to miss out on some of the most splendid flowers that April can bring.

American Narcissism II

Let me continue my tale of the Grant Mitsch daffodils. I confess that for a couple of Aprils I felt great pride of possession, taking a lot of satisfaction in the thought that I had daffodils like nobody else in town and maybe in the county, pitying the poor wretches up and down the street who had to get by with King Alfred while I had Festivity and Jetfire and lust in my heart for Impresario. But then the thought occurred to me that a yardful of daffodils in bloom gives pleasure to passersby as well as to the person who tends them. If my neighbors all grew Mitsch daffodils, I could see them everywhere. I wanted to know if Dutch growers planned to do anything about Grant Mitsch's superior cultivars. And I wanted to talk daffodils with someone, to escape the solitude of my own back yard for the fellowship of a like-minded soul. So I did two things. I wrote a very pushy letter to the Netherlands Flower Bulb Institute in New York, asking a lot of pointed questions. Had they ever grown, were they growing now, or did they intend to grow and market the Mitsch creations? If not, why not? Were they aware that by analogy they were like people who continued to tout wind-up Victrolas when digital sound systems were on the horizon? I also called Brent Heath, the owner of the Daffodil Mart in Gloucester, asking if I might pay him a visit.

Mr. Heath agreed, and so a few weeks later I was in the Tidewater area of Virginia, heading south on route 17 on a day in early July. There was little traffic, and the road dipped and rolled with the contours of the land, plunging into cool glens smelling of honeysuckle and then rising to sunny and torrid hilltops planted in corn or soybeans.

I arrived at the Daffodil Mart at noon and met Brent Heath at his packing shed. He introduced me to his wife, Becky, and then the three of us drove to the riverfront cabin they were living in temporarily while building a solar house several hundred yards away. Brent said we could have either crabs or trout for lunch, my preference. Crabs sounded just fine. The two of us climbed into a canoe, paddled offshore, and quickly hauled up more than enough for lunch. Then we picked sweet corn from a patch right next to the daffodil fields, which were entirely covered with immense tomato vines, perhaps a million of them growing in a tight tangle.

Indicating the lush stand of tomatoes, Brent Heath explained, "I covered the fields with treated sludge from the Gloucester sewage plant this spring. People down here eat a lot of tomatoes, but it seems that they don't digest the seeds especially well."

While the crabs steamed and the corn boiled in the kitchen, Brent told me about his family. I knew I was home again, back in the South, where even in the last quarter of the twentieth century friendships begin with conversations about one's people, kin who lived and died decades ago.

Brent's grandfather, Charles Heath, the dilettante son of a prominent family in Brookline, Massachusetts, lived in New York around the turn of the century. One morning Charles ate a cantaloupe so sweet and delicious that he asked his grocer to trace its origins so he could order a case a week during the season from the grower. The grower turned out to be Thomas Dixon, a wealthy gentleman farmer from Gloucester County and the author of a popular novel, *The Clansman*, on which D. W. Griffith based his controversial *Birth of a Nation*. When he heard of Heath's fondness for his melons, Dixon invited him down for a visit. Heath liked the area so much that he immediately bought 600 acres and an antebellum mansion.

Steaming platters of crab and buttered sweet corn arrived from the kitchen. Suspecting correctly that I was a novice at eating crabs right from the shell, Becky Heath provided instructions. The crabs were delicious, but getting at the meat was something like removing the grille of a 1952 Buick. The saga of the Heath family meanwhile continued, finally getting around to narcissus.

When Charles Heath moved to Gloucester County, there was a primitive local trade in the daffodils that had naturalized along the edges of woodlands—mostly *Narcissus obvallaris*, the Tenby daffodil brought to America by English colonists. Every spring, farmers picked the blossoms and took them for shipment by steamboat up the Chesapeake to Baltimore—the first cash crop of the year. Suspecting that there might be a profit in growing modern cultivars for the florist trade in the Northeast, Heath began importing bulbs from Holland and Great Britain, and encouraged many of his neighbors to join him in making Gloucester and adjacent Mathews County major producers of daffodils. It was a fortunate hunch on Heath's part. Business thrived, and the daffodil fields began to spread.

In the early 1920s, proud that the bulbs he grew seemed to be higher in quality than those he had imported from Holland, Heath wrote some Dutch growers to brag a bit. A little later, when it seemed that a United States quarantine would prohibit the importation of Dutch bulbs because of daffodil fly and eelworm infestation, the Dutch firm of M. van Waveren & Sons remembered Heath's claims and moved most of its operations to Gloucester County. But the Dutch managers and their American field workers didn't get along, so van Waveren hired Charles Heath's son George to run the farm. When the quarantine was lifted in 1939, George Heath bought van Waveren's land and stock, and founded the Daffodil Mart. It was a large operation, both in acreage and in the great numbers of cultivars grown. Because European bulbs were unavailable during World War II, Heath's business flourished—as did the commercial raising of daffodils for cut flowers in the area. Every spring, tourists flocked to the Tidewater Peninsula to see hundreds of acres of daffodils in bloom and to visit the Heaths' large display garden.

But in the middle 1960s the bottom dropped out of the Virginia daffodil business. It was an affluent time, and people who might have bought daffodils bought roses instead. West Coast bulb cooperatives offered serious competition for the Northeastern market—their blossoms lasted longer because of cooler growing conditions, and it was less expensive to airfreight daffodils from Washington State to New York and Boston than to truck them up from Virginia. Virginia growers resorted to refrigeration to keep the flowers in bud, an unfortunate practice, because when retail buyers brought them home they lasted only a day. Virginia daffodils became anathema to florists, and Tidewater bulb farmers plowed under almost a thousand acres of daffodils to plant soybeans.

Concluding the story of his family's eighty-year association with the daffodil, Brent Heath mentioned that in recent years he's cut back on his own operations. He grows only what he can harvest, store, clean, and ship with the assistance of his wife, his mother, a few teenagers during the busy season, and some very sophisticated digging and sorting equipment capable of being run by one person. For the naturalizing mixtures that make up the bulk of his business, he contracts with local farmers to raise bulbs and buys the rest from growers in western Washington and in Holland. He no longer has a display garden open to the public—and the tourists have stopped coming. On his own land he specializes in novelties—the best new hybrids from England, Ireland, New Zealand, and Tasmania.

The crab shells dumped on the compost heap, Brent and I nursed our beers on the grassy riverbank. "What do you think of Grant Mitsch?" I asked.

"There are some other daffodil hybridizers," he replied, "some in this country, like Murray Evans and Tom Throckmorton, some in Britain and Ireland, some in Australia and New Zealand. But I think I'd have to say that Grant Mitsch is the dean of American hybridizers. He's given us the American daffodil and it's a damned beautiful thing."

In the barn that serves as his office, he rummaged around on a shelf, found a small vial of daffodil seeds, and gave it to me. "I'm doing some hybridizing myself," he said, "but here, try your luck. Four years from now you might even have something worth looking at." Then he wrote an address on a scrap of paper. "If you want to know more about daffodils, you should join the American Daffodil Society. They publish a great deal of literature."

Two weeks later I was a member of the society and was confronted with a thick stack of printed matter: *The Daffodil Handbook*, published in 1966 by the American Horticultural Society in cooperation with the A.D.S.; several *Daffodil Yearbooks* from the Royal Horticultural Society; *Daffodils to Show and Grow*, a computerized printout of names, hybridizers, and characteristics of more than eleven thousand cultivars kept under electronic surveillance by the Daffodil Data Bank in Des Moines; and a great many back issues of *The Daffodil Journal*, the official publication the A.D.S. sends out regularly to its 1,600 members.

I was soon awash with daffodil information, much of it surprising and difficult to assimilate. Although my mind naturally turns to Holland when I think of daffodils, it might just as well turn to Great Britain, and not just because of William Wordsworth. The British raise far more daffodils than the Dutch; in 1965, the last year for which comparable figures are available, 4,159 acres in England were planted in daffodils for the cut-flower trade, 3,226 acres for the bulb trade. The same year, the Dutch had a combined total of 3,268 acres.

Furthermore, it is doubtful that daffodils would be so popular a garden flower and so important to the Dutch economy were it not for the passionate labors of several generations of amateur English and Irish hybridizers—many of them clergymen, and some of them eccentric—to develop superior cultivars. In the early nineteenth century they collected several species from the wild and began to cross them and intercross their progeny.

Although one daffodil, *N. pseudonarcissus* (the trumpet daffodil or Lent lily), grows naturally in the British Isles, most species (at least twenty-five of them, many with several subspecies) are natives of the lands surrounding the Mediterranean. Considerable variation of color, form, and habit is found among members of the genus. *N. asturiensis*, a yellow trumpet sometimes listed in catalogs as *N. minimus*, is extremely diminutive, growing only three to five inches tall. *N. serotinus*, *N. elegans*, and *N. viridiflorus* (which has green flowers) all bloom in the fall. Besides *N. pseudonarcissus*, the species most significant in the pedigree of modern garden daffodils are *N. cyclamineus*, a graceful, small plant so named because its sharply swept-back petals and sepals give it something of the look of a cyclamen; the intensely fragrant *N. jonquilla* and its various subspecies; *N. poeticus* (the poet's daffodil), a flower noteworthy for its mythological associations (apparently it was Narcissus's narcissus) and for its red-rimmed white cup, which may be the progenitor of today's pink- and red-cupped cultivars; and *N. triandrus* (angel's tears), which bears several nodding flowers, usually creamy white, to a stem.

The first serious British hybridizers to work with daffodils were Dean Herbert, Edward Leeds, and William Backhouse, but the crucial figure in the emergence of modern daffodils was Peter Barr, a professional plantsman. In 1874 he purchased a large collection of seedlings hybridized by Edward Leeds, who was in failing health. Barr kept half the seedlings for his own firm, selling the rest to British breeders and to a Dutch syndicate. Ten years later he persuaded the Royal Horticultural Society to convene an international conference on daffodils, which adopted the practice of giving hybrids simple vernacular names, rather than Latin ones—for example, Emperor instead of Barrii Conspicuus.

The Daffodil Handbook points out that after this conference Dutch and British growers began to move in quite different directions. The English and their followers in the English-speaking world concentrated on breeding flowers for exhibition and sought innovations in color and form. The Dutch turned to large-scale cultivation of a small number of cultivars known to be reliable and consistent performers in the cut-flower trade as well as in the home garden. Although some Dutch firms have bred their own daffodils, including Flower Record, Golden Harvest, and Unsurpassable, their fields have continued to be dominated by such British cultivars as John Kendall's King Alfred (first registered in 1899 and extremely popular through much of this century, though it now makes up only 1 percent of the daffodil fields in Holland), Guy L. Wilson's Broughshane, and Percival D. Williams's Carlton. (In 1975, 1,397 acres of the more than 3,600 acres devoted to daffodils in Holland were planted with Carlton, which was registered in 1927.)

Pondering the confusing material accumulating in my study, I began to see that the daffodil world was highly fragmented, actually several different worlds with limited communication among them. The devoted hobbyist who raises daffodils for exhibition is not the same as the gardener who just likes to have them around in the yard. A wide gulf separates the person who belongs to the American Daffodil Society and buys bulbs from specialty nurseries from the person who relies on large mail-order firms dealing in imported bulbs. This gulf cannot be narrowed unless the Dutch change their ways. Perhaps Grant Mitsch's daffodils, despite their American origins, will never be common in American gardens. Perhaps the Dutch simply aren't interested.

In due time, a letter arrived, forwarded to me from the Flower Bulb Information Center in Lisse, Holland, by the Netherlands Flower Bulb Information Center in New York, to which I had sent my pushy letter. The English was occasionally a little perplexing, but the letter explained that "up till now a new variety takes 20 to 25 years to grow from seedling to a commercially interesting quantity." There are, however, recently developed methods of rapid propagation that may reduce this time to five or seven years, by a process called twin scaling. American daffodils are not yet a significant part of propagation efforts in Holland, but expectations are high for several Mitsch cultivars: Accent, Dickcissel, Daydream, Jetfire, and Petrel.

The letter's mention of rapid propagation sent me back to some recent issues of *The Daffodil Journal* to read more carefully some articles on propagation I had barely scanned. Some dealt with twin scaling—dissecting a bulb into several fragments and then treating each chemically to encourage it to form bulblets. But much more exciting was a 1976 article by Professors Janet E. A. Seabrook and Bruce G. Cumming, two biologists at the University of New Brunswick in Canada, describing their success in adapting tissue-culture techniques of propagation (which already have proved useful with sugarcane, gladioli, orchids, and other commercially important plants) to daffodils. Twin scaling produces, at best, fifty bulbs in two years. In tissue culture, sterile daffodil tissue is dissected into extremely small pieces and cultured in jars of agar enriched with nutrients, hormones, minerals, sugars, and trace elements until small buds appear on the fragments. It is effective in turning one daffodil into a great many, because the material can be dissected repeatedly and recultured before the resulting plantlets need be placed in a different nutrient medium in which they can form roots and move out of the laboratory. Professors Seabrook and Cumming reported that in less than a year they can probably obtain twenty-five thousand plantlets from a single bulb. In their own words, "This is a tremendous increase over our present propagation methods."

Tissue culture of daffodils is an exciting prospect, something that might well bring together the fragmented daffodil world, as it has not been since that conference of 1884. It can shorten the time between the appearance of something rare and lovely in a hybridizer's seedling patch and its presence in the garden of a mild narcissomaniac like me. It can do away with the $100 daffodil.

After reading the article on tissue culture, I called Professor Seabrook. No answer. I called Professor Cumming to congratulate him on the greatest promise for daffodils since Peter Barr bought those seedlings from the ailing Edward Leeds. "You must spend half your time in Holland these days, consulting with the bulb growers," I said.

There was a somewhat sad sigh from the other end of the wire in Nova Scotia. "It's been several years since our research was published, not only in *The Daffodil Journal*, but in several scientific periodicals as well," he said. "I haven't had the slightest expression of interest from a single commercial grower. Say, do you perhaps know of anyone who deals with daffodils who might have some interest in this work?"

I gave him Brent Heath's address and I hope they managed to get together.

Minor Bulbs

No poet that I know of has ever bothered to sing the praises of winter aconites or of *Scilla siberica*, and history discloses no mad financial speculation in glory-of-the-snow, no great fortunes swiftly made in acquiring a handful of grape-hyacinth bulbs. Among spring flowers, the poetry belongs to the daffodil, which Sophocles, Shakespeare, Herrick, Wordsworth, and Amy Lowell have all celebrated in their turn. And the madness belongs mostly to the tulip, considering the strange aberration called "tulipomania" which swept Holland in the early seventeenth century, when otherwise sensible and solid Dutchmen put down the equivalent of $50,000 to own a single bulb of the variety Semper Augustus. (But something comparable happened on the West Coast of the United States between 1942 and 1947, when a boom in the Croft strain of *Lilium longiflorum*, the Easter lily, overcame a number of commercial growers with speculative fever, forcing many of them into bankruptcy when boom turned to bust.)

This poetry and this madness are easy to understand: between them, daffodils and tulips announce the departure of winter's harshness and the full arrival of spring's exhilarating instability. The glories of a hillside covered with golden daffodils have long been sung, and tulips come in such spectacular and incandescent colors—alabaster and vermilion and cerise and maroon, so many hues that no language can name them all—that most gardeners cheerfully forgive them their tendency to put on a disappearing act (sometimes sudden, sometimes gradual) after their first season of bloom.

I could not easily get through spring without daffodils and tulips blooming in my garden and filling a dozen vases throughout the house. But neither would I want to do without the steady procession of so-called minor bulbs which begins weeks and weeks before the daffodils and tulips break ground and which ends well after the last petal has fallen from the May-blooming lily tulips next to my quince tree. Why these bulbs have been lumped together under such an insulting and wholly inaccurate name, I can't imagine, except that they cost less than daffodils and tulips and offer gardeners the asset (and bulb companies the liability) of freely self-seeding themselves all over any garden where they're happy. Mail-order nurseries and local garden centers may describe them as minor if they wish, but the pleasures they bring and the aesthetic qualities they lend to the garden landscape from late winter to the verge of summer are both major.

The first of these bulbs to bloom is, of course, the snowdrop (*Galanthus nivalis*), which, I now recall, *has* been noticed by poets. Rossetti, observing that its blossoms were not precisely the clear white they seem on first glance to be, praised it for its "heart-shaped seal of green." Tennyson, looking for a simile for chastity, came up with these odd lines:

> *Pure as lines of green that streak the White*
> *Of the first Snowdrop's inner leaves.*

As it happens, I don't grow snowdrops at the moment. There used to be a small clump of them at the base of a little Colorado blue spruce by the sidewalk out front, a tree that I insisted to my wife some ten years ago ought to be removed, before it grew immense, engulfed much of the garden, and plunged our house into a Dantean gloom. I lost the argument. The spruce is now semi-immense, but it's far enough from our front windows that the house plants haven't yet died in the dark. But part of my prophecy was right on the mark. The snowdrops, engulfed, are no more. I mean to order their replacements but keep forgetting. My memory is always jogged in January or February, when I see them in someone else's garden, nestled in among damp oak leaves and often, true to their common name, dusted with snow or gleaming in a thin coating of ice.

Next, if I have the order down right, come the winter aconites (not members of the genus *Aconitum* at all but properly *Eranthis hyemalis*). They are perky things, bright golden buttercups only three inches tall at most, each blossom surrounded by a frilly collar of dark green, but it takes a great many of them planted close together to make much of a splash. Here I'll offer a concession to the people who write bulb catalogs: aconites *are* minor, no doubt about it, and if they bloomed in May instead of February, all the gardeners in America who would bother to grow them could meet in a public phone booth.

Need I mention crocuses? In the public mind, they are the bulb most associated with the coming of spring, for they appear at a time when it becomes reasonable to go outside in a sweater (some days) instead of Arctic outerwear. They are one of spring's brightest signs—what I used to call, until I was corrected at an embarrassingly late age, "harbringers of spring," by which I suppose I meant that they brought spring and a little "har" as well. At any rate, by all means let there be crocuses; crocuses in great masses at the edge of lawns and the base of hedges; purple crocuses and yellow crocuses and white crocuses and lilac crocuses; crocuses in clumps in odd corners of the garden; crocuses by the mailbox to greet the bringer of bills and 1040 forms; the delicate species crocuses such as *Crocus angustifolius* and *C. sieberi* and *C. versicolor*, all favored by the horticultural cognoscenti. And, yes, the Dutch crocus favored by the vulgar, including, I guess, myself, and by Henry Mitchell, who has spoken the definitive word in *The Essential Earthman*:

Let us have no more talk about "fat Dutch crocuses" or "fat Dutch hyacinths"—as if the better sort of gardener loved only the slender, elegant wild crocuses and hyacinths unfed, unbred, and untouched by the Dutch. The truth is that nothing is more sprightly to see than patches of fat Dutch crocuses in March, coming as they do to lift our spirits and amaze the young and simple.

Next, about the same time as the very earliest daffodils, such as February Gold, a fine quartet of predominantly blue (bluish-white through sky-blue through cobalt to bluish-purple) bulbs comes into overlapping bloom that can last a good month, unless there's a sudden and prolonged warm snap. These are glory-of-the-snow (*Chionodoxa luciliae*), striped squill (*Puschkinia scilloides*), Siberian squill (*Scilla siberica*), and grape hyacinth (several species of *Muscari,* including *M. botoroides* and *M. armeniacum,* as well as several named cultivars hybridized or selected by nurserymen).

If by some misfortune I were forced to grow but one of this quartet, it wouldn't take me a New York minute to settle on grape hyacinth and forgo the rest. For one thing, it's the only one of the four that has a place in my memories of childhood in Texas. We lived in a succession of houses, all of which had grape hyacinths growing in the yard—great dark-blue sheets of them that almost rivaled in their intensity of color the bluebonnets growing on the chalky prairie out in the country. Not forgetting snowdrops, I can't think of any other flower with so appropriate a common name, a name so right and seemingly so inevitable. Grape hyacinths do indeed have a sweet and grape-like fragrance, like ripe Concords on a vine in September. Held upside down, the clusters of flowers do resemble a bunch of dark grapes. (John Ruskin put it neatly, if in prose itself leaning from the blue to the purple, in describing grape hyacinths he found growing wild in southern France: "It was as if a cluster of grapes and a hive of honey had been distilled, pressed together into one small boss of beaded blue."

Glory-of-the-snow and *Scilla siberica* tie in my affections, coming in a very close second to grape hyacinths. One of the most beautiful springtime sights I've ever seen came early one May in upstate New York, when I drove down College Hill Road, a steep and twisting concrete lane leading from Hamilton College toward the attractive village of Clinton. As I rounded the final curve and reached the floor of the Oriskany Valley, I almost lost control of the car at the sight of a patch of woodland by a stream, where glory-of-the-snow had escaped from someone's garden and spread into a thick colony covering almost half an acre in a stunning deep-blue haze. *Scilla siberica*, I'm sure, would have brought a like lump to my throat. In my garden, I have concentrated most of my grape hyacinths, *Scilla siberica*, and glory-of-the-snow (punctuated by the lighter blue-and-white-striped flowers of *Puschkinia,* which I plant more sparingly) in adjacent, intermingled masses along the curved edge of a bed of lilies and periwinkle. There's also a band of fairly classy daffodils, but I've never thought of the *Muscari* and other small bulbs as being mere foreground for narcissus.

Skipping over *Iris danfordiae* and *I. reticulata*, which if I grew them would bloom earlier than my grape hyacinths, and the guinea-hen flower (*Fritillaria meleagris*), which would bloom about the same time, the last, and I think the most elegant of the bulbs some people stoop to call "minor," is the Spanish wood hyacinth, sometimes sold under the names *Scilla hispanica* or *Scilla campanulata*, although its true scientific name is *Endymion hispanicus*. In my experience, this lovely bulb stays put, not having the jackrabbit tendencies of some of the other small spring bulbs to be fruitful and multiply, popping up in every corner of the yard and in the middle of the lawn as well. It does, however, form larger and larger clumps over the years. It is extremely attractive, with sparsely set hyacinth-like blossoms of pastel blue, pink, or white nodding gracefully on tall, strong stems above a fountain of foliage. It enjoys shade. I have several clumps of it at the base of a wild cherry tree whose deep shade and cyanide-laced fruits discourage almost everything else from growing except some violets and an accidental clump of the hateful tawny daylily. On the other side of the garden, a dozen or so clumps are scattered beneath the lilac hedge, where they manage to rise a foot above the English ivy ground cover that has shouldered aside some less persistent bulbs, such as milla.

Since the Spanish wood hyacinth comes at the end of spring in my garden, I look on it as a "harbringer" of summer.

The Special Elegance
of Hardy Cyclamens

Early March is the season of my annual temptation by Mr. Royall W. Bemis, the proprietor of Blackthorne Gardens in Holbrook, Massachusetts. I've never met this gentleman, but from the picture in his annual catalog he looks as if he might be fun. The appearance of his advertising flier in my mail each year is as reliable a sign that spring is on its way as the first robin tugging on a worm in the back yard.

Mr. Bemis isn't the least bit shy about the plants he sells. His flier abounds in boldface type and multiple exclamation points ("You simply MUST have this one to highlight your garden THIS VERY YEAR!!!"). But I'm seldom put off by heavy doses of hyperbole in garden catalogs, and since the plants Blackthorne Gardens offers concide with my preferences—astilbe, bleeding heart, clematis, and so on through the floral alphabet—I often end up placing an order.

The last time his flier came, Mr. Bemis hooked me with his special offer of cyclamens. I'm especially fond of this most elegant and refined of winter pot plants. A large cyclamen from the florist makes a cheering sight on a gray day, with its profusion of graceful, pendant flowers of crimson, pink, or white, each blossom nodding on its own stem, held high above attractive, heart-shaped leaves all mottled and dappled like rainbow trout. These large cyclamens don't last very long for me. In better hands than mine, they may, but all too frequently I've come downstairs in the morning to discover that the cyclamen I bought the week before has suffered terminal nervous collapse. Lately

I've been buying the scaled-down version of the florist's cyclamen, which is fairly new on the market, about half the size of the ones I used to get, and blooms itself silly from late winter well into summer.

But I digress. Blackthorne Gardens' cyclamens weren't the tender, showy cyclamens florists sell, whether full-scale or half-pints. What Mr. Bemis was offering was a collection of seven hardy species collected in the southern Alps and the Middle East, providing a succession of pink and rose blossoms from early spring to late fall. None was supposed to grow more than six inches tall, some were said to be fragrant, and most of them were reported to have evergreen foliage, making them attractive subjects for use as a ground cover. For the benefit of people who might be intimidated by such botanical names as *Cyclamen coum* or *C. pseudoibericum*, Mr. Bemis provided new names, such as Rose Beauty and Crimson Velvet.

Whatever they were called, it seemed to me that I had just the right spot for a colony of cyclamens, a small bed at the base of a hedge, shaded by a venerable cedar. For years I had planted white impatiens there each spring, but no longer. I mailed off a cyclamen order, after doing some basic reading on the subject. I also bragged to a friend about the cyclamens I was going to have, persuasively enough that he decided to order a collection, too.

My new planting would do well, I figured, provided I followed instructions for its care. Since cyclamens are lime lovers, I would have to moderate my slightly acidic soil with some dolomitic limestone. The small tubers of cyclamens have eyes, and would have to be handled with care once they arrived. If the eyes were rubbed off from rough treatment, it would take a year or two for new ones to form and the plant to grow, a setback I wanted to avoid. It seems that the flat tubers of hardy cyclamens are highly displeasing to people with a low tolerance for ambiguity, since it is very difficult to tell which is the top and which is the bottom, so I would have to split the difference, planting each tuber no more than two inches deep and resting on its side, trusting that it would eventually right itself in a more comfortable position. I should not expect any miraculous display of blooms the first year; the tubers were coming a great distance, some of them by camel train, and it would take some time for them to acclimatize to conditions in my garden. I could, however, expect some bloom from *C. neapolitanum* (Pink Pearl) the first fall after it was planted. The others would probably bloom the following year. If they were especially happy with their location, they would self-seed and naturalize, but in any case, the bulbs would increase in size and number of blooms with each passing season.

In his flier, Mr. Bemis had written, "If you have never seen or grown these rare and glorious little charmers, it is impossible to imagine the joy that is in store for you." I dreamed of unimaginable joy while waiting for my order to arrive. Waiting and waiting and waiting. By early May my friend, who had also placed an order, called up to say, "Hey, what happened to that camel train?" Meanwhile, although I was eager to have wild cyclamens growing in the shade of that cedar tree, I was feeling the pangs of ecological guilt, having been told by a botanist who frequently chides me on just such matters that a great many species of cyclamen in Turkey and the Middle East are endangered species, that their collection is officially discouraged, and that I was probably an accomplice in the violation of a couple of international treaties. Telling myself that one sin does not a sinner make, I vowed that I would never order such cyclamens again.

At long last, the cyclamen bulbs—small and decidedly unimpressive—arrived, on the eve of a trip I was making to Costa Rica. I planted them hurriedly. There wasn't time to make a map telling me which species was which, but I figured I could determine that later on, when they bloomed, and I could consult the descriptions in *Hortus Third* (see page 242).

Spring turned to summer. July came and went. Not a cyclamen appeared. The friend who had bought some as a result of my bragging resorted to sarcasm over the telephone, calling me to report that he had about an acre of them in full bloom in his garden. Some volunteer white impatiens appeared in the bed where my cyclamens were apparently resting in final and eternal peace.

The impatiens thrived, at least until it was cut down by a hard freeze in mid-October. My wife went out to pull up the bedraggled, blackened plants and put them on the compost heap, while I sat at the breakfast table, drinking a third cup of coffee, reading Ann Landers, and pretending that there were no garden chores to do. My wife then rapped on the dining-room window and beckoned me outside to see our presumed graveyard for cyclamens.

I should, it seemed, have had more faith in Mr. Bemis. Here and there, concealed by the foliage of the impatiens, a good many clumps of cyclamen had sprouted during the early fall. Two of them—presumably *C. neapolitanum*, which taxonomists have now decided ought to be called *C. hederifolium*, by the way—were blooming, with several graceful, diminutive, rose-pink blossoms held about three inches above an attractive rosette of dappled gray-green foliage. I called my friend, asked him to go check his own planting, and stayed on the wire until he returned to announce that he'd be damned, he had the things after all, and some were blooming.

It is too soon to report in any final way that I've been successful with these cyclamens. They have returned for a second season, but various of them go in and out of dormancy, like a patient coming in and out of a coma. I have read encouraging reports by other gardeners who have great sheets of them covering the ground in dry and shady places, like my own spot. I am very, very far from being able to speak of having cyclamens as ground cover, and in fact they must constantly be rescued from the encroachments of some nearby ajuga which is greedy for the ground they occupy. But the cyclamens seem to be holding their own, and I have high hopes.

[1991: This essay needs an update. When it originally appeared in my column, I got a gentle but firm letter from Nancy Goodwin in North Carolina. She pointed out that hardy cyclamens were being collected in their native habitats so greedily that they were endangered. In the original edition of *Home Ground*, I added to the essay a vow not to sin again by buying tubers that had probably been collected. Soon, however, Nancy Goodwin founded Montrose Nursery, specifically to offer seed-grown cyclamens, so that Americans could enjoy them without contributing to their extinction in the wild. I regard Nancy as one of the true heroes of the gardening world today. Montrose continues to raise and sell cyclamens, but it also offers other rare and choice plants not to be found elsewhere.]

Broom and Wisteria

That field, perhaps ten acres of former woodland its owner cleared several years ago in hope of selling it to some developer who has yet to show up, lies between my house and the drugstore where I buy out-of-town newspapers, so I pass it several times a week, and always on Sundays. In any season it's a pleasant sight. It slopes gently toward the hedgerows that define the neighborhood bicycle path, and its unknown owner had the good sense to leave some fine oaks standing instead of converting them to cordwood when he brought in the bulldozer and the chain saws.

In compliance with town ordinances, most of the field gets mowed by the Fourth of July, so its vegetation runs chiefly to grasses and butterfly weed and black-eyed Susans, punctuated by patches of poison ivy that turn a glorious if deadly scarlet every fall. But in early May, part of that field always slows me down on the way to the drugstore and sometimes brings me to a halt. Just when the daffodils have quit and the azaleas are blooming like crazy in the front yards of half the split-levels within 350 miles, the field offers a sight that to my mind is worth most of the azaleas in town (and all its hydrangeas)—a strip of land some fifty feet wide, where the owner has held back the tractor that annually mows the rest of his property. Here, at the field's western edge, he has allowed a fine colony of self-sown Scotch broom (*Cytisus scoparius*) to develop, perhaps five hundred plants. Attractive all year round, because the stems of Scotch broom remain brilliant green even in the dreariest part of winter, these volunteer shrubs radiate a special, almost pyrotechnic cheer in May, when they burst into deep golden bloom. But what makes the field where they grow especially lovely is that when the broom comes into blossom, it is accompanied and complemented by the soft blue haze of another volunteer—wisteria vines (*Wisteria floribunda*, I think) that scramble over the dry, sandy slope and clamber to the tops of the nearby oaks.

Sometimes in May I do more than admire. I plunge into the sea of green and golden broom, dodge bumblebees seeking nectar, try to keep from tripping on the wisteria vines, and snip off a few branches of broom and some clusters of wisteria to bring home. Technically my act is theft, but I've always thought St. Augustine went on just a little too much about those stolen pears in his *Confessions*. There's plenty of both wisteria and broom in that field, and having arrived there on their own, they're really weeds. And if some ecologist took it into his head to chide me for disturbing the balance of nature, I'd chide right back. Neither Scotch broom nor *Wisteria floribunda* is native to our shores. Broom's name leaves its origins no mystery, and this particular wisteria is a Japanese import, although there are native American species. Certainly neither plant could be called an endangered species. "Endangering species" would be more apt. Broom, in its preferred habitat of sparse soil, spreads as quickly as a small-town rumor. Wisteria has engulfed whole pine forests in the Tidewater and Piedmont regions of Virginia, though it can't be mentioned in the same breath with kudzu, another import, which with some assistance from the manufacturers of polyester has just about toppled King Cotton in Mississippi and Alabama. I think I'm fairly sound on most environmental issues. I wouldn't dream of picking a lady's slipper orchid, much less digging it up and bringing it home. The one time I allowed myself to "rescue" a Turk's-cap lily from a roadside I felt remorse for a month. But picking some broom and wisteria from a vacant field troubles me not a jot.

A free, loose, and informal bouquet of wisteria and broom on a table flooded by the bright morning light of late spring offers an invitation to observe each plant for itself and then to attend to their differences and similarities. It also teaches something about the differences between poetry and science—and about their hidden common ground.

It will not do at all to speak of wisteria's "blue haze." To speak this way is to speak from a distance; we may be approximately correct but as far off the mark as congratulating ourselves for missing a plane connection by only a few minutes or referring to someone as being slightly pregnant. Blue is too simple a name for a cluster of wisteria blossoms, taken in hand like a bunch of grapes, slowly turned, and seen up close. I take one such cluster from the vase. It has forty-nine individual florets and buds, arranged in a spiral along its pendant stem. The twelve blossoms at the top, fully open, are multicolored, and none of their colors is blue at all. Each blossom has five petals. The topmost, which stands erect, is grayish-mauve, but overlaid with gold along a vertical crease at its center. Semitransparent, when held to the light it fades toward whiteness. The two middle petals, pointing outward and downward, are a deep violet purple, as are the bottommost set they protect, which point outward and slightly downward, are fused together at their bottom edge, and conceal within themselves stamens and pistil, the organs of generation. Below the twelve blossoms at the top of the cluster are nine others that have partially opened and are noticeably a darker purple. Below these, and darker still, seventeen buds show signs of swelling. Still lower, there are twenty-one small, tight buds, each one tinier in its turn down the spiral, each deepening from purple toward black. The final bud is a mere speck, no larger than the period that ends a sentence. Nothing here is blue; the blue is a trick of the eye and of distance. Furthermore, a cluster of wisteria has properties that utterly elude the eye. I shut my eyes, bring it to my face, and breathe deeply of a fragrance that I compare to that of violets and ripe grapes, though the comparison is crude.

At first glance, broom lacks the mathematical symmetry of wisteria's downward spiral. Its blossoms follow no apparent sequence, seeming to appear almost at random up and down the stem. There are blossoms open at the top of the stem, here and there in the middle, and at the bottom—and they are everywhere interspersed with swollen buds. Each blossom emerges from a point on the stem where it is accompanied by a pair of trifoliate leaves and a tiny bud that will bloom only when its larger companion has shattered and fallen. (The paired buds give broom a very long flowering season, well over a month.) All the petals of broom are the same color—an intense, saturated golden-yellow.

The differences between broom and wisteria are plain. Broom is upright and perky and straightforward, as emphatic as a manifesto. Wisteria is drooping and languid and complex, as indirect as a hint. Seen up close, broom's color is just what it seems to be from a distance; wisteria is more than it first seemed to be.

But surprises follow when you look even more closely at broom. The paired blossoms and buds and their accompanying leaves also spiral around their stem. And each blossom, like those of wisteria, has a top petal pointing up, two middle petals, pointing out and flanking two lower petals that point outward and slightly upward and that conceal stamens and pistil. Despite their differences, broom and wisteria are greatly similar one to the other.

Calling similar things by similar names is one of the most primordial of human acts, symbolized most profoundly in the story of Adam and Eve being given domination in Eden by the commandment to give names to the other living things they found there. Classification of things lies at the root of language and thus of culture, and it reaches its most advanced development and expression in science. Having looked closely at broom and wisteria on a bright May morning, having noticed the similarities that lie beneath their differences, I need words to name these things. I reach for the nearest botanical book at hand. Published in 1926 by a firm that no longer exists, it is very much out of date, being entirely silent on matters of molecular biology. But it serves my particular needs as regards the similarities of broom and wisteria, whose flowers show them to be indisputably kin, if not exactly kissing cousins.

Their top petal, I learn, is called a "standard." The middle petals are "wings." The bottom petals, fused into one, are called the "keel." I learn, furthermore, that both broom and wisteria are members of the vast numbers of genera and species that make up the legume family. Knowing this, I may also infer that, like all legumes, they have the power to transform nitrogen, to pluck it out of the atmosphere and fix it into the soil by interaction with certain bacteria. And thus I know that not only are those brooms and wisteria vines bringing beauty to that vacant field in May, they are also improving the fertility of the soil from which they spring. This knowledge is a matter of science.

But beneath the science there lies poetry. *Standards, wings, keel:* in naming the parts of these blossoms, we follow the path of metaphor into the poetic dimension that underlies all detailed observation and all science. We are comparing ultimately dissimilar things to one another, relating the parts of flowers to the banners that armies once carried before them into battle, to the means of flight in birds and butterflies, to the unseen, bottommost part of a ship slicing through the water.

And beneath the poetry? Here lies, I believe, finally a mystery. We cannot know the *Ding an sich,* the broom as it is in itself, the wisteria itself. These are instances of the unspeakable beauties of the things of this earth.

The Transience
of Columbines

Among the earliest lessons gardeners learn is that ornamental plants fall naturally into three categories: annuals, biennials, and perennials. Thus, we know that we have to plant marigolds and zinnias every year if we are to have them in our gardens, that Canterbury bells and lunaria are planted one year to bloom and then disappear the next, and that, once planted, hemerocallis and lythrum will long outlast us. But with experience we learn a second lesson that corrects the first: it ain't, as Ira Gershwin put it, necessarily so. Some annuals, such as moonflower vine, which is close kin to the sweet potato, may be killed by frost in temperate regions, but are perennial in their native habitats in the tropics. Other annuals self-seed so reliably and profusely that they might as well be perennials. Years and years ago I bought a flat of white sweet alyssum to edge a perennial border, and I haven't had to buy a single alyssum since. They spring up everywhere in mid-March; I transplant them where I like and give the rest to friends until I've run out of friends. From early June until the first really hard freeze they make a pleasant, fragrant mat between the lawn and the flower beds. And some biennials have the same self-seeding tendencies; anyone who ever plants lunaria had better really admire it for its purplish flowers in May and its round, translucent seed pods later in the season, for once it's planted, it becomes a tenacious, virtually permanent garden guest.

And as for perennials—some of them are so fickle or so finicky that they hardly deserve the name. When I was living and gardening in Texas and Virginia and other places in the South, Shasta daisies could be counted on to come back every spring, multiplying into huge clumps that had to be divided annually; not so in southern New Jersey, even though our winters are comparatively mild. They never last beyond a single season, and I can never seem to remember to do the right thing —dig them up and put them in a cold frame to nurse them through the winter. And delphiniums, no matter how they may behave in Great Britain and in the Pacific Northwest, are so chancy that I've learned to rejoice when one or two happen to make it beyond the first year and not to grieve when I lose the entire lot. The handsome, fairly short strain, Connecticut Yankee, bred by the photographer Edward Steichen, is somewhat more reliable—but the plain fact is that although last year I had it in my garden, this year I don't. Lilies also have, for me, a lamentable habit of sneaking off to Beulah land, except of course for tiger lilies, which increase so prolifically through the bulbils in their leaf axils that I suspect I couldn't dislodge them from my property unless I resorted to dynamite and Agent Orange.

But of all the perennials I grow that show tendencies toward transience, columbines are the most fascinating and ingratiating, for in their disappearance they also tend to leave other, often quite different, columbines in their place. I do have a stable colony of *Aquilegia canadensis*, commonly called the American columbine (although there are other species native to this country as well), which seems to be happy in its dry, shady spot beneath some white pines at the rear of my garden, where it produces a profusion of rather modest red and yellow flowers every spring. No other columbines have ever stayed with me beyond a couple of years, even though they all have left their progeny behind. Thus it happened with some potted specimens of the McKana Giants hybrid strain, which I picked out in bloom at a nursery in order to get the colors I wanted, a pale lilac and a deep rose-pink. It wasn't long before those original plants succumbed to the Lacy columbine curse, but their grandchildren and great-grandchildren are still with me—not a one of them pale lilac or deep rose-pink. Thus it happened with some columbines I grew from seed my friend Rick Hite collected in the Canary Islands when he was on sabbatical. He mailed them from Tenerife in May. I planted them in July, and when they bloomed the following year, I was in a state of columbine fever, for they were just about the most splendid things I'd ever clapped eyes on—almost three feet tall, floriferous enough to rival azaleas, loaded with masses of large, creamy-white, long-spurred blossoms, and possessed of attractive green foliage that had an unusual degree of resistance to leaf miners. Thinking I might have on my hands some rare species never grown in any American garden before, I sent seeds to a botanist friend in upstate New York and asked him to grow it and to see if he could identify it. He agreed, but he also warned me that the genus *Aquilegia* was notoriously confused and that various species had strong tendencies to hybridize among themselves, making identification sometimes quite iffy. Nevertheless, the following summer the word came back that my new columbine was definitely a white form of *Aquilegia chrysantha*, the golden columbine, a native of the Rocky Mountains. Probably some Spanish priest or explorer gathered the seeds and sent them home and they were then sent to the Canaries, whence they came to my garden for repatriation —a brief repatriation. A year later they had disappeared, although I occasionally think I can detect their genes in some of the seedlings that volunteer from time to time.

Now another changeling has appeared. I think I know its origins, but wherever it came from, it couldn't be lovelier. A few years back, just about the time that my Canary Island columbines were deciding they couldn't stand the idea of living in New Jersey, I tried some new ones. From seeds I grew a dozen or so plants of a strain called Fairyland, highly touted in a seed catalog for its dwarf habit (only fifteen inches tall) and for the wide range of color in its short-spurred, upward-facing blossoms. And from White Flower Farm I bought a single plant of a Japanese species, *A. flabellata* 'alba,' described as very attractive for its pure-white flowers and the bluish cast of its foliage. Fairyland was a bust. "Squat" says it better than "dwarf." Its blossoms, bunched together too closely at the top of the plant, were generally grotesque, their colors muddy, indeterminate pastel shades. I ripped them all up, except for one plant, a bit more graceful than the rest, with flowers an appealing shade of blue. It's gone now, of course. So is *A. flabellata* 'alba.' But in the bed where both once grew, a fairly dry and gravelly spot in the shade of a tall cedar tree, where now I grow mostly hardy cyclamen, I found this spring several appealing new columbines, all with the bluish foliage of the Japanese species and its graceful, nodding, downward-facing blossoms, and all with the blue color of that lone specimen of Fairyland I allowed a brief reprieve.

Columbine is an oddly named plant. Its Latin name, *Aquilegia*, puzzles me for its reference to eagles. Its English name means "dovelike," a reference, my dictionary tells me, to its presumed resemblance to a flock of pigeons. The nineteenth-century English poet, artist, and critic, William Morris, agreed with the dictionary, for he once advised his readers to "be very shy of double flowers; choose the old Columbine where the clustering doves are unmistakable and distinct, not the double one, where they run into mere tatters." In passing, I must say that the very idea of a double columbine, which I've never seen, is utterly repugnant, but I must also confess that my imagination summons up for me nothing of doves in the blossoms of columbine. I wonder if both the Latin and the English names might not refer instead to birds in general and to their transience.

Space in my garden grows limited. I have long reached the point—perhaps passed it—where any new acquisition means that I must get rid of something else. Nevertheless, I never seem to have enough columbines, and lately I've been carrying out a thought experiment that I might someday actually carry out, if I can find a place for it. I'd like to buy seeds of as many kinds of columbine as I can locate, wild species like *A. caerulea* and *A. longissima* and *A. vulgaris*, as well as hybrids like Spring Song and Maxi-Star and Snow Queen. I'd plant them intermingled, all together in the same spot. I know that like eagles or doves or hummingbirds or robins they would all soon fly away from my garden. But it would be fascinating to observe the odd permutations and changes among the progeny they might leave behind.

Plumbago Blue

Among the considerable numbers of things that separate Southern gardens and gardeners from their counterparts in colder regions of the United States is the prevalence of blue plumbago, or Cape leadwort, in Dixie and its pronounced absence up North. (I am referring here to *Plumbago auriculata*, which is sometimes called *P. capensis* and is a shrubby or straggling vine native to southern Africa, not to its distant relative, *Ceratostigma plumbaginoides*, which is sometimes called *C. larpentiae*, goes under the same common name as *P. auriculata*, and is a hardy ground cover native to China. I don't know of another flowering plant whose names are so confusing, and to make matters worse, no one is sure what it and lead have to do with each other.) Plumbago is widely grown in Florida, along the Gulf Coast, and in Southern California, where it is reliably perennial and may exceed 25 feet in height. In the upper South, where winters are too cold for it to survive, it may often be found in late spring at local nurseries, where it is sold as small rooted cuttings for use in window boxes or other containers in a sunny location.

Plumbago has no faults that I can think of. It blooms early and long. It grows rapidly. Its abundant soft green foliage, which is slightly glossy, is attractive. And its clusters of flowers are blue—a pale, pale blue, not the more saturated and intense blue of the cornflower. (There is also a white form, but I prefer the blue.) Its culture is simple, requiring only sunshine at least half the day, occasional fertilization to keep it in growth and in flower, and a heavy dose of water every day. (Plumbago is a very thirsty plant, and if allowed to dry out during active growth, it will never look the same again and may even refuse to bloom.)

There's really no reason, however, that Northern gardeners can't have plumbago and the cool touch of blue that it gives to the midsummer garden. It isn't much of a house plant by any means, but it is easily overwintered inside, until late spring, when it can be brought outside to a terrace or deck, where it will bloom unstintingly until early fall. I have four plumbago plants that I keep in 12-inch pots and that I bought years ago in Dallas as rooted cuttings. In early September I begin to withhold water, forcing them toward dormancy. Once the leaves lose their spunk and turn a bit yellow, I reduce the water ration still further and sharply cut their straggling stems back two to three feet, leaving one foot or so. Then the plants are brought upstairs to a table by a window on the north side of the house. They are watered infrequently, only about once every ten days, and very lightly. The trick is to keep them alive, but just barely. If they are overwatered, accidentally fertilized, or given any other sign of a lapse in benign neglect, they will spring back to life before the time is ripe, a disastrous resurrection.

The time is ripe in mid-March, when I sometimes divide my plumbagos to share with friends. With sharp shears, I cut the plants back almost to the ground, removing the top two inches of soil from their pots and replacing it with a rich mixture of compost. The fluorescent growing lamps above the plumbago are lowered and turned on, the pots are deeply watered and heavily fertilized, and by late April the plants are once again on our back-yard deck.

Northern gardeners who want to try plumbago may find them difficult to locate. Seeds are carried by Thompson and Morgan in Farmingdale, New Jersey, and plants are sold by mail by Logee's Greenhouses in Danielson, Connecticut.

Bearding the Iris
in Its Own Bed

Together with Oriental poppies and peonies, the tall bearded irises are in the eyes of many people the glory of the late spring garden. Hundreds of hybridizers, many of them amateurs working out of their own back yards, have labored since early in this century to improve this staple perennial, so aptly named for Hera's messenger and the symbol of the rainbow. Today's gardener has thousands of named cultivars to choose from, all much more spectacular than the old sweet flags our great-grandparents grew. By careful selection, the plant breeders have given us irises with larger flowers on taller and better-branched stalks. They have added touches of high fashion to their blossoms, whose petals are now often fluted or crimped or ruffled or flared, or all of these at once. They have achieved stunning innovations in color: clear, true pinks with red beards, rich claret purples, butterscotch ambers, and subtle blends that neither words nor camera can easily capture.

Nevertheless, I've come to a reluctant resolution: the tall bearded iris I grow must now find other homes. I can't bear to put them on the compost heap, but I'll give them to friends willing to put up with their bad habits. If need be, I'll put them out on the sidewalk in boxes with a sign—FREE IRIS. Thus will end my most ancient horticultural passion; the first plant I ever owned was a clump of a yellow iris called Happy Days, which I acquired during my stint in Mrs. Harkey's field when I was in the third grade.

I know that a great many gardeners are particularly devoted

to the tall bearded iris and that they will abhor me for my defection. Perhaps they'll come in a delegation up to my fence and waggle their fingers at me for having wandered from the path of true wisdom into the evil of apostasy.

I'm sorry, but a lot has happened to bearded irises in recent years, and much of it strikes me as bad. Lately I can't muster more than half a cheer for the people who bred the irises I've been growing, all fairly up-to-date cultivars. In their breakneck pursuit of immense blossoms in Technicolor hues, they seem to have forgotten that irises must live in gardens and therefore ought to behave themselves with some decorum.

Every year the same thing happens. In March, when leaves begin to grow at the base of last year's rhizomes, I look forward to the bright display coming in May. When the stalks begin to push up from the fans of foliage, my anticipation sharpens. And when the buds show color and the first blossoms unfurl at the top of each stalk, I tell myself that I really don't have enough irises, that I must remember to order some more and soon. Then come the disappointments. An iris stem with two or three blossoms open and the rest still in bud is lovely, but that same stem a few days later, when the first blossoms are spent but still cling on for dear life, is a disreputable sight. And the slightest wind and rain bring havoc to an iris patch, leaving the stalks leaning this way and that, toppling toward the lawn or sidewalk, the blossoms all bruised or muddy.

Furthermore, the plain fact is that for fifty weeks out of the year a clump of tall bearded iris is as homely as a starling. And often they're not healthy, since the bearded iris is much liable to affliction by borers, bacterial leaf blight, fungus attacks, scorch, and other loathsome maladies.

I will have no more tall bearded irises. The love affair has ended.

But I will still have irises—Siberian irises, to start with. A few years ago I bought three cultivars (Cambridge and Tealwood, both blues; and White Swirl, whose name tells it all) and stuck them in an odd corner of my garden, much to my later satisfaction.

My Siberians don't teeter and topple in a rainstorm, and their withered blossoms aren't especially obtrusive. They're as understated and elegant as their tall bearded cousins are overdone and tarted up. They're lovely when in bloom, of course, and their erect, narrow foliage remains an attractive accent in the border all during the growing season—something spiky to punctuate the more rounded forms of phlox and hemerocallis in midsummer.

I've also got my eye on some hybrids among three species of iris native to North America—*Iris brevicaulis, I. fulva,* and *I. giganticaerulea,* which are generally lumped together under the name Louisiana iris. I've known for some time that a great many hybridizers in that state and in Texas and California have been breeding them for decades and that several specialty nurseries offer a large number of named cultivars. I assumed, apparently wrongly, that the Louisianas weren't suitable for my Northern garden, until a recent announcement from the Geo. W. Park Seed Company in Greenwood, South Carolina, set me straight.

Park's now offers plants of what it calls American iris—Louisianas, in a variety of forms and colors, including blues and whites and reds and yellows. Bred by Carl Wyatt, a professional hybridizer in Marquand, Missouri, they are reportedly a new strain whose merits include freedom from pests and disease and a high degree of hardiness in most sections of the country.

But the announcement of these American irises has stirred up something of a ruckus among American iris fanciers. The July 1983 *American Iris Society Bulletin* reports that Park's

incurred the wrath of iris growers by introducing the strain of Louisiana iris they are handling as "American" irises. The term "Louisiana iris," [officials of the society state] is widely used and accepted in reference to these plants in all responsible horticultural literature. . . . It should also be pointed out that the Pacific Coast native irises, as well as *Iris cristata, Iris missourienseis,* and several other species are just as "American" as the Louisiana irises. . . . We do hope that the offending term drops by the wayside.

I have no intention of intruding myself into this controversy. It would seem that the A.I.S. has a valid point to make. Nevertheless, Park's did call my attention to something I didn't know—that Louisiana iris can be grown outside the Deep South and may make suitable things for me to add to the Siberian irises as substitutes for the tall bearded sorts that I now find so unsatisfactory.

Finally, although I'm ridding myself of all the tall ones, I will still have bearded iris. A few years back a friend with whom I shared my growing doubts about most of the iris in my garden told me about what he called "median" or "border" iris—bearded iris, yes, with the same hairy blotches high on the falls to point out to bees the shortest way to the nectar, but more compact, less ambitious to impress by immensity and flamboyance—economy models, not gas guzzlers, if you will. From a Midwestern iris nursery—Hildenbrandt's Iris Gardens in Lexington, Nebraska—I ordered half a dozen, with names like Carnival Glass, Dresden Frills, Frosted Crystal, and Plum Creek. They were inexpensive, under $10 for the lot. When they arrived in late summer, I didn't have time to take much care in planting them and I forgot to make a chart, so I haven't the faintest idea which is which.

But there's a purple one and a pink one and a yellow and a blue and a couple of blends, and they please me when they bloom in May. They behave themselves impeccably in my garden, and I'm not about to put them out in a box on the sidewalk.

Butterfly Weed

I don't know of another flowering plant that has gathered such an odd assortment of common names, ranging from slightly repellent to rather charming. The unpleasant names include chigger flower, Indian nosy, pleurisy root, pain-in-the-side plant, and fluxroot. I don't have any idea what the first two names refer to. Do chiggers find the plant irresistibly attractive, congregating on its leaves until some even more irresistibly attractive human passes by? Does "nosy" here mean prying and inquisitive, so that Indian nosy conceals a racial slur? Or is the word a corruption of "nosegay"? The remaining three names seem to imply medicinal properties, and in fact several of the wildflower guides in my library refer, somewhat vaguely, to such uses. Carolus Linnaeus, the great Swedish taxonomist, seems to have believed something of the kind when he named the genus to which this plant belongs *Asclepias* (this particular one being *A. tuberosa*). He derived the name from Asclepius, the Greek god of medicine, who was done in by Pluto out of jealousy over his skill at raising the dead. Nelson Coon's handy reference book, *The Dictionary of Useful Plants*, states that certain tribes of American Indians cooked and ate its roots and that others used it to induce vomiting, a claim that does not inspire me to add *A. tuberosa* to my culinary repertoire.

I prefer to call this highly attractive plant, which is a member of the milkweed family, by its more charming name, butterfly weed, which is also highly descriptive (unlike some other common plant names I could mention, such as hound's piss, viper's bugloss, and tinker's weed). Butterflies do, in fact, hover about its deep-orange clusters of blossoms during its long season of bloom, from June well into August. It's also by any reckoning a weed, for it's a lusty grower, springing up of its own accord along roadsides and in dry and barren fields everywhere in the United States from New England to Texas and westward to Arizona and North Dakota. If road crews mow it down in early summer, it regenerates as easily as poison ivy, quickly returning to bloom, as if nothing at all had happened to discourage it.

But for such a sturdy weed, it is also uncommonly polite. I don't know why, but it has never once appeared in any of the gardens I have had, although they've all had their dry and barren spots, the conditions it seems to prefer. And if it did show up in my yard, I'd probably let it stay, even though I'm not especially fond of orange-colored flowers. It has some sub-stantial virtues. Low-growing, seldom reaching two feet tall, it needs no staking. It has a graceful habit of growth, and when not in bloom, its foliage is attractive. Insects, as far as I can tell, leave it alone, except for bees and butterflies, of course. And it makes a fetching cut flower, long-lasting and lovely when ar-ranged loosely and informally in a wide pitcher or vase. It grows abundantly in a vacant lot by a grocery store in my neigh-borhood, a field where wild golden coreopsis also flourishes and where sea gulls congregate when an ocean storm is on its way, squawking nervously among themselves. Several times each summer I visit the field, gather an armload of butterfly weed, and bring it home.

I have heard that a yellow variant is sometimes found, and now I see that someone has taken it in hand and gussied it up a bit to make it more suitable for garden use. Carl Wyatt, the same Missouri hybridizer whose American iris caused such a stir, has just introduced, through Park's, a mixed strain of *A. tuberosa* called Gay Butterflies. In addition to the usual orange (which could be weeded out by those who don't like it), this strain comes in yellow, gold, pink, and deep scarlet. Since butterfly weed is an extremely reliable and sturdy perennial in most parts of the country, Gay Butterflies seems well worth a try, especially by gardeners who live where the soil is sandy and summer droughts are frequent.

The Glories of Hibiscus

Let's say that some kindly genie who specializes in granting the wishes of gardeners appears in a sudden puff of smoke and offers to rearrange nature more to my taste. Despite the fact that I live in the Northeast, where there are four definite seasons, including a winter whose gruff and chilly winds freeze the earth as hard as a bill collector's heart, my genie is capable and accommodating. He tells me I can pick one species of tender tropical plant, and he'll do what's needed to make it as hardy as a hemlock.

Bougainvillea, frangipani, and poinciana would all be tempting. I'd give some strong consideration to various of the heliconias, especially the lobster claw heliconia, whose huge red blossoms somehow suggest that it evolved on Mars. But my final choice would be unhesitating—*Hibiscus rosa-sinensis*, the Chinese hibiscus. It is one of the glories of the tropics and of the subtropical regions of the United States.

This hibiscus is a member of the family of flowering plants that botanists call the malvaceae. The malvaceae make up a large and useful tribe of some considerable economic importance, yielding dyes, fibers, foodstuffs, and gums. Cotton and okra are both malvaceae. So are hollyhocks and swamp mallows (from which, once upon a time, marshmallows were made).

But as far as I know, no one can eat the Chinese hibiscus, or spin with it, or do anything else of a practical nature. Its merit lies solely in its beauty, and that's enough, for it's an exceedingly handsome thing.

Of all tropical plants, the hibiscus is decidedly the most sensuous. Paul Gauguin could easily have collaborated in its creation. Everything about its blossoms, which are immense, is assertive. Sometimes they lie flat, but often they are strongly reflexed, bending backward, away from the dramatic, protuberant, slightly curved style at the center of the flower. (The hibiscus, I think, is not a plant for prudes.)

The rich palette of color in hibiscus beggars description. There are bold reds (some with a black sheen), glowing pinks and lavenders, pale lemon-yellows, and deep golden-apricots. Some flowers are selfs, meaning that they are more or less restricted to one shade, but others are blends of several colors, sometimes subtle, sometimes as brassy and overstated as an Arizona sunset. Often frilled and ruffled, the blossoms of hibiscus can be marked with blotches of contrasting colors, including a startling brownish-purple I've seen in no other flower.

I can think of only two faults in hibiscus. First, they are singularly lacking in fragrance. Second, the flowers last only a day. I don't take these complaints very seriously. What the flowers lack in fragrance, they more than make up for in dazzling color and in their sheerly opulent texture, which exceeds even that of the peony and the Oriental poppy. And the plants bloom so prolifically at their peak that it hardly matters that yesterday's blossoms are gone today, since new ones take their place. Furthermore, a hibiscus blossom can be picked early in the morning and brought inside, where it will last until evening without being put in water.

But I don't really need a genie. Despite winter, I have hibiscus, and they're quite glorious things. There are two reds, one bluish-pink blend that I call Baboon for reasons my wife says are vulgar, and a double apricot that I may give away, since I really prefer the single kind.

My four hibiscus live outside on the deck, which gets full sun most of the day, from mid-spring until fall. The rest of the year they serve as house plants—although, it must be said, very large house plants. "House shrubs" would be a more likely term, for I keep them about five feet high most of the year.

In the fall, they are brought inside, after first being placed in a sheltered location to allow the soil in their redwood tubs to dry out and reduce their weight for their difficult trip around to the front door and up the stairs to their winter location. They spend the winter in a cool bedroom (50 degrees F. at night, 60 degrees during the day) in front of large windows with an eastern exposure. Even though they are given a rest period (light watering only and no fertilizer), they will produce occasional winter buds, which should be pinched off for larger and more profuse summer bloom.

In mid-February the hibiscus are pruned according to a two-year sequence. One year they are pruned back very hard, leaving only two feet of woody stem and also removing the lower third of the root ball so that the soil can be renewed at the bottom of the tubs. The next year they are pruned more lightly. In March, they are watered thoroughly and frequently and fertilized with a 20–20–20 solution containing iron and trace elements. They go outside as soon as danger of frost is past— late April, where I live—and it is important to put them outside before the weather turns hot, in order to prevent leaf drop. Generally they stay in prolific bloom from June till October.

Hibiscus aren't commonly thought of as suitable house plants, and indeed they wouldn't be much good on a cramped windowsill in an overheated apartment. They're difficult to find in the colder parts of the country, but most people know someone who goes to California or Hawaii and who might be persuaded to stop off at a nursery specializing in tropical plants and bring back rooted cuttings of Chinese hibiscus.

All that's left then is to await the first bloom and the twice-yearly anxiety about getting the hibiscus in and out of the house at just the right time.

I should add, perhaps, some word to the effect that it's possible to have hibiscus without twice-yearly anxiety. *H. rosa-sinensis*, of which I have been speaking, is a woody shrub or small tree, most easily identified by its deep-green foliage, so glossy that it looks as if it's been varnished. It can survive temperatures that briefly move just below the freezing point, but only if it's in a protected spot or it's been wrapped or sprinkled with mist. There are, however, hybrids of several deciduous American species—*H. moscheutos* and others—that are completely winter hardy. They die back to the ground each winter, appear so late in the spring that most gardeners will have concluded that they were killed, burst into rapid vegetative growth when the weather turns hot, and bloom spectacularly for several weeks in late summer and early fall. Their foliage is dull, not glossy, and to my eye at least their huge blossoms—as much as a foot across—are crude. I grow a few, tucked away in a corner of the garden, but I have so modest an affection for them that I seldom pay them a visit. They just don't stack up against their charming Oriental kin.

Modern Daylilies

I would certainly hate to be told by some horticultural Big Brother, now that 1984 is upon us, that from now on I could either grow only one kind of perennial in my garden or expect an official midnight visit. But if I were forced to so painful a decision, my choice would require no deep soul-searching. I would settle immediately and unhesitatingly on modern daylilies, whose history is one of the great success stories of twentieth-century American horticulture.

Today's daylilies owe their existence to plant explorers working in Asia in the nineteenth century, who brought to American botanical gardens some sixteen species of hemerocallis, such as *H. thunbergii* from Japan and *H. multiflora* from China. (*H. fulva*, the tawny daylily so common in roadside ditches in this country, arrived much earlier. A remarkably sturdy and not especially attractive plant, its phenomenal spread across the land is all the more unusual in that it is sterile, propagating itself entirely by the aggressive stolons it puts out to form immense colonies.) The original species were fairly homely things scorned by discriminating gardeners for some obvious faults: narrow petals, insubstantial blooms that often turned to mush by midafternoon, unimpressive branching, and a color range restricted to yellow and hot or muddy orange. But their genes were extraordinarily rich in future surprises, and the ease with which they can be bred makes them the rabbits of the vegetable kingdom. Unlike some other plants that have attracted the attention of hybridizers, such as rhododendrons and peonies, they generally bloom from seed in two years. Furthermore, thousands of daylily fanciers have turned their hands to hybridizing. As a result of this collective effort, progress in their improvement has been rapid and dramatic.

I'm often far from sure that hybridizers should always be praised for the clever things they come up with, such as the inedible tomato and the rose that has no more fragrance than a piece of aluminum foil. They have developed pumpkins that can reach 225 pounds, without ever stopping to ask the pertinent question: *Why*, for heaven's sake? But in the case of the daylily, the hybridizers have produced a varied race of ornamental perennials of unsurpassed garden value.

The acknowledged hero of the daylily saga is Dr. A. B. Stout, whose name annually commemorates the best daylily of the year, as determined by the judges of the American Hemerocallis Society, a group of people who feel about daylilies much the same way that Romeo felt about Juliet. In the 1920s Dr. Stout built up a complete collection of daylily species at the New York Botanical Garden and began to hybridize them, offering his stocks to other interested breeders. A large number of later hybridizers followed in his footsteps, such as Elizabeth Nesmith, Peter J. Fass, Elmer Claar, and Edna Spaulding. New colors and forms rapidly began to appear. Then, in the 1950s, the day of the tetraploid began. (The earliest daylily hybrids were all diploids, meaning that they had a mere two sets of chromosomes. Tetraploids have four, thanks to a chemical trick played on them. In' the most usual technique for introducing tetraploidy, thousands of ordinary diploid seeds are washed with a solution of colchicine, a highly toxic and carcinogenic alkaloid derived from meadow saffron, or *Colchicum autumnale*, just as they are germinating. Most of the seedlings die. Some of the survivors remain diploids. But a few end up with an extra set of chromosomes, a trait they pass on to their own progeny.) Important breeders of tetraploids include Virginia Peck, Robert Griesbach, Hamilton Traub, and James Marsh. There is some debate among serious daylily people today about the virtues of diploids over tetraploids, but there was a time a few years back when daylily nuts like myself wouldn't even consider buying any daylily whose ancestors hadn't had their chromosomes successfully assaulted by colchicine. Some people claim that most tets look coarse and tend to cook in the afternoon sun; others claim that the extra set of chromosomes gives breeders more to work with in laying the groundwork for future surprises. I've decided to be a fence-sitter, to evaluate each daylily on its own merits, leaving others to worry about the number of chromosomes, if they so wish.

The virtues of daylilies are many and solid. They rapidly form sturdy clumps whose foliage discourages weeds and remains attractive all during the growing season. The existence of early, mid-season, and late varieties assures a succession of bloom from late May to late August. Some cultivars even bloom twice, with a resting period in between. A few, such as an admirable dwarf with miniature gold blossoms called Stella D'Oro, bloom continuously for two to three months. Some, the so-called evergreen sorts, which retain their leaves where the winters are mild, are especially suited to the Deep South; others, which die back entirely in the autumn, thrive best where the winters are tinged with ferocity. Except for thrips and a mysterious malady called spring sickness, which some people have compared to a hangover in that it seems much worse than it really is, daylilies are remarkably free of serious diseases and insects usually shun them, which is a bit odd, considering that most parts of the daylily are edible and have an honored place in Oriental cookery. (*Wyman's Gardening Encyclopedia* points out that *Gumtsoy*, the dried and pressed blossoms, are used by the Chinese to thicken soups. This encyclopedia also recommends deep-fried daylily buds in batter as a "tasty tidbit," and tells us that the first leaves in spring can be cooked and eaten in place of asparagus and that the underground tubers are notable for their "sweet nutlike flavor." I confess never having moved beyond daylily raising into daylily eating, and I haven't tried out the recipe I have for pickling daylily buds, which calls for one quart of them to be boiled with a cup of cider vinegar, a half cup of water, and small amounts of garlic, dill, salt, pepper, and mustard seed.)

The color range of the modern daylily is extremely wide. There aren't any blue ones or whites, but otherwise there's much to choose from—dark velvety reds, pale creams, clear pastel pinks, rich purples, a full complement of yellows and golds, as well as multicolors and blends and flowers with sharply contrasting eye zones. The blossoms of some daylilies can be immense. Six to eight inches across isn't uncommon, and I've seen reports, which I don't quite believe, that something named Yazoo Delta can reach a foot across. There are also miniature sorts—such as Lona Eaton Miller and Tinker Bell—which call it quits at one-inch flowers. Some daylilies are low-growing, and others have stalks that tower upwards of four feet, although most daylily fanciers prefer an intermediate height. It is possible to have a garden composed entirely of daylilies. Some people— the fully smitten—do. Others—the almost fully smitten—will raise other things as well, such as phlox and delphiniums and gypsophila, but the tip-off to the nature of their affections is that they call these "companion plants" and use them primarily as a foil for their daylilies.

But a major problem faces the gardener who wants to try modern daylilies and isn't lucky enough to have a daylily fanatic living next door: finding a good source. Almost all the large mail-order houses that sell daylilies are far behind the times. Some still tout a cultivar called Hyperion, a rather insubstantial light yellow long surpassed. Lately both White Flower Farm and Wayside Gardens have been offering some excellent recent hybrids, including tetraploids, but I find the prices way too high (although understandably so: the customer, after all, is paying for a full-color picture as well as a plant). I would suggest that in looking for up-to-date varieties, the gardener who wants to discover what's happened to the daylily since Hyperion really did rule the roost must turn to one of the smaller firms that specialize in daylilies, such as Tranquil Lake Nursery in Rehoboth, Massachusetts, to which I sometimes resort when I'm in a mood to add a daylily or two to my collection, since I have found the prices reasonable, the plants sturdy and healthy, and the catalog discriminating.

A daylily catalog, however, can be bewildering. The last time I checked, there were over 22,000 named cultivars registered with the A.H.S. Many of these, of course, have disappeared long ago, and by far the greater number probably weren't worth naming to start with. But it is undeniably intimidating for a novice to confront a list of hundreds of daylilies and wonder which to choose and how. Furthermore, it's startling to discover that some sell for $50 apiece or more. But Charles Trommer, a textile chemist who raises six acres of daylilies at Tranquil Lake

Nursery as an avocation, points out that price is a function of newness and scarcity, not an indication of quality.

"There's no reason whatsoever that most gardeners should go out and spend $50 on a daylily," he says, "unless they are hybridizers or serious addicts. As stocks build up by propagation, prices drop steeply. Last year Pride's Crossing, which I regard with the utmost admiration as being one of the finest daylilies yet, went at $50. This year it's $35. Before long it will be down to $3, just like Mary Todd, a yellow I highly recommend, or to $2, like a great many of the daylilies on my list."

But probably the best way to select daylilies is to go someplace where a lot of them are growing and blooming at the same time, and take down the names of those that speak to your heart, something daylilies have a way of doing. (Not long ago, I was easily seduced by a real sexpot with the unlikely name of Ancient Trail, an immense gold with a white margin around the petals.) The A.H.S. sponsors display gardens in several locations around the country, and most daylily nurseries don't mind visitors during the blooming season. Ancient Trail and I had our little rendezvous at André Viette's Farm and Nursery in Fishersville, Virginia, which is open to the public six days a week from mid-April to late September.

Daylilies are dangerous, however, and absolutely addicting, except to the occasional gardener with a will of steel and a heart of carborundum. Someone gave me one once and I was trapped. It's been my experience that most of the friends to whom I give a few come sidling up the next year to ask for more, perhaps even to get the address of the American Hemerocallis Society so they can sign up. If they do, they're probably doomed for life. The addiction may go into remission, but it never goes away.

Little Ado about Roses

My Grandmother Lacy used to say that no one could be considered a gardener who didn't grow roses, by which she meant hybrid teas, raised in formal, rectangular beds devoted solely to them, all neatly manicured and tended almost daily. Of course, she had the services of an almost-full-time gardener to do the manicuring and the tending. (The total absence of any such help in my own garden I take to be a grave symptom of downward economic mobility.) But she stopped growing roses in her garden in Dallas sometime around 1954, devoting herself instead to a crowd of azaleas in the spring and countless caladiums in the summer. Three decades later, she still doesn't grow roses. She also still considers herself, at ninety-three, a gardener. The lesson is clear—gardeners don't really have to grow roses if they, like Bartleby the Scrivener, prefer not.

I find that a relief and I shall be mercifully brief on the subject of roses. With one exception, which I shall get around to soon, I can't say that I grow roses. Roses grow in my garden, but that's a different kettle of fish emulsion. There's a vigorous and vigorously despised hedge of *Rosa multiflora*—which really ought to be called *R. horribilis*—that I mean to rip out one day and replace with something else. (I'd love to have a serpentine brick wall of the sort that Thomas Jefferson designed to keep students at the University of Virginia from stealing apples and cabbages from the gardens behind the faculty houses on campus, but bricks and bricklayers are expensive nowadays, and besides, I suspect my town fathers would frown on such a thing. I'll probably end up settling for a loose hedge of one of the larger cotoneasters, maybe *C. divaricata*, which I can easily grow from cuttings taken from a specimen I already grow. Or maybe I'll steal an idea from Rosalind Creasy's *Edible Landscaping* and replace the roses with a double file of blueberries, so I can munch my way up and down the hedgerow in June and July.) There are also two roses on either side of the front porch, whose names I have forgotten, an easy trick, since neither could be described as memorable under my care. One is pink, the other yellow. Each produces every year a single spindly cane, four blossoms, and a thousand aphids. The pink one is a constant disappointment to an adjacent white clematis, which would like to have something more reliable to climb in its ambition to reach the top of the porch.

As I wander about the front yard, I remember several spots where I planted some floribundas and hybrid teas ("plant box and all"). Nothing remains, and the boxes outlasted the rosebushes. At one corner of the property there's a plucky, amazingly sturdy Climbing Peace, much hated by the schoolchildren who must pass it each weekday morning and risk its thorns—unless, as they often do, they cut through my flower beds instead, increasing annually my misopaedia. Out back, in a neglected flower bed, there's a single Red Radiance, an old-fashioned rose that was planted by some previous tenant. It's lusty and thriving, but I take no credit for its success.

I don't plant box and all anymore. I can pass up the great numbers of boxed roses at the garden center in the spring without even glancing in their direction. I will leave roses to others, like my friend Royce Burton, who grows them beautifully in his nearby back yard and who looks forward to growing them even more beautifully a couple of years from now when he retires and moves to East Texas, a paradise for everyone who loves roses. To him I gladly leave all the feeding and mulching and dead-heading and disbudding and pruning and spraying and general fretting that's required of those who spend a considerable portion of their waking life in service to the rose.

Roses, to put it plainly, are too much trouble. This principle has a corollary: In every gardener's life there's room for a little laziness. Roses, to repeat and underline the point, are too much trouble.

True, I was almost convinced otherwise recently by a very

pleasant and ingratiating book by Roland A. Browne, called *The Rose-Lover's Guide: A Practical Handbook on Rose Growing*. Browne obviously loves roses, and he writes seductively on their behalf, arguing that the universality with which they are grown and admired worldwide suggests that they're not really at all difficult to raise, if only their particular needs and requirements are met.

I said almost convinced. I part company with Mr. Browne when I open the *Reader's Digest Illustrated Guide to Gardening*, a handy and forthright practical reference book, and read what it says about roses. It has a whole section entitled "What Can Go Wrong with Roses." It seems that eighteen separate things can go wrong, some of them simultaneously. These problems range from aphids to starvation. In between are such disasters as mottling, mildew, blasted buds and distorted flowers, Japanese beetles, off-color leaves—a long recital of possible woes. The names of their remedies are Diazinon, carbaryl, tetradifon, Captan, dodine, maneb, zineb, methoxychlor, nicotine sulfate, malathion, dinosept, Bacticin, Benomyl, and more. I don't like the sounds of the remedies. Impeccable logic tells me that I won't need the remedies if I don't have to treat the eighteen things that can go wrong with roses. So I don't grow roses. *Q.E.D.*

Now for that exception: I do grow rugosa roses (so named for their rugose or wrinkled leaves), two of them. A number of years ago, back when I was still planting boxes and all, I put in one plant of Max Graf, a hybrid whose parentage is probably *R. rugosa* x *R. wichuriana*. It's a low-grower for me, only two feet tall, and it's very much a wanderer, sending up its formidable, spiny canes everywhere along a seven-foot stretch of sidewalk. From late May to the middle of June, it's smothered in beautiful single blossoms of clear pink.

And out back there's another sturdy rugosa, a cultivar called Blanc Double de Couvert, which goes way back into the nineteenth century. I found it growing on a hillside at Weston Nurseries in Massachusetts three years ago and knew I had to have it. A mature specimen is a huge, spreading mass, five or six feet high and perhaps eight feet across, entirely covered with pure-white double flowers with a delightful fragrance too many roses these days utterly lack. I nursed it along for a couple of years, making sure that it didn't get clipped or bruised by the lawnmower, and now it has begun to exercise dominion over its corner of the garden, sending up sturdy new canes all around it. It blooms but intermittently after its first tide of blossoms in late spring, but it and Max Graf are both beauties. (And both form attractive large red hips in the late summer, which I leave for the birds, although I've heard they make a good jam.) Both my rugosas are also toughies. I haven't had the slightest need to get out the tetradifon.

A Damnable Vine's
Sweet Ambrosia

Few people plant it on purpose, but it grows so lasciviously almost everywhere in the United States that it appears to be as authentically American as New England asters, prickly pears, or poison ivy. But appearances are deceiving. Along with the tiger lily and the golden-flowered shrub he named *Kerria* for himself, William Kerr, a plant collector in the service of Sir Joseph Banks of Kew Gardens, brought it from China to England sometime after 1804.

He found it growing under cultivation just outside Canton at a fabled nursery which also gave Western gardeners invaluable species of azalea, chrysanthemum, camellia, and peony. Its botanical name is *Lonicera japonica,* and it belongs to a genus of more than sixty species of woody vines and shrubs, many of ornamental value, which are distributed throughout the Northern Hemisphere.

There's not a forester in this country who doesn't wish that William Kerr had taken one look at *L. japonica,* curled his lips in scorn, and left it behind in Canton instead of helping it migrate to the West. It's a terrible nuisance and a damaging one. I don't know in what American garden it first grew, but I do know that it soon escaped its confines to become one of our most invasive plants. Birds are extremely fond of its small black berries and spread it far and wide in their droppings. Given the slightest foothold, it can take over everything within its considerable reach.

Hortus Third, one of the most authoritative of all botanical reference books, is usually dispassionate and nonjudgmental in describing plants, but it minces no words with *L. japonica,* calling it "a serious woodland weed in the Middle Atlantic states," thanks to its peculiar habit of growth. In forests it trails thickly across the ground, forming new roots in the rich leaf mold as it goes. When it encounters a tree trunk, it climbs, spiraling upward in a clockwise direction until it reaches the bright sunlight above the forest canopy, when it begins to spread profusely. Its greedy habits make it a menace, for as its woody stems thicken, they girdle the tree that gave it access to the abundant light above the forest, eventually strangling it, which is no way to treat a host. Chemical warfare and hand-to-hand combat with shears and shovels seldom daunt it.

A damnable vine. A menace. A nuisance. A serious weed.

And yet I love this damnable vine with an affection I cannot manage for other weeds like crabgrass and chickweed and purslane, weeds in which I can find no redeeming social value whatsoever. *L. japonica,* you see, is also known as honeysuckle—a mellifluous word, a sweet fragrance on the night air, and a delicious experience for all small children who know the magical thing they can do with a cluster of ivory and white and creamy-yellow honeysuckle blossoms on a summer morning.

The trick is simple, but it requires concentration. Pinch off the green receptacle and ovary at the base of the long, trumpet-shaped flower, grasp the bottom of the pistil firmly between thumb and forefinger, and slowly pull it down through the tubular blossom until it emerges with a tiny, glistening drop of clear nectar to sip. And then another blossom, and another, each giving its perfume to the tip of the tongue. A child with a sufficient store of fresh honeysuckle blossoms becomes kin to the gods who feed on ambrosia, kin to the bee, the hummingbird, the lunar moth, to all the creatures of the air who pay their visits to this sweetest of all "serious weeds."

Even without sipping, children—and some grownups, too—find the mere scent of honeysuckle enough to make them happy, to glow with a sense of well-being and of belonging to the world. It's even better when it mingles with the other delicious and unmistakable odors of summer, with the scents of melting road tar, of new-mown grass, of mimosa trees nearby, of dusty roads after a sudden and brief shower of rain.

When my sons were very small, I took them aside to teach

them the magical thing they could do with a cluster of honeysuckle flowers. They already knew. They may have been self-taught in the matter. Children seem to learn some important things by themselves, with no formal instruction. I'm not even sure that anyone taught me this magic. I simply remember being three years old and standing by a dilapidated wooden fence covered with vines as I stole honeysuckle nectar drop by tiny drop from a handful of blossoms. That was a long time ago. By now I've acquired most of the bad habits of middle age. But when no one is there to see, I still know precisely what to do with a cluster of honeysuckle flowers.

A Flower Plucked
from the Devil's Kitchen

One August afternoon a neighbor from down the block asked me
to drop by to see some unusual plants growing behind her garage.
She said she'd never seen them listed in seed catalogs and didn't
know why they weren't, considering how handsome they were.
She had first grown them from seeds an aunt of hers had given
her many years ago, and ever since then she had saved the seeds
from one year to the next. She called them "moon lilies" and
promised to give me some seed if I liked them well enough to
try them.

They weren't lilies at all, and as soon as I saw them I knew
why they aren't generally listed in seed catalogs. But they were
unquestionably very handsome things, about three feet tall, with
soft and velvety grayish-green leaves. Each plant bore six or
more lovely, upward-facing flowers, huge white trumpets with
green throats and a faint blue cast to the petals, whose edges
flared out into odd little crescent-shaped hooks, giving each
blossom a pinwheel effect. They had a faint and musky fragrance,
something like that of a petunia, but bordering on being unpleasant.

I recognized them immediately from my childhood. One of my
grandmothers called them "angel trumpets," and grew them
along an alley fence. They are one species—which, I'm not exactly sure—in the botanical genus called *Datura*, and thus members of the solanum or nightshade family, which also includes
tobacco, potatoes, and tomatoes.

A Flower Plucked from the Devil's Kitchen

Although some daturas are homely, many species are among the most beautiful and striking ornamental plants on earth. One sort, which grows everywhere in the tropics and which botanists tell us we really ought to call *Brugmansia* rather than *Datura*, grows as small trees that can produce hundreds of blossoms at a time during their intermittent seasons of bloom throughout the year.

The blossoms of these tropical species face downward, like hanging bells. Their most usual color is creamy white, but there are attractive variations, including a clear pink and a subtle shade of melon-apricot. At night, the flowers become more strongly perfumed, giving them the name they sometimes have in Latin America—"La Reina de la Noche," Queen of the Night.

I admired my neighbor's daturas and told her so, for they brought a fine tropical touch to a garden in New Jersey. I also told her that since she had grandchildren who might be tempted to pick the blossoms or to collect the large, sharply spoked seed pods in the fall, which look a bit like hand grenades and seem just the thing to attract a child's curiosity, she should immediately root these plants out, destroy them, and relentlessly hoe up any seedlings that might come along later.

The fact is that in addition to being utterly beautiful, some species at least, daturas are extremely dangerous and often deadly plants to have around, as some British soldiers found out in the spring of 1676 in Virginia when they picked the first green shoots of a plant that looked succulent and appetizing and then made them into a "sallat." They got a bit more than a salad. Some thirty years later, a historian of Virginia wrote that they had hardly finished their meal when they

turn'd natural fools . . . for several days. One would blow up a Feather in the Air; another would dart Straws at it with much Fury; and another stark naked was sitting up in a Corner, like a Monkey, grinning and making Mows at them; a Fourth would fondly kiss, and paw his Companions, and snear in their Faces, with a Countenance more antick, than any in a Dutch Droll. In this Frantick condition they were confined, lest they should in their Folly destroy themselves; though it was observed, that all their Actions were full of Innocence and good Nature. Indeed, they were not very cleanly; for they would have wallow'd in their own Excrements, if they had not been prevented. A Thousand such simple Tricks they play'd, and after Eleven Days, return'd to themselves again, not remembering anything that had pass'd.

The scene was Jamestown, and what the soldiers had in-gested was *Datura stramonium,* a species with unattractive flowers and an odor that has given it part of one of its common names—"raving stinkweed." This episode in American history gave the plant another common name, "Jamestown weed," which was in time corrupted to "jimsonweed." Like all daturas, every part of the jimsonweed contains extremely potent and potentially lethal toxic alkaloids such as atropine, hyoscine, and hyoscyamine.

As Amos G. Avery pointed out in the first chapter of the standard scientific work on this genus, *Blakeslee: The Genus Datura,* the history of the daturas is long and often grim. Among the Arabs of the eleventh century it was used in tiny doses as a hallucinogen and in larger ones as a poison. The Aztecs, who called it "ololiuhqui" (magic plant), regarded it as sacred, and used it to communicate with the spirit world. The Indians of western South America gave it "in large doses with tobacco to women and slaves to deaden their senses before burial alive with their dead husbands or masters," according to Professor Avery.

And Berton Roueché tells in his fascinating book *The Medical Detectives* the tale of a man in eastern Tennessee who had the bright idea of grafting a tomato plant onto the rootstock of jimsonweed, thinking that it might enable him to have tomatoes before any of his neighbors. The experiment was in part a suc-cess, in that he produced some phenomenally early and very juicy tomatoes. But he and his family came close to perishing after eating just one fruit, unusually delicious but also loaded with toxic alkaloids.

Datura has its uses, of course, besides turning soldiers into natural fools and inducing people to let themselves be buried alive. Chemists and pharmacologists have found its alkaloids worthy of close study. But it's not a good plant for the home gardener. The angel's trumpet was concocted in the devil's kitch-en. It is a good reminder of a truth as ancient as Eden: There are some lovely and appealing things we owe it to ourselves to leave strictly alone.

The Considerable Virtues
of Alstroemerias

Despite their dandy virtues as winter cut flowers, alstroemerias aren't nearly as widely known in this country as they deserve to be. Maybe it's their formidable name, which sounds as if it might refer to some dread disease of the gastrointestinal tract, that's earned them so much neglect.

Also called Inca lilies and Peruvian lilies, although like agapanthus and clivia (blue lily of the Nile and Kaffir lily) they're not lilies at all but members of the amaryllis family, these sightly natives of South America appeared in Spanish gardens soon after the conquest of the New World, as missionary priests brought them and many other beautiful or useful plants back home with them. In the eighteenth century Claes Alströmer, a Swedish naturalist noted mainly for his deep interest in the principles of sheep breeding, spotted them blooming in a courtyard in Cádiz. He sent a few seeds to his countryman, the famous botanist Carolus Linnaeus, who repaid him in the coin of horticultural immotality by naming the genus *Alstroemeria*, which *Wyman's Gardening Encyclopedia* informs me should be pronounced "al-stree-MEER-ia."

Alstroemerias are new to me. I'd never heard of them until one recent November day when my wife threw out the last withered remains of the chrysanthemums she'd picked from the garden ten days previous and asked me to get some flowers from Granny's Greenery, our neighborhood flower shop, which despite its name is run by a burly young fellow named Ed.

I had gerberas in mind, or maybe freesias, but a wedding had just cleaned Ed out of both. Nothing in his display case offered the faintest temptation. Chrysanthemums from a florist shop, in or out of season, are as boring as mud. Carnations bring to mind a date I had in high school who once ate her corsage, ribbon and all. Roses, considering what they cost, give up the ghost far too soon.

I asked Ed if he didn't have something else in his back-room cooler—something a bit unusual.

He returned with a bucket of bright crimson anthuriums, a flower that I have always considerd a shocking lapse in good taste on the part of evolution. All garish and glossy, anthuriums have an artificial and nonbiodegradable look to them, as if they had been extruded from heavy vinyl. Unmistakably phallic, they don't really belong in a good family flower shop named for someone's grandmother.

Back went the anthuriums and out came another bucket, this one filled with the first alstroemerias I'd ever seen—entirely admirable things, with long stems like those of tiger lilies, each one bearing a loose and graceful cluster of ten or more blossoms and buds. The blooms, creamy pink with glowing yellow throats and attractive stipples of dark maroon and light green on their petals, much resembled azalea flowers. The fat buds, like tiny balloons, were the color of crushed raspberries.

Alstroemerias, I could see, were paragons of elegance and also, at $1.25 a stem, a great bargain. When I took them home, just three stems filled a vase very nicely, in a pretty, informal arrangement that lasted almost eleven days. The leaves went a bit sallow toward the end, but the flowers were persistent and new buds kept opening.

Soon I was back at the flower shop to get more alstroemerias and to pester Ed for whatever information he could give me about them. I learned that there are other colors, including a burgundy-red and a clear lilac-pink. I also found out that these days alstroemerias are real gadabouts, floral members of what used to be called the jet set, before everybody's Aunt Gertrude and Cousin Billie Sue took to the skies and People Express came along.

Raised from seed in Portugal, they are shipped as small plants to greenhouses in the Netherlands, where growers adore them because they can be kept on the cool side to save energy costs. Six months later, when the first buds show signs of opening, they are harvested and rushed to auction. Those destined for retail sale in the United States cross the Atlantic by jet transport, in an operation so swift and well oiled that the blooms I buy on Tuesday were probably growing under glass in the Dutch town of Aalsmeer the previous Saturday. (The same thing, incidentally, is true of gerberas, freesias, white lilacs, and many other cut flowers American florists sell in the winter. The patrons of florist shops in the largest American cities have enjoyed these imported blossoms for over a decade, but these days the Dutch have penetrated our hinterlands, including my hometown.)

Now I've got in mind trying to raise some of these things out in my own garden. I've tracked down two sources of seed. Park's offers one species, *A. aurantiaca* (which sounds a bit too torrid-looking: "great sheaves of golden orange"), and a strain called Dr. Salter's Mixed Hybrids (which sounds better: "color from salmon-pink, cerise, flame, to deep red"). Thompson & Morgan offers the same two, except that it's Dr. Souter instead of Salter, and it also sells the Ligtu Hybrid strain and a whiskered one it warns to be of questionable hardiness.

Cultural information about raising these perennials under American conditions is scanty and confused. *Wyman's* claims that they are hardy only in the South and that Northern gardeners should lift and store their roots over the winter. But the Park catalog states that the two sorts it offers are reliably winter hardy as far north as Philadelphia. The British garden books I own recommend putting alstroemerias in a very dry and sunny location, and utter stern imprecations against trying to transplant them or otherwise disturbing their roots. I'm puzzled by the conflict between *Wyman's* and the British experts about disturbing their roots.

As for the British recommendation to grow them dry and sunny, I suspect this is merely one of many pieces of horticultural advice that works well in the English damp but is a recipe for catastrophe in America, except for gardeners in the Pacific Northwest. When I get around to trying them, my alstroemerias are going to get some light shade and moisture against those blistering summer days when the road tar melts.

Meanwhile, there's always winter—and the alstroemerias at Granny's Greenery.

A Paean to
the Fussy Oriental Lily

From early summer onward, there's a steady, predictable, and entirely satisfying parade of hybrid lilies in my garden. In June the easy and reliable Asiatic hybrids arrive, such as Enchantment and Harlequin and Parfait, all fairly carefree plants, seldom exceeding three feet in height, whose wide range of both bright and pastel colors combines well with white Shasta daisies and blue Connecticut Yankee delphiniums in the perennial border.

In July the Asiatic hybrids give way to the taller, more assertive Aurelian hybrids like Black Dragon, Moonlight, and Pink Perfection. Often reaching six feet, and much benefited by staking, they add a touch of drama and accent to the border just when it can stand some—and take my mind off the remarkable success the crabgrass is usually having by that time of year.

But in late summer the truly glorious climax of the lily parade arrives. The Oriental hybrids come into bloom, and nothing I know can match them. They are as intricate as a Persian carpet, as improbable in form as a Gaudí cathedral, as lavish and bold in color as an Henri Rousseau painting.

The Oriental hybrids owe their spectacular color to two equally spectacular Japanese species, *Lilium auratum* and *L. speciosum*, which were extensively collected in the wild earlier in this century and exported to Europe and North America, where they often failed badly because of virus disease and the weakening of the bulbs during their long voyage. (Unlike daffodils and tulips, lily bulbs never go entirely dormant. It is essential that they suffer no dehydration, that they remain out of the ground only briefly, and that they be replanted with healthy roots still attached beneath the loose cluster of scales making up the bulb.)

Working with these and other Japanese species, a number of American hybridizers, most notably Jan de Graaff, have produced a great many varieties, such as Empress of Japan, Imperial Gold, and Crimson Beauty. I have no favorites; I grow some fifteen sorts, chosen for a succession of bloom from early August to mid-September, and it is impossible to choose among them. I love them all, so much so that as each one starts to open I snatch it inside. They are cut flowers par excellence. A single blossom in a bud vase is enough to brighten a room. A cluster of three or four (on a stem cut as short as possible, to keep from robbing the bulb of the photosynthesis it needs to bloom next year) is awesome.

The Oriental hybrids may have flat, saucer-like flowers, or bowl-shaped ones, or recurved and swept-back ones, depending on the particular kind. The waxy, long-lasting petals are often translucent and suffused with an uncanny glow when strongly backlit from a sunny window. The edges of the petals, often white and contrasting with the deep colors at their center, may be twisted and fluted. Many of these hybrids are oddly spotted with deep purple and russet. Usually the blossoms have green, star-shaped nectaries radiating out from their centers, guarded by strange tufts of what I can only call "lily hair." All of them are intensely fragrant, especially at night. Even if unseen, these lilies immediately announce their presence to anyone who enters a room where they are, for there is nothing the least bit subtle or shy about their heavy aroma—a sweet and delicious odor tinged with the scent of cloves and somehow tropical in character.

I can think of only two things to say against the Oriental hybrids. First, they are a little more expensive than other lilies, averaging $3.50 a bulb. Second, they aren't as foolproof as the earlier Asiatic hybrids. I've never lost a great many Oriental hybrids all at once, but some springs I've been sharply disappointed to discover a blank space where a lily ought to be. (A blank space doesn't necessarily mean that a plant has disappeared; some of these bulbs have restless and nomadic tendencies and a way of springing up a couple of feet from the spot where they grew the previous season, which is an excellent reason not to hoe a lily bed, even if the bulbs were marked with stakes the fall before, until all the lilies come up in the spring that are going to come up.)

Until recently, I attributed the occasional vanishing of a lily or two to some failing on my part—ignorance, perhaps, or a character flaw. My spirits brightened somewhat when I read in Eleanor Perényi's *Green Thoughts: A Writer in the Garden* that in her opinion Oriental hybrids have decidedly fickle ways. She quoted an English writer who called them "the world's most expensive annuals," but went on to console herself that florists charge immense prices for just one blossom and that a bulb that disappears after one year still costs less than four packs of cigarettes and is a far healthier investment.

But I've got a lily-loving friend who insists that the Oriental hybrids aren't fickle at all, just fussier than other lilies. He says that they will thrive perfectly well if their special requirements are met. They should be planted a little more deeply than other lilies (as deep as eight inches in sandy soils), fertilized only in the spring, and kept in a shady location, *never* in full sun. He may be right, for all my failures have been in a flower bed that gets direct sunlight from early morning until late afternoon and really cooks in August. One of these autumns, once the foliage has yellowed, I mean to move them all to another spot, where the light is filtered by some nearby trees.

Oriental hybrid lilies turn the rag end of summer into a feast and a celebration, but acquiring them calls for a bit of caution. All lilies are poor travelers, especially the Orientals. They end the lily season and are thus the last to ripen sufficiently for harvest and shipment to customers. Many of the bulbs imported from Holland—the most likely ones to be found in neighborhood garden centers—are dug prematurely, and their roots are often trimmed to reduce weight and transportation costs. I've had some bad experiences with some mail-order houses dealing in Dutch lilies, paying a stiff price when the lilies bloomed poorly, failed to live, or turned out to be so virus-ridden that I had to dig them up and destroy them to protect my other lilies from infection. I have, on the other hand, the utmost respect for Rex Bulb Farms in Port Townsend, Washington. Their thick, full-color catalog is wonderful winter reading, and they have always shipped me very fresh bulbs, as plump and succulent as artichokes, with the roots still firmly attached.

As I think about Oriental hybrid lilies, I discover only one real problem with them. I don't have enough to satisfy my greedy gardener's heart. But to achieve such satisfaction, I'd have to reckon my garden in acres, not square feet.

An Impulse toward Grass

The Spanish philosopher and novelist Miguel de Unamuno once said that in their thoughts and actions human beings could be divided into two mutually exclusive categories. Some people are viviparous, others are oviparous. The viviparous people are impulsive and full of surprises, even to themselves. Their words and deeds spring into being without forethought or warning, fully born, as it were. Oviparous people, on the other hand, hatch what they mean to do and say long before they do or say it. They are arch planners and worriers. They are easily persuaded to buy life insurance. They keep an eye on their retirement plans when they are still in their twenties. If they haven't eaten octopus before they are seven, they will probably never eat it. I'm pretty sure I belong among the oviparous of this earth, even if I did eat octopus for the first time when I was thirty-six. (I was in Spain, it was fried, and I thought it was onion rings.)

For about four years now, my mind has kept returning to the subject of grass, but it's neither the kind of grass that people smoke nor the kind they mow and try to keep out of the flower beds. The grass I'm thinking about is the kind people put *in* their flower beds—the very few people who have become enlightened enough to realize that a good many grasses are damned handsome things and considerably more elegant than, say, a pink petunia.

The impulse toward raising a little grass hit me on a bright early morning in mid-December as I drove to work. The temperature was down near zero, and a stiff breeze was making the barren branches of willows and alders dance a jig. There had been heavy frost, and as I turned a corner, I passed a clump of tall roadside grasses, waving in the wind and all golden and honey-colored in the sunlight, glistening and diamond-dusted with frost. That afternoon the frost had departed and the wind had died down, but the grass again caught my eye as it stood in its spot at a break in a hedgerow, backlit by the final slanting rays of the setting sun. The thought struck me that that clump of grass had a lot of dignity, somehow, and that it might look really splendid out in our side garden, where we could see it from the window at breakfast. I considered gathering some seed and planting them at home, but ultimately rejected the idea because, being a native to this area, it might turn into a terrible pest.

But I still had grass on my mind, and I began to pay more and more attention to nursery catalogs that list ornamental perennial grasses, such as *Festuca glauca*, Job's tears, and fountain grass. These grasses come in a variety of colors. *F. glauca*, or blue sheep's fescue, is, as the name suggests, deep blue-green. Some of the eulalias, or miscanthuses, are green, but the variety 'Zebrinus' or zebra grass has intermittent golden stripes horizontally across the leaves. And they range in height from eight inches (*F. glauca*) to six feet (*Miscanthus sinensis* 'Giganteus'). I'd never actually seen any ornamental grasses, except for the immense plumed clumps of pampas grass that were so much a landscaping cliché during my childhood in the neighborhoods where I lived that a gaucho would have felt perfectly at home. But the more I read, the better they sounded. They would look fine in the summer for their foliage. They wouldn't mope or scream and stage wilting tantrums if I forgot to water them during a drought. Unlike other perennials, they wouldn't have to be cut down in the fall, and during the winter their dry leaves, tassels, and plumes would add something worth seeing to an otherwise dead garden. The winter wind swishing through them would probably be pleasant to listen to, a reminder of pleasant walks on the beach through dune grass. Their foliage and seed stalks would look good in tall vases inside the house.

I don't know why it took me so long to get around to acquiring some ornamental grasses. Perhaps it's that my lust for buying plants is usually triggered by actually seeing something and deciding that I must have it, rather than by just looking at its picture or reading a description of it in a catalog. Perhaps it's that no one in my neck of the woods has any of these grasses in his garden, and I didn't want to alarm the neighbors by making them think I was taking up pasturing on a suburban lot. Perhaps it was my oviparous nature, the best friend a gardener's bank account has. But recently I saw a fine collection of ornamental grasses, superbly grown, at Longwood Gardens, in Kennett Square, Pennsylvania, and I was hooked. A few weeks later I saw an equally fine collection, all growing in containers, irresistibly ready and handy to be bought and carted home, at a nursery in the country, and I was landed and netted. They're still growing in their containers until I get around to planting them, but I know just what I'll do with them.

I've got one flower bed that hasn't pleased me much in recent years. Triangular, bordered on one side by a hedge, on another by a fence, and on the third by a lawn, it was the first bed I dug when we moved into our house years ago. The best thing it contains is a fair-sized collection of tall, July-blooming Aurelian hybrid lilies, whose stalks rise as if in disdain high above the other perennials and the usual weeds. Except for those lilies, there's nothing there whose presence I would miss. In my mind's eye I see just what I want to have—an underplanting of the low, gray-blue *F. glauca* at the front, with clumps of taller grasses at the rear, and the lilies rising high in July, like Roman candles of color, a brief and sudden festivity in a planting designed to bespeak dignity and restraint the rest of the year.

I also know precisely where I'll put the tallest grasses, the several types of miscanthus—way at the end of another flower bed by the front gate, just across from some bayberry bushes, in a spot that's been devoted to some straggling clumps of veronica that never have amounted to much. The miscanthus will be perfect there, tall and noble, marking the place where my property ends and the street begins.

Onopordums:
Formidable Friends

Of late, I show signs of becoming a curmudgeon, or at least a grump. I get annoyed with computers that ring me up and ask nosy questions about my buying habits. I don't like the plastic mesh bags grocery stores pack grapes in these days. And I'm not at all sure it was a good idea to buy a house on a corner lot, particularly one that lies on the shortest route between an elementary school and a candy store fully equipped with the latest video games. I think of my flower beds as places to grow flowers. A good many kids think they make a fine shortcut to get to school. Apparently they see nothing wrong in stumbling over my chrysanthemums, liatris, and sedums when they're running late, meanwhile scattering candy wrappers and aluminum cola cans in their wake.

When I catch one of the little urchins in the act, I say something grumpy. I seldom get an apology or a vow to cease and desist henceforth and forever from trampling my flowers. Often I get a withering verbal blast that shows how early the schoolchildren of today master the art of obscenity.

Late last spring I tried to put an end to their trespassing and my grumpiness by installing a chain-link fence along one side of the yard to replace an old picket fence that had gone to rot and ruin. I hoped the new fence would keep the little intruders at bay and dramatically reduce the number of empty potato-chip bags that collect in the shrubbery. But the fence wasn't as effective as I had hoped, thanks to town ordinances specifying that the first 15 feet nearest the street be no more than 30 inches high, a height easily vaulted by any fourth-grader who's just heard the school bell ring down the block.

I discussed the weak point in my defenses with the man who installed the fence. He made four suggestions. The first three I rejected instantly. I may be grumpy, but I don't hate children. Barbed wire, electrification of the fence, and a row of sharpened bamboo sticks all seemed extreme. His fourth suggestion had more appeal—coating the top of the fence with axle grease, so as to stain the trousers of the malefactors and get them in trouble at home. But I didn't have to buy any axle grease. I found a better solution in *Onopordum acanthium*—the Scotch thistle.

Like everyone else, I'd heard of these thistles. They're as closely associated in my mind with Scotland as Robert Burns, bagpipes, plaid kilts, and malt whiskey. But I never actually saw any until last summer, when I was visiting some friends at their country place in Virginia. Avid bird-watchers and bird lovers, they had put in a long, wide planting of tall grasses, fruiting shrubs, and brambles to attract birds, offering them both food and shelter. The most spectacular sight was a colony of Scotch thistles at the far end of the planting.

I knew instantly that I had precisely what I needed to keep uninvited guests out of my garden—something that besides being utterly beautiful was also formidably armed. The Scotch thistle is impossible to overlook. It spreads wide and high, over eight feet high and four feet across. Its purple flower heads and grayish-blue foliage are lovely and distinctive. Also, it's no plant to trifle with. Widely branched, like a candelabrum, it is wonderfully covered with bristles, prickles, and thorns. Anyone who leaps a fence and tangles with a Scotch thistle will instantly repent of the deed.

But before gathering some seed—carefully, with a pair of tongs—I had some second thoughts. Was I perhaps introducing something into my garden whose presence I would live to regret? Would I, in time, have a house in a thistle patch?

My bird-loving friends reassured me, just as they had reassured the dairy farmer next door, a man already beset by the Canada thistles and bull thistles contending to take over his pastures. He had appeared on their doorstep when he first spotted their giant thistles and demanded their removal. His alarm was understandable but mistaken. The thistles that plague farmers are either perennials or annuals, and their tiny seed floats freely in the air on thistledown, spreading far and wide. The Scotch thistle's seeds, beloved of finches, are large and heavy. They fall to the ground instead of taking to the air. Furthermore, unlike its troublesome kin, it is a biennial. In its first year it forms a low mound or rosette of leaves that attracts little attention but is easily hoed out if it has taken root where it isn't wanted. It doesn't put on its spectacular show until the second season, after which it dies.

Just this side of my new fence there's now a row of *O. acanthium*, ten neat little unobtrusive rosettes of prickly blue-gray. Next spring the pupils at the Bellhaven School will mend their ways when they discover my new friends—plants that are even grumpier than I. Next fall I'm hoping to have goldfinches.

Rudbeckia

Every issue of the magazine *American Horticulturist* includes near the end a two-page pronunciation guide for the scientific names of all the plants mentioned in articles. I'm grateful that its editor is so helpful and I think I know why she provides this feature: the second-worst embarrassment a gardener can experience is finding out, years too late, that he or she has been getting the names for things all wrong, saying "FICK-us ben-ja-MEE-na" for *Ficus benjamina* instead of hitting the bull's-eye with "FY-kus ben-ja-MY-na."

It's no wonder that many of us prefer to use common names whenever possible. There's many a trap in botanical Latin and Greek, and I've discovered that my three years of high-school Latin and my one, inconclusive year of college Greek aren't much help at all. I always get the cold shivers when I hear another gardener more knowledgeable than I pronounce a plant name in a way that's new to me. Not long ago I rushed to the nearest garden encyclopedia on my shelf after hearing someone refer to the aloe, getting three syllables out of a word I'd always gotten two from, and making it rhyme with "Galloway" instead of "tallow." (In this instance, we were both right. The genus's scientific and common names coincide; if you're speaking Latin, it rhymes with "Galloway," but the other way is fine in English.)

So much for the second-worst faux pas a gardener can commit. The worst is not only to mispronounce something but also to misspell it. And I fear I owe a deep apology to the two professors Rudbeck, father and son, eighteenth-century Swedish naturalists for whom Linnaeus named an important North American genus of wildflower. The plant is called rudbeckia. For more decades than is pleasant to consider, I have pronounced it with an extraneous syllable, an "i" between the "d" and the "b." And I have written the word thus: rudibeckia.

I learned of my long-standing error much the same way that the emperor in Hans Christian Andersen's tale learned the shocking facts about his wardrobe. A friend, new to gardening, asked me what she could plant in a dry, sunny spot in her yard, something easy that would provide cut flowers for the house.

"Get some rudibeckia seed," I said. "They're in the Burpee catalog."

She telephoned me a few hours later to say Burpee sold rudbeckias, but she couldn't find rudibeckias.

"Same thing," I muttered, covering my mistake by saying that in Texas where I grew up everybody pronounced it with an extra "i" in the middle, one of our little quirks of language, like still calling refrigerators iceboxes, years after the iceman no longer cometh.

I'm glad I got their name straight finally, for these many species of North American annuals, biennials, and perennials and the ornamental cultivars derived from hybridizing them are extremely valuable for producing the most splash in the garden with the least amount of care and work.

Some rudbeckias, those derived from the reliably perennial *Rudbeckia fulgida*, have a rather stiff and formal elegance. Cultivars such as Goldsturm and White King may be purchased from any number of mail-order nurseries specializing in perennials, as may Bright Star (a maroon) and White Lustre, which used to be considered hybrids of *R. purpurea*, until botanists decided, as botanists are always deciding, to reclassify them in a separate genus, *Echinacea*, from a Greek work for hedgehog.

But the most rewarding of all the rudbeckias are the Gloriosa daisies, real triumphs of plant breeding involving the manipulation of chromosomes in *R. hirta*, the ordinary black-eyed Susan that brightens American fields and roadsides throughout the summer with a cheerful golden glow.

It isn't necessary to seek out mail-order nurseries in order to have Gloriosa daisies. Since they were introduced to the market after World War II, most seed catalogs have listed them in several sorts—doubles, singles, and semi-doubles; golds and oranges and mahoganies; Gloriosas with brown eyes and those with green ones at the center.

There's some question about exactly how to classify the Gloriosas. Some people call them annuals that sometimes hang around for longer than a year. Some say that they're pretty much biennials, but biennials that bloom the first year as well as the second. Some call them perennials, but iffy ones. It doesn't really matter, for they self-seed themselves so generously that once you've got Gloriosas out in the garden, they're with you forever— undemanding, carefree flowering plants that are in copious bloom from early summer to the first frost, that resist drought long after less tough perennials and annuals have called it quits and that offer bouquet after bouquet of cheering color for inside the house.

Feverfew and Nippon Daisy

Two of the flowering plants that please me the most when they're in bloom are chrysanthemums, though few people would recognize them as such on first sight and no one would ever call them "mums"—a hideous word whose use the late Katharine S. White quite properly excoriated in *Onward and Upward in the Garden.* The autumn-blooming garden and florist chrysanthemums developed in China and Japan over the centuries have come to usurp the name of the entire genus to which they belong, so that we often forget that Arctic daisies, costmary, and painted daisies are equally entitled to be designated as species within the genus *Chrysanthemum.* For that matter, the popular Shasta daisy is really a chrysanthemum, bred and selected by Luther Burbank at his Sebastopol farm in California in a complicated program of hybridization using *C. maximum* and *C. lacustre* and other species as parents. But the species I'm referring to as personal favorites are feverfew (*C. parthenium*) and Nippon daisy (*C. nipponicum,* also sometimes popularly called Montauk daisy or Norfolk daisy).

I first encountered *C. parthenium* in one of the pleasanter gardens on this earth, the Bonnefont herb garden at The Cloisters in Manhattan's Fort Tryon Park, on a fine day in late May when I was enjoying being shown around the place by Susan Leach, the museum's head (and often only) gardener. I didn't know what the plant was, but it was so attractive that I knew I had to grow it—tall and commanding, almost shrub-like, with ferny leaves of soft green and a profusion of white single flowers like small daisies. Ms. Leach cheerfully identified it for me, and I wrote the name down on a scrap of paper and stuck it in my wallet so I wouldn't forget.

Back home, I consulted John Lust's *The Herb Book*, which described *C. parthenium* as a "carminative, emmenagogue, purgative, stimulant, tonic," mentioned that it was hard to find, and recommended a warm infusion of its blossoms as wonderful stuff for treating "colic, flatulence, indigestion, colds, and alcoholic d.t.'s." Clearly it was a plant with a lot going for it in addition to its striking beauty—and just the thing in the unlikely event that I need an emmenagogue and don't have one in the medicine chest.

But when I searched through a dozen seed catalogs, I was stymied, learning just what Lust meant by "hard to find." I found several species and hybrids of *Matricaria* listed as feverfew, but no *C. parthenium*. So I wrote Susan Leach a pleading letter asking if she might perhaps be willing to send me a few seeds. A month later, near the end of July, an envelope arrived from The Cloisters containing enough almost infinitesimal seeds to plant a football field with this sturdy perennial. I filled a dozen small plastic pots with milled sphagnum moss properly moistened, sprinkled a few seeds on each, and set them in a shady spot to await germination.

I didn't have to wait long; *C. parthenium* wastes no time coming up. Within thirty-six hours, the first leaves appeared, and I believe it possible that every single seed germinated. I thinned the seedlings, kept them well watered, and gave them weekly doses of weak liquid fertilizer to make up for the absence of nutrients in sphagnum. By September 1, I had a dozen stocky plants ready to go into the perennial border, where I planned to use them in groups of three among the phlox and hemerocallis and lythrum.

But something nagged at me as I considered my plans. I recalled the breakneck speed with which my feverfew had sprung to life. I remembered other plants that had liked my garden a little too well, so much so that they quickly changed from welcome guests to pesky nuisances. I got on the phone and rang Susan Leach to ask if *C. parthenium* had invasive tendencies.

"O Lord, yes!" she replied. "Didn't I warn you? They come up here everywhere by the thousand, in the flower beds, amid other herbs, in the least little crack in the pavement. I spend hours every year yanking up feverfew."

I put the feverfew instead in a small triangular bed in the side yard, to let it fight it out with the tiger lilies and the star-of-Bethlehem that had already invaded that spot, and it seems to have worked out. The star-of-Bethlehem rules the roost through its season of bloom in mid-May. Then the feverfew takes over for a month of spectacular bloom, after which time I cut it back (being extremely careful not to put the old stalks and their enormously viable seeds in the compost heap), and let the lilies take over in July. Then the tiger lilies, which are tough, get cut back. In September there's usually a second burst of bloom from the feverfew's pure white stars.

Feverfew is something of a newcomer in my garden, but *C. nipponicum*, the Nippon daisy, is an old friend and not at all invasive. I believe that it is self-sterile, for I've grown it over a decade now and never once seen a seedling. But it is so easy to propagate both by rooted cuttings and by dividing the plant's crown into several pieces each containing a bit of root and stem that I've shared it with gardening friends all up and down the eastern seaboard from Norfolk to Boston. In coastal areas it is perfectly reliable and hardy, though I've got a hunch that it would be doomed in Woodstock or Utica.

There's something a little strange about the Nippon daisy, as if it had been put together by two designers, each of whom had different ends in mind. It's woody, so that new growth appears every year on old wood, as in the hydrangea, but it also can be cut back almost entirely to the ground in the spring, after which it quickly becomes a bush some two feet high or higher. From spring to mid-fall it functions in the garden landscape as a small attractive shrub whose leaves give it a strong resemblance to pittosporum. Then, late in the fall—very late, after most of the garden chrysanthemums have faded, the perennial asters have been cut back to the ground, and the maple leaves have turned and started to fall—the Nippon daisy changes from shrub to flowering plant, when large single white flowers much resembling those of the Shasta daisy (in whose complex ancestry *C. nipponicum* is thought by some to figure) appear at the very tips of the stems. The flowers and the leaves, to my eye, don't really seem to go together. In bloom it seems almost as if someone has come along with a bunch of Shastas and wired them, one by one, to a pittosporum. Nevertheless, I have no complaint. It's nice to have something blooming when everything else has ceased for the year and when the snow geese are flying overhead to escape the approach of winter.

Clock Plants

I'm trying to be crabby about the new strain of portulaca called Afternoon Delight, for I have some extremely pleasant recollections of portulaca in my childhood and I'm of an age when I'm getting protective about all such memories. I wouldn't dream of trying to make some ice cream according to an ancestral recipe that calls for enough pure whipping cream to delight several dairy farmers and uses almost a pound of peppermint sticks, crushed fine. I'm afraid that I might find that Baskin-Robbins tastes just as good as the ice cream my Grandmother Lacy used to make for those hot Sunday afternoons in July when the entire tribe assembled at her house to eat what she called "peppermint cream" and listen to my grandfather cuss out the Democratic Party.

Everyone raised portulacas out in the country where I lived for most of World War II, except that no one called them that. They were called either moss rose or rose moss. People grew them in rusty metal washbasins sitting on tree stumps, in whitewashed rubber tires they used to outline the course of their driveways, and in coffee cans up and down the edges of their front steps.

Those old-fashioned moss roses had much to recommend them. They would take the sweltering Southwestern heat better than any other annual flower, thanks to their succulent stems and leaves and their thrifty use of moisture. They thrived right up to Labor Day, when the zinnias were long gone and even the marigolds had turned sullen. Drought didn't faze them. They came in a bright range of colors that should have clashed but didn't— cerise and orange and maroon and apricot and gold and creamy white. They were also prolific self-sowers, reliably returning each spring to their customary rubber tires and coffee cans and usually producing a second crop in the fall from seed formed in midsummer.

It may be that the grownups among my people lamented the fact that these moss roses flowered only briefly, opening as soon as the warm sun touched them in the morning and closing before noon, when their petals turned to mush. I don't know. What I do know is that, for a child, portulaca and some other plants were living clocks that gave a summer an order it would otherwise have lacked.

In childhood, before we grow up to live in history, by watches and calendars and schedules and appointments, before we come to the realization that our personal span of years on this earth is fleeting and insufficient for the accomplishment of our desires, time seems eternal and life an endless waiting. It is a miracle that Christmas ever comes or that another birthday rolls around. The notion of a year is so vast as to be incomprehensible. If it is summer, then it seems that it has always been summer and that it will remain so forever. Even a day can seem interminable, unless it can be broken down into smaller moments and events.

I know of no better description of childhood's battle waged against time's petty pace than the one in Annie Dillard's *Teaching a Stone to Talk*:

You are young, you are on your way up, when you cannot imagine how you will save yourself from death by boredom until dinner, until bed, until the next day arrives to be outwaited, and then, slow slap, the next. You read in despair all the titles of the books on the bookshelf; you play with your fingers; you revolve in your upholstered chair, slide out of the chair upside down onto your head, hope that you will somehow damage your heart by waiting for dinner in that position, and think that life by its mere appalling length is a feat of endurance for which you haven't the strength.

But plants, like us and other animals, are temporal creatures. They have their own processes of development from infancy to maturity and finally to senescence and death. Some plants are extremely short-lived, such as the desert annuals that must germinate and blossom and set seed within a very restricted period of moisture in the spring. Others may live for centuries, even millennia, such as the bristlecone pine. Different plants respond in different ways to the seasonal variations of the year. Chrysanthemums are triggered into bloom by the shortening days of late summer and fall. The increasing warmth of the soil in late spring sends beans and corn into active growth and also signals daffodils and tulips to go dormant until late summer, when root growth begins again. And in a fascinating phenomenon known as synchroneity, every individual member of certain species of plants may blossom simultaneously all over the world in a rhythm that seems to have nothing whatsoever to do with the seasons of the year. In *Ever Since Darwin*, Stephen Jay Gould writes:

A bamboo bearing the formidable name *Phyllostachys bambusoides* flowered in China during the year 999. Since then, with unerring regularity, every 120 years. *P. bambusoides* follows this cycle wherever it lives. In the late 1960s, Japanese stocks (themselves transplanted from China centuries before) set seed simultaneously in Japan, England, Alabama, and Russia.

(Gould also tells us that once they have set seed, they die, and that this long cycle of 120 years gives them an evolutionary blue chip, by preventing the co-evolution of predators specializing in the consumption of this particular kind of bamboo.)

These larger rhythms of plant growth and life are important to understand, but they have scant interest for children, at least not in comparison with the shorter, much more visible rhythms of plants that change in response to the immediate time of day, of plants that claim but a few hours for themselves, flowering briefly and then closing.

First come the early risers, the plants of the morning. Soon after sunrise, with the first warming of the air, the Heavenly Blue morning glories open, more and more blossoms appearing each day, until by summer's end the blue radiance of the fences where they grow outdoes the sky itself. In roadside ditches, bindweed, the morning glory's humbler kin, blooms pink and white, somehow demure, despite bindweed's thoroughly deserved reputation as a weed. In fields the delicate blue blossoms of blue-eyed grass (not a grass at all but a member of the iris family) lift their morning faces. And in their old tires and coffee cans and discarded washbasins the fat buds of portulaca open to reveal the colorful taffeta petals within.

By noon, the morning show is over. It is time for lunch, and then the afternoon lull, a quiet time for napping or reading or just sitting quietly, listening to the distant din of katydids and watching the faint, almost imperceptible fuzz from cottonwood trees float slowly through the still air until it comes to rest on the window screens. The sky goes white-hot and hazy. Nothing moves; nothing is happening. But then the quiet time ends. A faint breeze stirs with the promise of evening. In the kitchen there are the sounds of supper being made, the clinking of a spoon and of ice in a pitcher of tea, the frying of bacon to be used for wilted lettuce. Outside, by the kitchen door, the four o'clocks have opened, and they are wonderfully various, since the same bushy plant can produce several different colors of blossoms—pink or red or yellow or white, as well as mixtures of several of these in one flower.

But the finest of the day's procession of clock plants comes last, at dusk, when the moonflowers open, each bud swelling and puffing up like a small balloon until it unfurls, visibly, in a matter of seconds, to become a pure-white saucer with a sweet fragrance that delights both man and night moth. And then, soon after the moonflowers appear, it is time for all children to be put to bed. One more summer day has passed, its hours told by the plants that blossom and fade in succession.

Nevertheless, despite my memories of portulacas that called it quits by late morning when I was a child, I have a large pot of Afternoon Delight, eight plants growing thickly together in a bright assortment of colors, and they please me. Their flowers are showy, mostly double or semi-double. The pot sits on a table on the deck, and the blossoms linger well into the time for gin-and-tonic. I'm older now. I don't take naps. I know that the summer is barely begun before it comes to an end, that Christmas always comes, and that birthdays roll around with a ferocious speed. I live by calendars and watches. I don't need plants to help me tell time, to mark the passing of the hours. It doesn't much bother me that the hybridizers have worked on the portulaca, extending its life span. But I very much hope they keep their hands off the morning glories and the moonflowers.

A Garden
That Welcomed Strangers

I do not know what became of her, and I never learned her name. But I feel that I know her from the garden she so lovingly made, over many decades.

The house she lived in lies two miles from mine—a simple, two-story structure with the boxy plan, steeply pitched roof, and unadorned lines that are typical of houses built in the middle of the nineteenth century near the Jersey Shore.

Her garden was equally simple. She was not a conventional gardener who did everything by the book, following, for example, the common advice to vary her plantings so there would be something in bloom from the first aconites in the spring to the last chrysanthemum in the fall. Hers was a summer garden, where bloom started in late May, continued until early September, and then ceased, except for an occasional sporadic blossom out of season. I don't know why. Perhaps she lived somewhere else most of the year. Perhaps she simply didn't like spring and fall. And she had no respect at all for the rule that says tall-growing plants belong at the rear of a perennial bed, low ones in the front, and middle-sized ones in between. Nor did she seem to think much of the views of those horticultural theoreticians who hold that perennial borders ought to be home to a large number of different kinds of plants.

In her garden everything was accent, everything was tall, and the evidence was transcendently plain that she loved three kinds of plants and three kinds only: clematis, roses, and lilies, intermingled promiscuously to pleasant effect but with no apparent design at all.

She grew a dozen sorts of clematis, perhaps fifty plants in all, including *Clematis* x jackmanii, Duchess of Edinburgh, and Ramona, of the ones I could identify. All were planted at haphazard intervals through the border, trained and tied so that they clambered up metal rods of the sort used to reinforce concrete. Each rod was crowned intermittently throughout the summer by a rounded profusion of large blossoms of dark purple, rich crimson, pale lavender, light blue, and gleaming white.

Her taste in roses was old-fashioned. Not a single modern hybrid tea rose or floribunda in sight. Instead, she favored the roses of former years—the York and Lancaster rose, the cabbage rose, the damask, and, in several varieties, the rugosa rose so well adapted to her sandy soil near the seashore. She propagated her roses herself in an old-fashioned way, sticking cuttings directly in the ground and then covering them with upended gallon jars to serve as individual greenhouses for moisture and protection.

Lilies, I believe, were her greatest love. Except for some Madonna lilies, it is impossible to name them, since the wooden flats placed casually here and there on the lawn or in the flower bed, all filled with the dark-green leaves of lily seedlings, and the occasional paper tags fluttering from seed pods with the date and record of a cross, combined to suggest that she was an amateur hybridizer. Judging from most of the lilies in bloom, she was especially fond of tall trumpet lilies of a warm muskmelon shade or a pale lemon-yellow.

She believed in sharing her garden with both friends and strangers. By her curb there was a sign: THIS IS MY GARDEN AND YOU ARE WELCOME HERE. TAKE ALL THAT YOU WISH WITH YOUR EYES, BUT NOTHING WITH YOUR HAND.

Until five years ago, her garden was always immaculately tended, the lawn kept fertilized and mowed, the flower bed free of weeds, the tall lilies carefully staked, and the clematis tied up. But then something happened. I don't know what (everything about that woman is unknown to me except the garden she made), but the lawn was mowed less and less frequently, then not at all. Tall grass invaded the roses, the clematis, the lilies. Honeysuckle intruded from a vacant lot next door. Soon there were bindweed and bittersweet. The elm tree in her front yard sickened and died, and when a coastal gale struck, the branches that fell were never removed.

With every year, the neglect has grown worse. Sumac, ailanthus, poison ivy, and other green invaders joined the honeysuckle and the bittersweet in threatening the few lilies and clematis and roses that still struggled for survival in the developing thicket.

Then the house itself went dead. The front door was padlocked and the windows covered with sheets of plywood. For over a year there has been a FOR SALE sign out front where another sign once invited strangers into the woman's garden.

I drive by that house almost daily and have been tempted to load a shovel in my car trunk, stop at her curb, and rescue at least a few lilies from their smothering thicket of weeds. The laws of trespass and the fact that her house sits right across the street from a police station have given me the cowardice to resist temptation. But it bothers me to see her garden in its decline, for its lesson is that all gardeners and the gardens they create are fragile things, creatures of time, hostages to chance and decay. Most gardeners are extremely conscious of their mortality. We hope that our gardens will outlast us, but we know that they well may not.

Last week, the FOR SALE sign out front came down and the windows were unboarded. A crew of painters arrived and someone cut down the dead elm and carted it away. This morning there was a moving van in the driveway unloading a swing set, several bicycles, a barbecue grill, a grand piano, and a whole houseful of what looked like sensible, unpretentious furniture. A young family is moving into that house.

I hope that among their number there's a gardener whose special fondness for old roses and clematis and tall trumpet lilies will mean that everything else is put aside until the garden is restored to something like its former glory.

May White

Just when the first of the two dogwood seedlings I rescued some years ago from a tangled hedge reaches a height of eight feet and puts on a fairly respectable show in mid-May, its dazzling white bracts glistening in the morning sunlight, swaying in the faint breeze so that it seems from some distance away that a flock of white doves is hovering about the tree in search of a momentary place to perch, I pick up the Arts and Leisure section of the Sunday *New York Times* to glance at the garden pages in case there's something I have missed. There's news, it turns out, and it isn't good news for my dogwood: all up and down the eastern seaboard a blight has been attacking the native American dogwood (*Cornus florida*), causing a great many specimens of this tree, which is lovely in woodlands (and on front lawns as well, thanks to its manageable size), to sicken and die a lingering death. A quick walk through my neighborhood confirms this evil bit of intelligence. Pink and white alike, at least half the dogwoods within a half mile have what looks like the sickness unto death. Bloom is sparse, particularly on the lower branches, many of which have failed even to leaf out.

I won't mourn the loss of the pinks, especially. May's a month with a trifle too much pink in it already, to my mind. The mats of pink and mauve *Phlox subulata* are still in bloom in too many of my neighbors' gardens, and masses of pink and red and purple azaleas assault the eye from every shady spot. As the last tulips fade and the temperature begins to rise toward summer, what I want to see and to see most abundantly is white, the white of

May White

May—lily of the valley, white lilacs, my beloved but endangered white dogwoods, mock oranges, even the clusters of star-of-Bethlehem, whose tufts of foliage are otherwise such a nuisance in my lawn and which only a fool would knowingly introduce into a garden. If the dogwoods go, they are irreplaceable.

Well, almost irreplaceable. There are some good candidates to take their place. First among these, I'd say, is an extraordinarily handsome and carefree large shrub that's been greatly overlooked by American gardeners, *Viburnum plicatum* cv. 'mariesii,' which many good mail-order houses still list under the name *V. tomentosum* cv. 'mariesii,' a mistaken appellation according to both *Wyman's Garden Encyclopedia* and *Hortus Third*, to which I gladly defer. I bought one, whatever it's called, by mail order in 1973, and the next spring it bloomed as if it had grown in my garden for years. This particular viburnum lacks the delicious fragrance of some of the other species in this genus of ornamental shrubs, such as *V.* x burkwoodii and *V.* x carlcephalum (both hybirds of *V. carlesii*, a Korean native), but it commands much attention when in bloom. Reaching ten feet in height, it spreads as wide. Its horizontal branches are hung below with heavily ribbed, bright-green, oval leaves. Above them, in double file, like white satin roses on the sleeve of an old-fashioned wedding gown, perch rows of glistening flowers, twelve to twenty to a branch. Seen from afar, these blossoms give an effect of simplicity, purity, and virginal whiteness; up close, they have a much more complicated architectural form. The apparent "flowers"— really sterile bracts, five to eight per inflorescence—surround clusters of tiny, creamy-yellow true flowers, branching twice in a starlike, five-pointed pattern rising at the very center for a slightly rounded look. The effect is as elaborate and studied as a bridal bouquet.

Which statement brings me by a bumpy transition to the second possible replacement for dogwood's white in the May landscape, bridal wreath or *Spirea* x vanhouttei, a late-nineteenth-century hybrid of *S. cantoniensis* and *S. trilobata*. A favorite garden shrub since late Victorian times, bridal wreath is as apt to be well known to beginning gardeners as *V. plicatum* is unfamiliar. I'd place a fairly large bet on its being one of the first shrubs purchased by new houseowners who suddenly realize that the house they've just bought sits naked on its lot, that they've got to buy "some bushes" to supplement the symmetrical pairs of junipers and arborvitae the builder put in as "foundation plantings," to satisfy the requirements of the FHA. (The other shrubs are forsythia and weigela, in case you care to bet.)

I'd also mention mountain ash, which can be grown either as a shrub or as a small tree. Its clusters of white flowers in May are almost as attractive as the deep-red clusters of fruit that follow them in late summer, except that ash has one of the nastiest odors I've encountered in a flower this side of skunk cabbage or carrion flower, smelling something like I imagine a bathroom cleaner factory might smell.

Finally, there's another dogwood that may turn out to have the stamina to resist the blight that's attacking our American *Cornus florida*, namely *C. kousa* 'chiniensis,' which was imported to the United States via the Arnold Arboretum in 1907. The bracts of its blossoms are pointed, rather than rounded, and it blooms later than our American dogwood. The long-lasting blossoms appear in late May, but they do not really qualify as "May whites," since they are green and inconspicuous at first, becoming white and large only in mid-June. This Chinese dogwood has the added dividend of producing sizable round fruits the color of crushed strawberries, reputed to be highly regarded by birds.

I can still have my white in May, no matter what. But I hope the *Times* is dead wrong about our native dogwood.

A Taste for Tamarisks

Gardening is in large part a phenomenon of attention and perception, by which I mean that one is constantly learning things one ought to have known long ago, suddenly seeing things that were there all along, though they went unseen. I have three recent examples to offer from my own experience.

The first is a matter of spelling. A well-known taxonomist with whom I am on good terms read something I wrote in which I made mention of gingko trees, and repeatedly. He sent me a note, gently telling me the bad news, that the preferred spelling is "ginkgo," not "gingko." Although it strikes me as an outrageous injustice that the word should be spelled that way, the dictionary tells me that he is correct.

The second example concerns a shrubby plant with the jaw-breaking Latin name of *Leptospermum scoparium*, which, it seems to me, I'd never seen or even heard of until last March, when a fine specimen knocked my eyes out at the Philadelphia Flower Show. I spotted it from sixty feet away and dashed over to find out what it was, suspecting it was an unusually good flowering almond, five or six feet tall, with dime-sized double blossoms of a pleasant reddish-pink fairly covering its graceful, upright branches. The label it bore proved me wrong about its being an almond, but the blue ribbon the judges had awarded it confirmed my judgment that whatever it was it was wonderful. And once I became aware that *L. scoparium* is one of the lovely things this world happens to contain, I began seeing it everywhere both in print and in person. I've seen it by the bucketful in florist shops, I've seen it mentioned in several garden books and magazines, and a picture of it grown in tree form has led me to Allen Haskell. He's a specialty nurseryman in New Bedford, who doesn't ship by mail or UPS but who has agreed to save me a good-sized specimen to be picked up the next time my brother-in-law drives down from Boston. From what Mr. Haskell tells me, it will grow just fine in our cool but well-lit entranceway, giving a prodigal display of blossoms throughout the late winter. I look forward to having a *Leptospermum* for my very own, but I rather regret the many years I've wasted in ignorance of its existence.

Finally, there's the matter of tamarisks. I've known about them as long as I can remember, but it now turns out that I didn't know enough about them. One species of tamarisk, *Tamarix ramosissima*, may well be the first plant I knew by name, although I didn't address it in Latin. It grew in my Grandmother Surles's garden in Wichita Falls, Texas, where I sometimes spent much of the summer when I was growing up. She called it salt cedar, like everybody else in Texas, and she valued it for its graceful, deep-rose haze of flowers in midsummer. I called it the switch bush, because although Grandmother was basically kind and doting toward her grandchildren, the notion that kids might be brought up without corporal punishment and not turn into bank robbers and ax murderers as a direct consequence was alien to her system of beliefs. Transgression of her rules (if detected) brought swift retribution. The advantage of salt cedar in administering a licking to a young malefactor was that its supple branches stung fiercely but couldn't actually maim.

I leave it to Freudians to determine whether these childhood punishments have anything to do with the fact that an inventory of the flowering shrubs and small trees in my garden reveals a conspicuous absence of *T. ramosissima*, although it can be a splendid summer sight, especially when planted near *Cotinus coggyria*, the smoke tree so beloved by our Victorian ancestors for its light-pink or purple panicles of bloom. But the real point about tamarisks is that for reasons I fail to understand I have been spectacularly inattentive to the existence of another species that isn't my old switch bush at all but *T. parviflora*, the small-flowered tamarisk. All of a sudden this past May I realized that it was growing in many of my neighbors' gardens and that it's a ravishing sight in full bloom. It has a great deal to commend it, being a graceful fountain of pink some ten feet high, swaying in the slight breeze, all ashimmer in the slanting golden light of early morning. *Wyman's Gardening Encyclopedia* touts it highly, especially for dry and sandy soils near the seashore, which is precisely what I've got.

I answer to being middle-aged; some who are near and dear to me point out that I'm set in my ways, and that not all of these ways are entirely praiseworthy. There are many things I have failed to notice that I should have noticed. The Book of Common Prayer has my number exactly, for I have done those things that I ought not to have done and I have done left undone those things that I ought to have done. (Some of them, anyway.) But as a gardener I can still learn. I will possibly never write "gingko" for "ginkgo" again. That pot of *Leptospermum* will be on its way from New Bedford one of these days. And next May there will be a tamarisk blooming in the garden, my own fountain of delicate pink in the early-morning light.

Magnolias, Gardenias,
and Crape Myrtle

Although when most of my friends down South think of New
Jersey they probably think of it as being way up North, my
particular part of New Jersey isn't all that far away. The map
shows that I live considerably south of Philadelphia, even if in
my mind Philadelphia is due west. I'm not very far from the
Cape May peninsula, and in degrees of latitude I tend my sandy
soil just a smidgen northward of Baltimore. As a consequence,
I can grow some things that aren't really hardy "up North," as
well as plants that can't take the Southern heat. I could grow
white birch trees, though I don't. I could grow crape myrtles,
probably, but I haven't tried and I have my reasons. As a transplanted Southerner, I find myself longing to have growing in my
garden a number of the plants I was raised with—but I'd want
them to do just as well here as they did down South. And there's
the rub.

The three kinds of plants I most miss and long for—and
always greet with a deep sense of homecoming when I'm visiting there—are gardenias, magnolias, and crape myrtle. In one
of the houses in Dallas where I lived when I was growing up,
there was a hedge of gardenia or Cape jasmine (*Gardenia
jasminoides*). Although it sometimes died back, if the winter was
fiercer than usual for Dallas, most years it thrived as if it were
native to the area, although it originated in China. Its glossy,
deep-green leaves were almost handsome enough in themselves
to make it something to prize, but as anyone who has ever stood
downwind of a gardenia bush when it's in full bloom on a sum-

mer evening knows with absolute clarity, it's the sharp, sweet fragrance of the double white flowers that makes gardenias so marvelous. There's nothing I can think of to match it.

Except of course *Magnolia grandiflora*, the bull bay or Southern magnolia, one of the finest contributions of the native flora of the southern United States to the world's horticulture, for gardeners who live in suitable climates. In my senior year at Duke University, where I had a room on the third floor of a pseudo-Gothic building known as the Few Quadrangle, my desk overlooked the very top of a tall magnolia of this species. It was handsome in any season for its large, dark-green, glossy leaves (whose undersides were fuzzy and reddish). In May, when the huge white blossoms, almost a foot across, opened, the indescribable lemony sweetness of their fragrance made it impossible to study and almost impossible to think about sex.

But the crape myrtle, which people can call *Lagerstroemeria indica* if they feel so inclined, is also matchless. No fragrance here, but it doesn't matter. Whether grown as large bushes or as small trees, crape myrtles are among the loveliest of flowers, with their billowing masses of clusters in colors that might have been invented by Renoir on one of his better days—rosy lavenders, winy purples, pinkish-white and pinkish-pink, soft whites with hints of gray and blue, blends and particolors, and best of all, a red like the inside of a vine-ripe watermelon. I defy anyone on earth to go to Norfolk, Virginia, a city extravagantly blessed with crape myrtles, in late July and early August, when they are in full bloom, and try to think of somewhere else he'd rather be—despite the sweltering heat and the withering humidity.

Gardenias don't grow in southern New Jersey. They're not hardy enough. I'm not sure what the northernmost edge of their range is, but it's probably somewhere between Durham, North Carolina, and Washington, D.C. I grow one gardenia as a house plant, but it's *G. thunbergii*, a smaller species than the Cape jasmines of my childhood and a native of southern Africa, not China. It is a mere token of what gardenias ought to be, and to speak frankly, spider mites like it far too much.

Of course, crape myrtle and Southern magnolias do grow here. Barely. A block or so away, there is a crape myrtle tree about twelve feet high, which struggles into bloom late in August. A couple of miles farther up the same road, there is a magnolia, which obviously isn't destined to reach the hundred feet the tree can easily attain down South. It blooms some years, in mid-July, producing no more than three or four blossoms, which scarcely call to mind Vita Sackville-West's wonderful description in *Vita Sackville-West's Garden Book* of the magnolia flowers in her garden at Sissinghurst, which reminded her of "great white pigeons settling among dark leaves."

I'm not tempted to try crape myrtle or magnolias here. Survival is not enough. The few that I've seen around the neighborhood seem out of their element, shy and deeply uneasy, like wedding guests who realize too late that they've found the wrong church and are attending the wedding of strangers. I leave them, and real gardenias, too, to the friends I left behind in the South.

Dr. Abel's Amiable Shrub

Just down the street there's a garden I don't especially admire. For one thing, its owner asphalted his lawn a few years ago, turning it into a parking lot for his VW bug, his old Cadillac (pink and finned), and his speedboat. For another, his horticultural tastes run almost entirely to cannas, rather too many of them, planted just south of the Cadillac's usual parking spot, in garish reds and oranges that clash with themselves, not to mention the car. Nevertheless, I admire him for one thing: the hedge of glossy abelia that runs all along one side of his "garden." (Here, I think "yard" is the better term.)

Much planted in the 1940s, when it enjoyed a certain vogue that made it almost a horticultural fad, the glossy abelia has now fallen on days of entirely undeserved neglect. Botanically known as *Abelia* x *grandiflora* (oddly so, since anyone who could call its blossoms large must be a descendant of Pinocchio), it is a hybrid between *A. chiniensis* and *A. uniflora*, two species collected in China by Dr. Clarke Abel, a British naturalist who botanized there (rather lackadaisically, it is said, because of his delicate health) for the East India Company under Lord Amherst shortly after the Battle of Waterloo.

Neglected it certainly is. Few of the better mail-order nurseries list it or some of its close kin, such as the cultivar Edward Goucher, which was developed by the U.S.D.A. early in this century. I've never seen it being unloaded in early spring at local garden centers when the trucks arrive from Monrovia and other wholesale nurseries in California—aucubas, yes, and potentillas and yews of course, but no abelias. Except for Mr. Asphalt down the street, almost no one else in my town seems to grow it, at least not on the customary routes I take to buy groceries, cigarettes, stamps, brandy, and other essentials. The one abelia in my own garden, growing out by the mailbox by the front sidewalk, came from an out-of-the-way nursery deep in the country, where I snatched it up on sight and expressed my loud disappointment that it was the only one the owner had.

For overall garden value, I would class the glossy abelia as an almost perfect plant. It is happy in full sun, but doesn't seem to mind partial shade. Its foliage, which is semi-evergreen in the South, is highly attractive, a deep and shining green that takes on a dark-purplish cast in late summer. Its pale-pink blossoms appear in profusion from midsummer until early fall. It is tolerant of drought and August heat waves. Except for bees, insects leave it alone, and it seems immune to diseases such as the powdery mildew that makes lilac hedges a sorry eyesore by midsummer. It is said to be so easy to propagate that the fact I haven't tried to do so by taking cuttings in July is testimony to my dedication to the fine art of procrastination. It makes a wonderful hedge, and a single plant is lovely and graceful for its slightly arching foliage. Its blossoms are agreeably fragrant, though no competition for honeysuckle.

The abelia has only one fault that I can think of. In regions north of Philadelphia it may suffer a partial die-back during an unusually harsh winter, which means that it makes a shorter hedge up North than it does in the South—typically four feet rather than six. But it springs back quickly in late March, and since it blooms on new wood, a pruning in late winter, whether by the gardener's hand or by nature's hand, increases summer's bloom. Dr. Abel's amiable shrub deserves much more attention than it's getting at the moment.

Copper Beech
and Blue Atlas Cedar

I can never remember whether there are sermons in stones and lessons in brooks, or the other way around, but there's a cautionary tale in the front yard of a neighbor a couple of blocks east of my place, in the form of the two copper beeches planted there, about forty feet apart on either side of the sidewalk from the street to his front porch. It's a reasonable bet that whoever owns that house didn't plant those beeches, for they grow slowly, I hear, and these particular specimens, at least fifty feet tall, have entered their maturity. My guess would be that they were planted in the 1930s sometime, by someone who admired them as saplings for the solemn dignity of their dark foliage and who thought that one simply was not enough. I hope my neighbor isn't inclined toward gardening, because if he is he's out of luck, unless he's got some sunnier space out back than he has in the front. The beech trees have grown almost as wide as they are tall, and they have gobbled up every inch of his front yard, plunged his front porch into gloom deep enough to gratify trolls and troglodytes, and probably limited his choice of house plants inside to things that have little need for much light, like aspidistras and mother-in-law's tongue and vinyl geraniums from Mr. Big.

I never pass that house without looking at those copper beeches and what I can see of the dwelling they so obscure, and longing to be able to pluck them up and transplant them to the city park a couple of blocks farther down the street. No one ever planted beech trees in the park, and it could stand some. The lesson here is that too often home gardeners plant trees without asking some fundamental questions of the nurseryman: How big will they get? And how soon? We rush out lusting for beech trees or weeping willows or sugar maples, all monsters that eventually bully their owners and dominate the gardens they occupy—or prevent. Copper beeches and other large trees are grand opera; what people with small gardens need is chamber music, small and graceful trees like oxydendron and redbud and Japanese maples of any sort at all.

I don't see many people planting copper beeches these days, but there's another menace on the scene: the Blue Atlas cedar, a native of North Africa which apparently loves the northeastern United States. It's become so popular among the goodly number of people with not a lick of training in horticulture who nevertheless buy trucks and announce their services as "landscapers" (meaning that they hire crews of high-school kids in the summer to mow lawns and that occasionally they'll plant a tree or two) that I predict that when my retirement rolls around early in the next century, I'll be living in a forest of North African cedars.

It's easy to see why someone would want a Blue Atlas cedar around. All year long, they're most attractive trees, with interesting sculptural shapes, thanks to branches that seem undecided about whether they want to grow up or down instead, and which consequently bend and alter their direction. The color of their foliage is an excellent gray-blue, far bluer than is found on all but truly exceptional cultivars of Colorado blue spruce. (I have some feeling that people who a decade ago would have planted spruces are now planting cedars instead, but I can't document it statistically.) Even when they are small, only six or seven feet high, they have a touch of elegance and drama about them. They have pizzazz. And so the trucks of "landscape experts" ply up and down the streets of my neighborhood, dispensing Blue Atlas cedar, as often as not planting them right next to houses, just under the eaves. I don't think there's more than one dentist's office within forty miles that doesn't have several of the things.

The problem is that they don't stay small very long. Their height at maturity hovers between 65 and 75 feet, and a particularly robust specimen can top off at 100 feet. Furthermore, no less than the copper beech, they spread out as they mature. Again, they are beautiful trees—for parks and very large estates. Their scale is utterly wrong for a small or even a medium-sized garden. I know better, of course, than to plant a Blue Atlas cedar too close to my house. I planted mine, about eight years ago, too close to the front sidewalk and the power lines instead. It won't be long before the utility company comes in with a truck and a cherry picker and probably presents me with a bill for chopping out the top of my tree.

The Fruits of Mr. Downing

My friend Bill Lubenow thought I might like it, when he came across the book for just 79 cents in a bin at a junkstore in Philadelphia. He said he knew it wasn't for him, since his botanical knowledge is limited to being able to identify rhubarb and mushrooms in the produce section of a grocery store and since his most recent horticultural triumph was managing to kill twenty-two house plants, including some cactus.

Bill was right about my liking it. I have a passion for old garden books of any sort, and this one was a pip, weighing in at over four pounds on my kitchen scale and running to 1,098 pages printed in type small enough to make me consider visiting an optometrist. The title page alone was worth the price: *The Fruits and Fruit-Trees of America, or The Culture, Propagation, and Management, in the Garden and Orchard, of Fruit-Trees Generally; with Descriptions of all the Finest Varieties of Fruit, Native and Foreign, Cultivated in this Country.* Now, that's a title to reckon with. By comparison, most of the other titles of books on my garden shelf are as laconic as Gary Cooper.

The author of what I will call *The Fruits and Fruit-Trees of America*, for short, is listed as a Mr. A. J. Downing (Andrew Jackson Downing, 1815–52), who is identified as "corresponding member of the Royal Botanic Society of London, and of the horticultural societies of Berlin, the Low Countries, Massachusetts, Pennsylvania, Indiana, Cincinnati, etc." Presumably to establish the author's credentials as a literary gentleman as well as a practical scientist, there follows a quotation from Andrew Marvell:

> *What wondrous life is this I lead?*
> *Ripe apples drop about my head;*
> *The luscious clusters of the vine*
> *Upon my mouth do crush their wine;*
> *The nectarine and curious peach*
> *Into my hands themselves do reach.*

A note below the quotation indicates that while the book was originally published in 1845 in New York by John Wiley & Sons of Astor Place, the copy I have is the second edition (1870) of a revised version prepared by one Charles Downing after the death of his brother.

In his original preface to *The Fruits and Fruit-Trees of America*, A. J. Downing showed himself to be a man of firm moral convictions about human beings and fruit. "He who owns a rood of proper land in this country, and, in the face of all the pomonal riches of the day, only raises crabs and choke-pears," he wrote, "deserves to lose the respect of all sensible men." He also showed himself to be a patriotic man, in pointing out that although America is a *"young orchard . . .* there are more peaches exposed in the markets of New York, annually, than are raised in all France . . ." and that "American apples, in large quantities, command double prices in Europe." Downing was also well versed in the botanical theory of his day, explaining at some length the theory of a Dr. Van Mons, a professor at Louvain, who "devoted the greater part of his life to the amelioration of fruits," and who believed that fruit breeders should use only young plants as parents, since older ones gradually decide that producing luscious fruit isn't worth expending the necessary energy, so that they concentrate on producing mere seeds instead. Gregor Mendel and his successors in genetics have shot Van Mons's ideas to earth, but there was no reason for either Van Mons or Downing to know about Mendelianism—and certain analogies with human beings may have made Downing think that Van Mons was on the right track. Finally, the preface, like the title page, shows the author's literary knowledge, in a wonderful quotation from Dr. Johnson, who gave this advice to a friend: "If possible, have an orchard. I know a clergyman of small income who brought up a family, very reputably, which he chiefly fed on apple dumplings."

Downing's book is admirably thorough. He devotes his first eight chapters to the care and culture of fruits and fruit trees generally, to cross-breeding, grafting, layering, suckering, pruning, training, transplanting, and fertilizing. An entire chapter is given to "general remarks on insects." Here he advises orchardists to get after the caterpillars when they are small and to seek them out in their nests before 9 a.m., when they are still groggy and lay-abed, crushing them individually between forefinger and thumb. (Downing is bound to delight organic gardeners, and to give little pleasure to the manufacturers of agricultural chemicals, who have managed to spread wide the notion that before we had DDT and its successors in our arsenals we had no fruit to eat.)

But Mr. Downing's book gets down to his obvious first love only with Chapter IX, which deals with the apple—the apple in general and then specific varieties of apple in particular. I'm not about to sit down for half a day and count the number of apples he lists and describes, starting with Abbott and concluding with Zoar Greening. Suffice it to say that the descriptions of apples that he gives occupy a full 342 pages of his text. Only very few of the apples listed, such as the Grimes Golden, Jonathan, and Winesap, are known today, except through Downing's painstaking descriptions of each, his history of its origins where known, his evaluation of its flavor, keeping quality, best season for eating, and suitability for commercial use by large growers. Here's what he has to say about King of Tompkins County, a variety also known as King Apple, Toms Red, and Tommy Red:

Origin uncertain; said to have originated with Thomas Thacher, Warren County, N.J. A valuable market fruit. Tree very vigorous, spreading, an abundant bearer annually. Young shoots very dark reddish brown, quite downy, especially toward the ends.

Fruit large, globular, inclining to conic, sometimes oblate, angular. Color yellowish, mostly shaded with red, striped and splashed with crimson. . . . Flesh yellowish, rather coarse, juicy, tender, with an exceedingly agreeable, rich, vinous flavor, delightfully aromatic. Very good to best. December to March.

Downing on the subject of apples is quite overwhelming, but I love to browse through these pages, like a deer browsing in an orchard, savoring the poetry of the names of these apples. Here's a sampling of names, and some of Downing's commentary on each: Catface ("from Kentucky"), English Beauty ("almost very good"), Hay Boys ("good to very good"), Krauter Reinette ("a German apple, highly praised in its own home"), Red and Green Sweet ("good for baking and stock feeding"), and Yellow Bellflower ("thrives in the sandy soils of New Jersey").

Although Downing really knows his apples and lavishes the greater part of his attention on them, he doesn't neglect other fruits. Almonds, apricots, blackberries, currants, cherries, cranberries, figs, grapes, melons, mulberries, nectarines, peaches, plums, pomegranates, quinces, raspberries, nuts, even oranges and olives—each sort of fruit is described in turn and its varieties sorted out, its recommended culture discussed in full detail.

To tell the truth, this book saddens me somewhat, giving me the uneasy feeling that my life is a little poorer for not being able to comfort myself with most of the apples Downing lists—to bite into a fine specimen of King of Tompkins County, refreshing myself with its exceedingly agreeable, rich, vinous flavor, its aromatic delight. By allowing grocery stores to provide us with most of the apples we eat now in our lifetime, we've probably lost something. And who among us now knows how to make his own cider from his own apples?

My sadness, however, takes on a touch of jealous rage when I read Downing on the subject of gooseberries. I hardly have room for an orchard in my small garden, but I can grow gooseberries—and I do. I am much taken with the argument of Rosalind Creasy, in her book *The Complete Book of Edible Landscaping*, that by planting edible plants with attractive ornamental qualities instead of things like euonymus and yew, we can add an extra dimension to our gardens. (As Downing put his somewhat similar version back in 1845, "In one part or another of the Union every man may, literally, sit under his own vine and fig-tree.") But Ms. Creasy in her discussion of goose-berries could come up with only three varieties, including Pix-well, the one I grow and virtually the only one sold by most mail-order nurseries. (Forget trying to buy gooseberries of any sort, even Pixwell, in your local garden center!) Now, I know a little bit about gooseberries, though I didn't learn until the summer of 1970, when I strolled around the small garden of Oma and Opa Engel, a charming elderly couple in Nordheim, West Germany, who are distantly related to my wife. In their shady yard—front, side, and back—the Engels grew goose-berries: red ones and purplish-wine ones and green ones and golden ones and white ones; gooseberries for tarts, gooseberries for jams, gooseberries for plucking right off the bush and eating from the hand. Invited to sample the gooseberries, I sampled; permitted to gorge on them, I gorged, savoring their odd sweet sharpness, their hints of honey and lime. Later that summer in England, I continued to sample and gorge on red ones and purplish-wine ones, small ones and large ones, and so on.

I know that the gooseberries I raise here on my own home ground are inferior, mere reminders of gooseberries, nothing like what I mean when I say—as I would if by some miracle a pint of the Engels' gooseberries were to appear on my kitchen coun-ter—"*Gooseberries!*" My gooseberries, I know, are to the real thing what Plato believed the tree in my back yard is to the Platonic Ideal of the Tree Itself. My gooseberries are hardly better than imitations, simulacra. I turn in my discontent to *The Fruits and Fruit-Trees of America* and learn that in 1845 over 149 named varieties were grown in Great Britain, especially in the vicinity of Lancashire, whose weavers took special interest in growing and hybridizing them. Downing lists 41 varieties from Britain—10 red, 8 yellow, 13 green, and 10 white—which were being grown in America when he wrote. He calls gooseberries "luxury for the poor," because they are easily grown in the small confines of a dooryard garden and because they are delicious in vast disproportion to the care they require and the space they occupy. He admits that some English gooseberries don't take well to the American climate, but he also discusses six varieties, bred in America, which grow vigorously and produce fruit that he rates as very good to excellent. Pixwell isn't among them, and I suspect it would receive a rating of only fair, perhaps even his contempt. The six he mentions are Downing, Hobbs Seedling, Houghton's Seedling, Mountain Seedling, Pale Red, and Smith's Improved. All originated in the Northeastern states, from Pennsylvania to Vermont. None to my knowledge is still known or sold. But if I ever manage to locate any of them, a gooseberry named Pixwell will be promptly evicted from my yard, and I'll thank Bill Lubenow again for that book.

In Praise of Privet

Its very name comes from the same Latin word that gave us "privacy," and it's easy to understand why common privet (*Ligustrum vulgare*) is the most widely used plant in America for hedges. This sturdy shrub, a native of the Mediterranean basin, grows rapidly, seldom turning temperamental. It's inexpensive and easily available in bundles of twenty-five plants from garden centers in early spring. All the standard books on gardening agree that it has an amiable tolerance for conditions that would drive less sturdy plants to destruction. And my friends Anne and Ray Birdwhistell agree. Their small back yard, which is separated from the waters of Brigantine Bay only by a bulkhead, contains just one shrub, a huge privet that has remained healthy and beautiful for over ten years, despite repeated drenchings with salt water during hurricanes or fierce northeasters.

Above all, privet is submissive to human beings wielding pruning shears, even if their knowledge of the art of pruning is so rudimentary as to be well-nigh nonexistent. For anyone who understands that a hedge should taper slightly toward the top so that it receives even sunlight, privet makes a very decent screen, thick and uniform from spring to fall. For those whose creative impulses so move them, privet makes an easy subject for topiary art.

But I'll confess it here: I don't really think much of privet hedges—for several reasons.

First, they call up some faintly unpleasant childhood memories of a garden surrounded by a privet hedge infested by wasps. Every August they turned mean and angry—I was stung often, and these stings were the first evidence I can recall that the natural world offers not only pleasure but also pain, sudden and unsought.

Second, privet is a fast grower. A fast-growing hedge is one that must be sheared several times a season. The garden tasks I like least are those that must be done repeatedly. Mowing the lawn and doing a quarter of my share of weeding the flower beds are enough of such tasks.

Third, in horticulture I admit to more than a touch of elitism. Democracy is fine in politics. It should stay there, and we need more of it. But its political virtue is no reason to practice it in the garden. I like to grow things that are unusual, and privet hedges are simply too common up and down my block to excite my admiration.

Nevertheless, one of the plants in my garden that I most admire happens to be a privet—one I almost dug up and threw away over ten years ago, when, at a fairly advanced age as such things go, I became a mortgage payer.

Our house, as I've already mentioned several times, is very old. It never had much in the way of a garden, except for a lilac hedge, that hedge of *Rosa multiflora*, and a few admirable trees. Before they placed it on the market, the former owners spruced it up a bit, inside and out. The outside sprucing up took the form of "landscaping," meaning that they bought some humdrum bushes from the closest garden center and sprinkled them about the yard in dreadful symmetry: here a yew, there a yew; one juniper here, another over yonder; a clump of privet out front in the left corner of the yard, another in the right; a blue Colorado spruce planted too close to the north side of the sidewalk exactly matched by another one too close to the south side —and everything pruned into little cones, like gumdrop shrubbery.

Once we moved in, I ripped out most of this unimaginative landscaping, made out huge and impossibly expensive lists, pared them down to size, and began to order things more to my taste—viburnums of several sorts, ditto cotoneasters, hazelnuts, Japanese maples, Chinese flowering dogwoods, and so on. I took out every other yew, leaving them in a nonsymmetrical arrangement, and determined that I could let them grow un-clipped as far as possible. By the time I'd met the first mortgage payment, one of those two privet gumdrops was out by the curb for the garbage men to pick up. My plan was that the other would join it shortly.

But the weather turned hot, the beach beckoned, and pro-crastination set in. The privet, I thought, could have a slight stay of execution. And then, on a hot July afternoon, I happened on a farmer's field a few miles away that many years ago had been outlined with a windbreak of privet, privet that had never known the bite of pruning shears. It was a truly beautiful and arresting sight—a handsome billowing hedge, thirty feet high, its leaves a deep and glossy green in the glaring sunlight, its branches swaying slightly in the faint warm breeze. Left to itself, I learned, privet could achieve a splendor I had never suspected possible. I came home resolved to live with my one remaining privet, to let it grow unrestrained and unpruned in its corner of the yard.

No garden visitor has ever bothered to praise my privet, but its gifts are not to be despised. I have given it no attention at all. I have neither fertilized it nor treated it to some of my precious compost nor watered it except incidentally, when it caught some spray from a sprinkler set to water something else. But it has thrived. It has grown 20 feet high and almost as many feet across, giving us a sense of enclosure and shelter from the street. In June it blooms for two weeks, with hundreds of creamy spikes made up of tiny flowers that sweeten the air in a way that I find pleasant, though some people might think that it is slightly cloying. The bees love it, and some of its nectar may have found its way into the honey made by a neighbor who keeps bees. So far, it has not attracted wasps in search of a place to build their nests; they far prefer the eaves just above my study window.

Now its tangled branches have grown into a small thicket where robins nest each year in the spring and sparrows and finches perch in the winter to rest before making another pass at one of our bird feeders. Two years ago, the ground beneath it was home to a mother rabbit and her offspring. Two nights ago a raccoon and I met in wary mutual surprise at the thicket's edge before he finally backed off. The privet has become the token wild place in my garden, something that links it with the rhythms of the larger order of nature. This fall, like every fall, the abundant blue-black fruits of my privet will feed some of the birds that live year-round in the neighborhood and some of the other birds that gather briefly here before resuming their annual migration southward. Left to itself, with no intention or planning on my part, the common privet turns out to have uncommon quality.

Swamp Maple

The time may not be far away when I will wake up one morning to find that the immense old swamp maple in my back yard is no more. A hurricane or a coastal gale will have taken it down during the night, leaving a shambles of branches, twigs, and leaves. I have friends with chain saws who love them the way some other people love high-speed, precision automobiles. They will help me clean up the debris, rending the neighborhood air with the piercing whine of their gasoline engines. In short order the tree will become cordwood.

That maple tree has its best days behind it. Its massive triple trunk is full of hollows. A number of large branches are dead; some have already fallen in windstorms. There are clear signs of rot, and recently the gypsy moths worked their damage. Ten years ago the tree might have been saved for the next quarter of a century at least, if I had noticed the first symptoms of decline and called in a tree surgeon to prune, to paint the wounds, to fill the hollow places with cement, and to cut away the rot to clean tissue. I will not call him now, for fear that he will shake his head slowly, pronounce the case hopeless, and advise turning the tree to firewood. It's probably foolish of me, since the tree could do considerable damage if it fell, but I can't yet justify the wise thing, the rational thing, of having it cut down now by professionals. I would rather that it die what seems to me a nobler death, going down before the force of the wind, succumbing to something elemental and unforeseen.

I am quite sentimental about that tree, but sentiment does

not blind me to its faults, which are grave enough that I would never replace it with another of its kind. A swamp maple is not appropriate for a garden of modest size like mine. It is shallow-rooted and a voracious feeder. The grass within its shade is weak and unhealthy, and there are several large spots where nothing will grow but small weeds. Its roots spread into every corner of the back yard. In the spring I must spade up our small vegetable patch and cutting garden to sever and pull out the great tangle of maple roots that have invaded since I did the same thing the year before.

Moreover, the maple is uncommonly messy. In early spring its sticky sap covers the cars parked nearby. Soon afterward, its red blossoms fall, catching in the sap and making it a bitch of a job to wash the cars. In mid-May the abundant crop of maple seeds pours down. They usually clog the gutters. Whenever they fall to the earth, they germinate immediately, bringing a pointed invitation from my wife to leave my study (where, at the moment, I am at the typewriter telling you about my swamp maple) and join her in an arduous session of weeding the flower beds out back lest we soon find ourselves living in a jungle of swamp maples.

Furthermore, the tree's location is all wrong. Someone planted it—or it came up on its own—perhaps a century ago, in what is now the exact center of my back yard. Trees should grow at the edges of a garden; what I want at the center is a clearing, an open place where ever-changing shadows and patches of sunlight mark the passing of hours and days and seasons.

Still, that maple is, for all its flaws and all its woes of age, a handsome thing. In summer it gives a cooling shade. Most autumns it flames into a more than satisfactory shade of crimson. And now, in its decline and decay, it offers a home to other living things. Last spring, before it came into leaf, a pair of woodpeckers built a nest high in its trunk. Taking advantage of a small cavity, they set about enlarging it, flinging so many wood chips to the ground that it looked as if a carpenter had set up shop there. In a hollow branch some raucous starlings have taken up residence. There are robins, too, and a chipmunk burrow at the base of the trunk, half hidden in a clump of periwinkle.

I am, of course, resigned to the inevitable, but I hope this will not be the year when the tumult of a hurricane is followed by whining chain saws out back. As I think further about that maple, I believe I'll call a tree surgeon, after all. If he says it's a hopeless case, I'll go for a second opinion.

Harry Lauder's Walking Stick

From the time its leaves first appear late in April until the last tenacious leaf falls before November's blast, it's the homeliest shrub I grow, except of course forsythia. During the spring and summer its leaves are coarse and unattractive, and they don't bother to produce a lick of color to add to autumn's show. Although it's a hazelnut, it produces no nuts, since its blossoms seem to be exclusively male. Being noticeably less vigorous than the understock it's grafted on, it gives me the constant chore of removing a great many suckers during the growing season, lest they take over and crowd it out of my garden. Its common name —Harry Lauder's Walking Stick, after the great Scottish comedian whose trademark was a gnarled and twisted cane—conveys little real meaning to most gardeners today, since Sir Harry had his heyday in vaudeville at the turn of the century; so we're left with its Latin name—*Corylus avellana* 'contorta,' which translates roughly as the screwy filbert.

Despite its many liabilities for half the year, our screwy filbert has been dear to all in my household ever since it arrived in a spring shipment of bare-rooted plants ordered from Wayside Gardens eight or nine years ago. Well, not exactly "ever since." We liked it on sight in its leafless state, but as soon as its foliage appeared we decided that we were mistaken in buying it and even more mistaken in giving it a prominent spot near the front door, a location that meant we had to pass it several times a day. But when winter came we were again delighted; all thought of yanking the thing up and relegating it to a remote corner of the yard vanished with the departure of its ultimate leaf.

Its beauty lies, first of all, in the structure of its twigs and branches, which have all the restless vitality of Martina Navratilova's tennis game. Twisting and retwisting back on themselves, moving now left and now right, now up and now down, according to no perceptible pattern, describing a variety of arcs and ellipses like some odd vine twining itself around the empty air, they delight the eye, much as an especially apt joke at just the right moment delights the mind. *Corylus avellana* 'contorta,' Harry Lauder's Walking Stick, or screwy filbert, it's my favorite plant in the garden half the year. I've never been much taken with the notion of decorating the shrubbery at Christmas with strings of colored lights, but my son Michael came up with a splendid idea when he offered the opinion that our screwy filbert would be really fine to look at if we draped it with several strands of tiny Italian white lights. It was the start of a family tradition that we remember to follow at least every other year.

But there's much more to say about that filbert, for it reminds us that winter, too, is a season of growth and not of death. On even the darkest winter day, photosynthesis still takes place, although at a much reduced rate. Growth also takes place, and noticeably so, in the scores and scores of male catkins that first appear in early November—small, slightly elongated, pendulous buds, a dark olive-green with a slightly waxy feel. By Christmas the catkins have lightened in color and reached a length of an inch. During late winter, growth continues, accelerating with the first warm days of early April, when the catkins, hanging gracefully in clusters of two or three, reach four inches and begin to display their golden pollen. No other sight in my garden, not even the daffodils in a bed out back where they can be seen from the kitchen window, pleases me as much as this filbert near the front door on an April day, when its pendant blossoms are backlit in the early-morning sun. On such a day, at such a sight, I forget the April all around me, overtaken by the unseasonal longing for November and the return of the strange and skeletal beauty of this screwy filbert.

II. PETS, PEEVES
& CONFESSIONS

A Dream Garden

We tell ourselves, and sometimes our friends, that when we moved into this house there was no garden here, as there is now, over a decade later. There was a front yard and a back yard and two side yards merging imperceptibly into both, but no flowers to speak of or shrubs of any particular interest. Today there are flower beds in respectable bloom from March till September. Some cotoneasters that I planted have now grown immense. They are a fine sight in early summer, when they bloom, attracting honeybees by the thousand and filling the garden with a sweet scent that stops just this side of sickening. Some of them have clusters of creamy flowers resembling bridal wreaths, except for being a kind of semi-virginal off-white; others bear much sparser clusters of tiny pink flowers that never fully open and that exude a sticky nectar enjoyed by several kinds of ants. It was a fine idea to plant crimson clematis beneath the cotoneasters, for they have clambered through the intricate architecture of their inner branches to emerge triumphantly on top with a profusion of blossoms in May and June and intermittent bloom thereafter. I gladly take credit for my quince tree, though I'm not so happy with the two mock oranges I bought from the same mail-order nursery. Alleged by the catalog to be both double and extremely fragrant, they are unarguably single and have no more scent than cardboard. One of these days, when it stops sulking and begins to grow, I can show garden visitors a fine Japanese red maple. And most years, when the daffodils bloom I turn into a complete exhibitionist, inviting all the neighbors in to see them and coming close to putting up a sign in the street demanding the attention of strangers, too.

But the fact is that most of the decisions that have affected the character of my garden were made by other people, long before we bought this house. I did not plant the swamp maple that dominates the back yard, or the two old cedar trees that rise like exclamation points by the driveway and in the southwest corner of the front yard. The location of the perennial beds was determined by the sidewalks and hedgerows and fences that were already here when we moved in. Like many gardeners, I have a lazy streak. I wouldn't mind it in the slightest if some distant, unknown, wealthy kinsman should pass on to glory and leave me a sizable sum of money in trust, with the strict provision that it should be used only for hiring help to tend to the necessary chores in my garden. Anyone who says he actually likes weeding or mowing the yard either lies or has deficient powers to discriminate between what is irksome and what is pleasurable. In my garden, I have generally followed the path of least resistance—working with what I've got, rather than engaging in grand designs and then laboring long and hard to bring into being something that would be intentionally and perennially splendid, instead of just occasionally and accidentally fairly handsome.

Of course, the character of my garden is also determined by things beyond any human decision, mine or anyone else's. Geography and geology command that I must garden in sandy soil on terrain that is absolutely flat.

I am generally well pleased with the garden I have made along the path of least resistance. But lately I've been musing a bit about that imaginary kinsman and benefactor. What if he gave me not only a payroll to hire a crew of crabgrass vigilantes and lawn wizards who would turn my scruffy turf into an emerald putting green but also underwrote the cost of making whatever garden I would like to have?

Here's the garden I would have if I could.

First, its very existence could not be suspected from the road. There would be a large white house near the edge of the road to conceal it, and it would be further concealed by the terrain, which would slope down sharply from the rear of the house toward a distant stream, itself sloping down sharply toward a valley floor several hundred feet below. A side path would lead from the house toward a hemlock hedge, one of four enclosing the main part of the garden in a long and fairly narrow rectangle. You would enter the garden through an arch cut in the hedge, but still not see the garden as a whole, because of a diversion, a walled and sunny area with long benches against the walls and with two raised beds made of stone, displaying a fine collection of alpines and other rock-garden plants. Beyond this walled area, situated so as to be comfortably warm even in very early spring, some wide stone steps would lead to the garden proper, a place of simplicity, formality, and symmetry. On either side, there would be tall, immaculately clipped hemlock hedges, serving as dark-green backdrops for well-planned perennial borders. In the borders would be peonies in May and early June—great billowing clumps of both single and double herbaceous peonies in shades of ruby and rose and white. There would be tree peonies as well, especially golds and creams. Later there would be martagon lilies, planted in vast drifts, their tall stems leaning at a graceful angle to display their lovely tiers of blossoms. I would have delphiniums, of course, tall ones, discreetly staked, massed together for emphasis, their rich blues and deep purples set off by the soft gray foliage of nearby artemisia and by white clouds of baby's breath. A great many astilbes, mostly white and apricot-pink, would occupy the shadier nooks of the border, along with purple aconites, dark and sinister for their hint of poison. In midsummer there would, of course, be foxgloves and phlox and a multitude of daylilies. In September great masses of perennial asters would glow in rich purples and pinks as the garden moved toward its sleep of winter.

I have already spent many thousands of dollars, but it's not my money anyway, so I shall proceed.

This garden, as I have described it, would be lovely, but also claustrophobic. There must be some means of escape from symmetry into informality, from artificiality into nature, from order into wildness. So I would make my garden not a destination in itself but an entrance into something other than itself. It would have two exits.

The first would be an archway, invisible from the top of

the garden, cut into the right-hand hedge of hemlock, at a momentary break in the expanse of perennial border. It would lead to a curving path through a damp and shaded garden where primroses grow—not the polyanthus or cowslip kind, but the tall Himalayan sort, with their blossoms in tiered whorls at several points along the stem—to an open meadow where wild tulips, naturalized from seed collected in Turkey, bloom in May. Eventually the path would curve back on itself to the primroses and the secret arch in the hedge.

The second exit would be a parting of the hedge down at the bottom of the garden, where shade trees grow and where there would be a bench, with hostas planted around, on which to sit and contemplate the garden above. From below I would hear the inviting sound of a stream tumbling over massive granite boulders down to the valley. A stone bridge, arching the stream, would lead to a wide path up the hill through a woodland of hemlocks and beeches and oaks to places where wild trilliums and lady's slippers grow, a retreat from all symmetry and formality.

It's a lovely, almost perfect garden. But I can take no credit for it, for it isn't at all the product of imagination. It is a garden remembered, and like all memories, this one may not be exact in its details. There may have been no aconites.

It is—or was—Grace Root's garden, also known as the Root Glen. It was—or is—a real garden, in Clinton, New York, brought into being over many decades by Mrs. Root, the closest thing to a dowager empress I've ever known. I met Grace Root in 1967, when I moved with my family to a rented farm in Clinton, New York, having been chosen a charter member of the faculty of Kirkland College, the brand-new sister institution to Hamilton. Mrs. Root, a trustee, invited me for Sunday dinner. I declined, fearing that if I somehow displeased her—and she had a reputation for eccentricity—I would be out of a job. The next Sunday she again invited me and I again declined. The following Monday the president of Kirkland told me that I would again be invited to have dinner with Mrs. Root and warned me that *no one* turned her invitations down, certainly not three times running.

The next Sunday at noon, my wife and I arrived. My fears

turned out to be groundless. Mrs. Root, who had moved out of the big white house after turning it over to Hamilton for an art center, greeted us warmly at the door of the rambling, one-story cottage formerly occupied by her head gardener. Although she was badly afflicted by arthritis and needed a cane to walk, she was lively in mind and spirit.

"Please sit here with me," she said. "I hear you are a gardener. Tell me, do you also like dry vermouth? If so, I think we shall get on very well indeed."

It was the first of many visits. We drank more dry vermouth than I like to confess—or than I found comfortable the next morning. She told me that she had been friends with Edmund Wilson, Dorothy Parker, and Alexander Woollcott, who is buried in the cemetery at Hamilton College. She talked about his funeral. Through some mistake, his body had been shipped not to Hamilton College in Clinton, New York, but to Colgate College in Hamilton, New York. It took hours to correct the error, and when the coffin was lowered, it slipped, splattering mud on the mourners, causing Dorothy Parker to remark, "How like him— throwing dirt until the very last." Somewhere in the middle of our fourth vermouth, Grace was no longer "Mrs. Root," and she was telling me about the time she and her late husband went to Turkey and collected wild tulip seeds for the Glen. She mentioned along the way that a preacher in Clinton had once denounced her as "the scarlet woman of College Hill," adding, "You cannot imagine what satisfaction I take in the fact that his church has now been turned into a town art center."

After dinner Grace Root invited us to survey the garden from the walled area at the top, as she told us its history. She mentioned that she feared that on her death Hamilton College would want to take it over and turn it into a ski slope.

"But that won't happen," she said. "I've spent a lifetime making this garden, and I've seen to it that my death won't be its undoing." She spoke of foundations, trusts, complicated legal strategies with only one purpose—the perpetual care and tending of her garden, which she had already opened to the public.

During my three years in Clinton, I visited her garden a great many times. There were other Sunday dinners and much more vermouth. We corresponded from time to time after I moved away, but her handwriting grew increasingly faint and spidery. Then one day I heard that Grace Root had died in New York City, where she always spent her winters.

I trust that her legal strategies worked, that her garden is still there, as lovely as ever. If it isn't, I don't want to know.

Clubs for People Who
Fall in Love with Plants

Amateur gardeners have the reputation of being generally sensible and reasonable people, partly because if our gardens are to work at all, we must keep our lives in harmony with the seasons. When it's time to prune, we prune. If we don't get the chickweed in time, it will get us. To have tulips in the spring, we must order them in the summer and plant them in the fall. We patiently build up piles of lawn clippings and fallen leaves to make compost to enrich our shrubbery and perennial borders. Surely we are solid, well-balanced souls—aren't we?

I don't think so. Amateurs are by definition lovers, and our deepest thinkers have long and repeatedly warned us that lovers usually act irrationally. Plato pointed out in his *Symposium* that we constantly forgive conduct in lovers that we would condemn in people in their right minds. José Ortega y Gasset likened love to a kind of disease of perception, which narrows its focus on a single object and attributes to it enormous merit and beauty, much of it fictitious.

Plato and Ortega were talking about the love of persons for persons, but it's certainly possible to fall in love with some particular kind of plant. I know. I've been there. For iris, for hemerocallis, and for daffodils, all in their turn, I've felt the same sudden and inexplicable attraction that knocked me off my feet in the ninth grade, when a girl named Della asked me to sit by her on a piano bench and turn pages while she played Mendelssohn's *Rondo capriccioso*.

Here's how it happens. One moment an iris (or some other

plant, and almost any will do) is just an iris. The next minute it seems changed into something more wonderful than anything else on earth. You're hooked. Ravished by an infatuation that may last a lifetime, you can't help yourself. Addicted to iris or peonies or camellias, you can think of little else.

People who fall in love with one kind of plant undergo visible changes of behavior. They send for catalogs from nurseries specializing in the object of their devotion. When the catalogs come, they pore over them for hours, like religious scholars trying to put the proper interpretation on a difficult text. They make long lists of the plants they mean to order, and they often end up ordering far more plants than they can use and spending far more money than they had intended—or than they will admit to their spouses. They bore their friends with unintelligible raptures over whatever orchid or amaryllis or oleander they've just added to their collection.

Their conversation takes an odd turn. Since individual cultivars of various kinds of plant are often named after people, some of the things plant lovers say can sound quite alarming to outsiders. A daylily aficionado, for example, might be overheard saying that J. Edgar Hoover looked better than ever this summer, that he's just given Lucretia Borgia a dose of insecticide for mites, or that he must remember to put some cow manure around Sir Patrick Spens.

People who feel unusually deep affection for the same things often seek each other out, so it isn't at all surprising that there are a number of societies or associations dedicated to particular plants or particular kinds of gardening. As a member of several such societies—and a former member of several others, where passion has waned—I can testify that they offer their members a great deal for very little. For anywhere from $2.50 (the American Gourd Society) to $20 (the American Orchid Society), the specialized plant lover can find and enjoy the company of like-minded folk.

Until just recently, I hadn't the faintest notion how many such plant societies there are in this country, but then I discovered the reference guide *North American Horticulture*, published in 1982 by the American Horticultural Society. It devotes an entire chapter to plant societies—some fifty-five in all.

These organizations have much in common. Generally they publish quarterly newsletters or bulletins, sometimes an annual yearbook. Many sponsor regional meetings and annual conventions, so that daffodil people may gather one April in Williamsburg, the next in Nashville, while the daylily crowd takes in Dallas in late May one year, Chicago in mid-June the next, for several days of visiting gardens, looking at slides, listening to lectures, and above all enjoying being with others who understand their passion. Plant-swapping programs are fairly common. Usually a society will have a registrar to keep track of named cultivars, to ensure that two different hibiscus, for example, don't turn up both called Glenn Gould. Some cater to members with a scientific interest in the plant they promote, others to hobbyists, and some to a mixture of both. The publications of the American Hemerocallis Society, for instance, are remarkable in the way a highly technical scientific article about the induction of polyploidy in hemerocallis may appear cheek by jowl with a sentimental poem addressed to daylilies in general.

Some of the societies are large and fairly old. The American Rose Society, with 16,000 members, dates back to 1899; the American Orchid Society, with 23,000 members, to 1921. A number of common and familiar plants have their societies—for example, the African violet, the peony, the lily, the iris, and the dahlia. But there are also societies whose members are dedicated to more unusual interests—the International Carnivorous Plant Society, for one—and to styles of gardening, such as bonsai and rock gardening, rather than to a single genus of plants.

Almost all these societies are amiably democratic in their qualifications for membership. An interest in the plant they promote and the payment of dues are all that's required. But the Herb Society of America, an organization of 1,500 members founded in 1933 and headquartered in Boston, is something different. It lists no dues, but its rules sternly exclude neophytes by requiring that prospective members be sponsored by at least two other members willing to attest to their seriousness of purpose and their prior achievements in raising herbs.

That strikes me as elitist, but when I said so to one of this society's members, she corrected me gently by explaining that the rules are meant to exclude herb kooks (she said "eccentrics") who run around making wild claims that borage will cure cancer or that basil is an unfailing remedy against flatulence and other distressing disorders.

Maybe so. But isn't there some pleasure in belonging to an organization that isn't open to just anyone with the money to buy his way in?

Garden Advisors

It's high time for me to offer thanks—and a bit of confession—to those dedicated, wise, and gently chiding souls who write garden columns in almost every American newspaper. What Ann Landers is to heartbroken adolescents who fear they've got terminal acne, and to women in Sacramento who find lipstick on their husbands' jogging shoes, these garden columnists are to us readers who need advice and who also can stand occasional prodding to tend to our horticultural chores at just the proper time.

They answer our questions, and it usually turns out that we are in even worse trouble than we suspected. We write to tell them that we are vaguely alarmed about something a bit odd happening to our aspidistra, that we fear some strange goings-on among our clematis vines, that there's something terribly the matter out in the peony patch. The columnists may not comfort us, but at least they give us names for our malaise, letting us know that we're cursed with scale, scab, scald, or smut, that nematodes or grubs are afoot, or that the lantana cannot possibly survive its latest attack by white flies or red spider mites.

Sometimes they offer us remedies.

Question: I have just noticed some tiny purple spots on the stems of the dieffenbachia in my living room. They have no legs or wings, but they move around like crazy anyway, so what should I do?

W.C.L. *(Lindenwold, N.J.)*

Answer: Your dieffenbachia is infested by artichoke mites, very small insects with microscopic legs. Unfortunately, they carry Herpes IX, a virus which spreads rapidly to apple trees, juniper, sedum, delphiniums, zinnias, and humans, where it causes impotence, a yearning to travel to places you can't afford, and sometimes an untimely death. Burn your house to the ground immediately, see a physician, and make certain that you have a valid will.

But usually, by the time someone writes a garden columnist for advice it's too late. The squash borers have already done in the zucchini, botrytis has decimated the lilies, slugs have ruined all the tomatoes, and the old lilac hedge might just as well be bulldozed and replaced by a fence. The problem with much good advice is that it can't be retroactive.

These columnists, however, provide a valuable second service. Week by week, all year long, they tell us what we must do *now*, before the moment passes and it's too late. In November they remind us to clean, sharpen, lubricate, and store our tools, and they harp on us to be sure to drain our gasoline-powered lawnmowers and weeders to avoid clogging the lines with varnish and gum. In December they tell us to order seed catalogs. In January they tell us to clean, sharpen, lubricate, and store our tools, in case we weren't listening to them in November. In February they inform us that it's almost too late to order seeds, and they suggest that we try some Oriental vegetables so that we won't be stuck next summer with the same old boring fare of tomatoes, peppers, and squash. In March they insist that we get to it and apply dormant oil spray to our fruit trees, and in late April they warn us that unless we dead-head our daffodils immediately to remove spent blossoms, there'll be much skimpier bloom next spring.

And so it goes, throughout the gardening year. As faithful as the alarm clocks that scold us awake each morning, these writers are constantly there with excellent and timely advice. They tell us what we need to know precisely when we need to know it. But whenever I consider the debts I owe them for all their sage counsel, I get what my people in Texas used to call "the willies"—that plaguing feeling of guilt that I have neglected my duties and failed to honor those who pointed out to me the paths of righteousness.

In June I finally go, shears in hand, to dead-head my daffodils, only to discover that they have already lapsed into dormancy. Their scanty bloom next year will be my punishment. In July, huge colonies of crabgrass scuttle across my lawn, luxuriating in the fertilizers I put down last spring. I would have a thick turf of desirable grasses like Kentucky bluegrass and fescue if only I had applied pre-emergent crabicide when the Sunday paper advised it, back in April. I tell myself the lie that I didn't do so because I've reached a higher level of ecological consciousness. My neighbor's lawn is enviably velvety, without a sprig of crabgrass in sight. When he walks past my yard, he tries not to look; if we meet on the sidewalk, he smiles, but I can sense his inner sneer.

The damage the gypsy moths did to my trees is partly my fault. I should have searched my property, as I was told in midwinter, to locate and destroy as many of their egg cases as possible.

I yawn when I walk into my vegetable garden. It's thriving, but it's the same old deadly bore, an unimaginative collection of tomatoes, peppers, and squash. I could have had snow peas, bok choy, Japanese black radishes, and Chinese cucumbers. I might have planted some of the celeriac I like so much, cooked and served German-style, cold, with a dressing of oil and vinegar. I could have had some arugula or Malabar spinach or parsnips for the winter. I might have had some of the new melons from Israeli breeders. I was given good advice, but ignored it, to my loss.

I tell myself that I will do better in the future, but I know I won't. The columnists who give garden advice seem unanimously to believe that gardens are made by rational foresight, prudent planning, and prompt attention to the right thing at the right time.

My garden whispers something else in my ear. It has come into being through sudden impulses, happy mistakes, and unfortunate accidents, and my own enduring willingness to tolerate ambiguity and to practice procrastination whenever possible. The gypsy moths and I love it.

Keeping Record

There's one simple garden tool that often goes unmentioned by newspaper garden columnists, never needs oiling or sharpening, and is truly indispensable. It is the garden journal—a sturdy book of blank pages in which to record the ongoing history of the particular corner of the earth we happen to occupy and tend.

The reason for keeping a garden journal can be summed up in a single word: time. Some arts, sculpture and architecture for instance, are spatial. Others, like music, are purely temporal. But gardening, like the dance, is both spatial and temporal. A garden fills a three-dimensional space, but it also grows, changing with the seasons and the years. We plant tulips in autumn, anticipating the bright resurrection they will bring to our gardens and our spirits come spring. We set out small Japanese maples, knowing that we will be ten years older before they look like much. We plant oaks, aware that they are our gift to future generations. Sometimes we survey our gardens, making an inventory of our regrets and our satisfactions. We should have been more generous with peonies. We never should have left that yew so close to the house, letting it grow as it pleased, cutting down the light the house plants need. It was a fine idea to plant bayberry and beach plum and rugosa rose out by the garden gate, to make that bed of vinca by the deck, edged in a broad band of muscari and chionodoxa in the spring, with tall lilies towering upward in June and July.

Gardeners are forgetful. Even a modest garden is a complicated venture, and memory alone is insufficient to keep track of it all. Without some written record to aid remembrance, a garden may in time become so filled with vexing puzzles that it is tempting just to pave everything over with concrete and take up tennis instead.

When it's time to prune clematis, you need to know the names of the clematis you've got. *Clematis* x jackmanii blooms on new wood and needs to be cut back severely in early spring. Other cultivars, such as Nelly Moser and Ramona, bloom on mature wood and require only light pruning, just enough to keep them shapely and in bounds. When it's time to cultivate the perennial border, you need to know where you planted the lilies last November, so you won't decapitate them with a hoe before they break through the ground in April.

The fancier stationery shops sell impressive garden journals made for the purpose—leather-bound, with the words *Garden Journal* and even your name stamped in gold leaf on the cover. But a plain, clothbound ledger from the nearest office supply store will do just as well. The one I have cost $3.99. Its 200 pages have lasted me over ten years, but before long I'll have Volume II underway.

What should go into a garden journal? Journal-keeping, like the diaries of Casanova and the lists Leperello kept of his master Don Giovanni's seductions (". . . and in Spain, 1,003!"), is an entirely personal pastime. There are no real rules. I don't keep mine in any slavish way. I lack the dedication my mother had for three years in the early 1930s, when she recorded every event in her life during the time she was waiting for my father to propose—and then trying to decide whether to accept or not. Sometimes I go for months without writing anything down, sometimes I've written at least once a week. I make lists of plants I've ordered by mail or bought from local nurseries. I make maps of daylilies and daffodils, so I'll know what they are when they bloom and so I won't buy new ones that duplicate those I've already got. Occasionally I paste in photographs, so that I can trace the way the garden has developed over a decade, the changes it has seen. I usually manage to record the more spectacular storms—the hurricane that damaged the wild cherry trees in the side yard in 1976, the blizzard in February 1978 that trapped my family inside the house for three days. Sometimes I mention the animals hereabouts—the nest of baby rabbits we had by the spruce tree in April 1980, the chipmunks by the back door last year, the raccoon that took up residence in the hollow branch of a maple tree. The latest entry in my journal notes that on June 20, 1983, the sixteen-year-old collie-shepherd, Heidi, who grew into senescence from puppyhood, even as my sons grew from childhood into manhood, suffered a terrible stroke and had to be put to sleep. The inevitability of this loss did not ease my grief, or my wife's and our sons'.

My journal is a fair record of many of the things that have taken place on my home ground.

But it also has its share of mysteries, thanks to terrible handwriting that sometimes baffles even me. In December 1974 I wrote: "Be *sure* to order glmpks from R.O." Who or what R.O. might be and what one does with glmpks, I really can't say.

Wonderful Stuff:
The Joys of Compost

I've never been an Organic Gardener of the Strict Observance, although I lean more and more in that direction and I'm increasingly bothered by the knowledge that the amount of pesticides used in the United States soared from 200,000 pounds in 1950 to roughly 1.6 billion in 1976. But even when I was blithely using all sorts of chemicals to keep things going in the garden as I thought they should, I was devout in my admiration for compost.

I still am. It's wonderful stuff. I like the look of it when it's finished and has turned dark and crumbly. I love the smell of it, its heavy earthen aroma like a woodland clearing after a summer shower. I like the things I know it does for my garden, the improvement it works in my sandy soil, the way it stores up precious moisture against drought. And there's great satisfaction in the thought that compost takes what would otherwise be only trash and garbage—dead leaves and lawn clippings, lemon peel and watermelon rind, coffee grounds and the remnants of salads —and turns them into something of great value. Making compost, like making good wine, is horticultural alchemy.

But the problem with compost is that there's never really enough of it to go around. One year the entire pile goes to my small garden, where I spread it several inches thick and then till it into the soil just before it's time to plant the first crop of lettuce. Another year it will mulch a section of the perennial border. I can always use more than I have.

A couple of summers ago I set about to solve my problem of the compost gap. My older son, Paul, had just taken a summer job working for his friend Bob, a rising young entrepreneur in the lawnmowing trade. Every week Bob and his crews mow and trim lawns for almost ninety regular customers. Several times each day his trucks drive to a dump four miles outside of town to get rid of the clippings.

I had an inspiration. Bob could save a little gasoline and I could get all the compost my heart desired if he'd just dump a few loads in my yard. Bob was agreeable to the idea, so one Sunday I laid the foundations of a compost heap of monumental proportions, one that would dwarf every other compost heap in town, and maybe in the county. I bought fifty feet of heavy metal fencing and wired it together to produce a circular crib five feet high and a little more than fourteen feet across.

The next day Bob made four trips with his truck and dumped the clippings next to the curb. Layer by layer I added the clippings, occasionally throwing in a little dirt and wetting each successive layer with the garden hose. By standing on a ladder for the final layers, I managed to fill the crib to overflowing, and then some. By eight that night the work was done. I knew that I would pay for my labor the next day with a spectacular backache and cramped knees, but it didn't matter. I was happy at the thought that soon the compost would start to work as millions of bacteria began to break down the material. As the pile settled I would add another truckload of clippings, and then another. Maybe I'd even build a second crib—why not a third?—to take full advantage of Bob's generosity. Next spring would be rich with compost; I might even be able to spare some for the neighbors.

I contemplated my compost heap with satisfaction, little knowing that I was about to be repaid for my overweening pride. The clippings gave off the sweet scent of new-mown hay. The bacteria began their work. The next morning the top layer of grass was warm to the touch, and that afternoon, when I climbed the ladder to stir the clippings a bit with a pitchfork, a cloud of steam rose in the air, rich and yeasty in the nostrils.

All was well until the fourth day, when things took an ugly turn. I noticed an odd smell—like nothing I had ever encountered with compost heaps of more modest dimensions. The odor was faint, a mere hint of something nasty, but it was definitely coming from the compost heap. And with every hour it grew perceptibly stronger. There was trouble in my biomass. I could find no analogy in my experience to describe the odor, but I suspected that factories making dioxin probably smelled like that.

By the dawn of the fifth day, my wife had closed all the windows overlooking the back yard. The swimming pool next door, usually filled with giggling preteens, grew suddenly silent. Our family dog whined and refused to go out the back door.

The air grew poisonous, and so did my relations with other people. My wife took to the beach with an Agatha Christie mystery in German translation. It may have dealt with someone who murders a husband who deserves it. My sons bitched that the smell was enough to gag a maggot, and they decided to sleep over with friends on the other side of town. My in-laws were advised to postpone their impending visit. My neighbor with the swimming pool left a note in my mailbox saying that whatever I was brewing at my place had just lowered property values by 50 percent. That evening when we passed on the sidewalk, he shot me a glance that would have laid flat a forest.

I had been undone by simple greed and by inattention to a fundamental biological fact: the difference between aerobic and anaerobic decomposition of organic matter. One set of bacteria presides over decay when there is oxygen present, another when there is not. In a modest-sized compost heap, properly turned and aerated with a fork from time to time, there is no unpleasant odor to assault the nose and upset the neighbors. But in my lust for compost I had created a Frankenstein monster, a compost heap so large that there was no way to turn it. When the oxygen was exhausted deep within the pile, anaerobic microbes took over, and the result was evil-smelling gases, foul enough to have been concocted by Lucifer himself.

There is no known way to deodorize a compost heap gone wild. We had to last it out, and it took two weeks for the odor to start subsiding. Finally, the organic meltdown in my back yard cooled off. My wife opened the back windows. I admired the tan she had acquired at the beach. My sons stayed home at night, and laughter returned to the swimming pool next door.

When we met on the sidewalk, my neighbor managed a faint smile.

I have continued to have a compost heap where I put lemon peel and watermelon rind, coffee grounds and the remnants of salads, and lawn clippings. The clippings come from my lawn and my lawn only.

The On-Growing Crimes of Budding and Liebig

For some time now I've been increasingly convinced that the world would be a better place for gardeners if Edwin Budding and Justus Liebig, two nineteenth-century gentlemen with bright ideas, hadn't let these ideas loose in public. Budding, an English engineer, invented the lawnmower, a device to keep grass short. Liebig, a German professor of science, invented chemical fertilizer, a means to make it grow faster.

A moment's reflection is all it takes to see that these two ideas are at odds, but I reached my forty-eighth year before I suddenly perceived their contradiction. I was caught up in that most common and pervasive of all American suburban superstitions, the belief, as Henry Mitchell has put it, that the lawnless life is not worth living.

Each spring I did homage to Justus Liebig—and increased the profits of those who manufacture and sell lawn fertilizers—by peppering the lawn with nitrogen, phosphorus, and potassium. And as often as twice a week, unless I could persuade one of my sons unto the task, I honored the memory of Edwin Budding by revving up the mower to attack the lush growth of fescue, bluegrass, dandelions, crabgrass, chickweed, and purslane.

Last year I began to feel some of these nagging doubts about my behavior that seem to go along with attaining middle age—or maturity and wisdom, as I prefer to call this condition. Was the lawn serving me, or I it? Did I need a lawn at all? If so, how much? Just down the street, someone else apparently was asking the same questions and coming up with a radical answer. One day there was a lawn there, the next day a vast expanse of red pebbles, hemmed in by railroad ties.

I considered all the gardens I had heard about or seen that make no use of neatly clipped grass. The painter Claude Monet made do for several decades at Giverney with a few fruit trees and a lot of water lilies. I've heard people go into rhapsodic ecstasy over Japanese gardens made of raked pebbles, two or three half-buried boulders, a handful of moss and lichen, and maybe a little bamboo. When I visited the Alhambra, I heard the sounds of fountains splashing and tourists' cameras clicking, but no power mowers.

Lawns, after all, are by no means universal in the history of gardening, and they have no special antiquity. They are British in origin, evolving in the eighteenth century, partly from the bowling greens of English villages (which were cut painstakingly by hand), partly from pastures and meadows. The first lawns worthy of the name were vast expanses of grass on the estates of English gentry, and they were kept mown by cattle and sheep. These animals, which also provided fertilizer, were kept in their proper places by the invention, late in the eighteenth century, of the "ha-ha," a deep concealed trench surrounding the immediate grounds of the country house to prevent sheep from nibbling on the roses and cows from adorning the terraces with dung.

Mr. Budding, it seems, didn't invent the lawn: he democratized it by giving the world mechanical sheep. His mower was a monstrous contraption of clanking metal reels, cutting bars, and wheels, inspired by the machinery used in British textile mills to cut the pile on thick fabrics. So heavy it required several men to pull it, it was one of the first contributions of the Industrial Revolution to the serious gardener—to the serious gardener, that is, who could find some other people to help.

Then, some weeks ago, I saw it: the cure for my malaise over my lawn and my first step into a new, post-industrial style of gardening. It was a veritable mountain of shaven cedar bark, on a back road deep in the country, next to a sawmill that specializes in fence posts.

When I talked to the mill's owner about the bark, he was amiably inclined to sell me as much as I wanted, at a price so low it was evident the news about what mulch was bringing these days had somehow not reached his ears. I didn't want to smother my entire yard in bark—only half of it, a side yard and a part of the front yard where the growth was patchy despite my chemical homage to Herr Liebig each spring. I calculated that it would take eight cubic yards to do the job, so I ordered sixteen out of lifelong devotion to the principle of going to extremes whenever possible. At $80, it was a bargain.

The next day when the truck arrived I had two surprises. The first came when I saw how the abstraction "sixteen cubic yards" looked when it became a concrete reality. I had my own mountain of cedar bark now, so imposing that the cat hissed at it in alarm while I knit my brows and tried to calculate how many wheelbarrow loads it would take to get it spread out and to consider ways to inveigle my family and friends to help with the task.

The second surprise came when the truck started to back out of the yard and got too close to an abandoned cesspool. The earth trembled like gelatin all around the cesspool as its brick walls buckled and collapsed. A chasm six feet across and eight feet deep opened up. If the truck had been two seconds later in pulling away, it would probably still be in our back yard, its front wheels high in the air, its rear wheels hopelessly stuck in a huge hole.

The mulch turned out not to be such a bargain, after all, considering the $150 worth of dirt it took to fill in the old cesspool. But all the cedar bark is spread now. I am much pleased by the way it gives a sense of unity to a rather haphazard and unplanned part of my garden. Although it will pack down considerably come winter, right now it's spread some twelve inches deep. It has a satisfying woodsy feel underfoot and a zesty cedar spice just after a sudden summer shower.

What's left of my lawn now takes just forty-five minutes to mow—hardly time enough to raise a decent sweat or to work up a proper resentment of those two nineteenth-century gentlemen whose bright ideas so long enslaved me to too much turf.

The Cutting Garden

Without any statistical or historical evidence to back me up, I would hazard the guess that the market pack, a plastic or fiber box the size of a brick containing six to eight annual bedding plants already blooming, has much transformed the habits of home gardeners since the end of World War II. I clearly recall the day when there were only two ways to get bedding plants. Some things, like alyssum and candytuft, you could buy in wooden flats filled with dirt. The plants were always quite small, certainly not blooming size. Most other things, especially flowers that transplant poorly, such as larkspur and poppies and zinnias, had to be planted from seed—the soil was cultivated, string was stretched out to mark the rows if you were the tidy type, the seeds were sown and watered well. Then you waited for them to come up, meanwhile keeping the packets with their little line drawings showing what the small seedlings looked like, so you wouldn't pull up the calendulas and keep the ragweed. This kind of horticultural practice, doing it yourself instead of resorting to ready-made, produced a particular kind of garden—rows and rows of zinnias and marigolds and scabiosas and sunflowers and cosmos, all in a bright crazy quilt of colors to which the word "subtle" just didn't apply. Such a garden was nice to look at, but its primary purpose was to produce an abundance of cheery cut flowers for the house.

I still see the packets of zinnias and so on in the racks at the grocery store and the garden center. Someone must buy them, but the fact is that I don't see them and other annuals growing for cut flowers in my neighbors' gardens these days. What I see instead are the instant gardens that miraculously appear hereabouts every May 1, when, like lemmings, we all head for the local garden center to fill up our car trunks with market packs of begonias, petunias, dwarf marigolds, red salvias, and especially impatiens. There's nothing wrong with any of these plants, except that it gets boring to see the same old things in every garden in town and that none of them is worth a damn as a cut flower.

For some time now, my wife has insisted that we simply had to do something about keeping her supplied with cut flowers. I insisted right back that we had a pretty good perennial border, but when I thought further about the matter, I realized that it had its drawbacks as a source of flowers for the house. Many of the flowers it contains—daylilies, shrubby potentilla, and monarda, to name a few—are no more suitable for arranging than are petunias and wax begonias. Some, like delphiniums (those years when I've got some), are suitable, but I tend to resent their disappearance out in the yard.

This year we worked out a treaty in which I ceded her some territory out back, a piece of land with a little history to it. Originally, when our sons were smaller and we first moved in, it was a basketball court, made of the golden-red sandy gravel that lies about six inches below the thin topsoil in this part of the country. A couple of years later, pointing out to my sons that there was a much better concrete court two doors down at the junior high school, I took it over for a vegetable garden, although it took two years more before it raised very much in the way of vegetables. I made it the sole beneficiary of our compost heap, and I dug in bushels and bushels of leaves every fall. I planted winter rye as a green manure and dug it in each spring. In time, the soil in my vegetable patch turned rich and brown.

Now I've handed over most of that piece of earth to my wife to use as a cutting garden. To be absolutely truthful, I wasn't much of a vegetable gardener, anyway. I never got it weeded in time. I never thought about staking the tomatoes until it was far too late. I never remembered to plant vegetables that aren't available at our grocery stores or roadside stands. The vegetable garden was a living testimonial to my deficiencies, so I gave it away with good cheer, holding back just enough to keep us in chives and lettuce and parsley.

I like the result. Where untidy tomatoes once sprawled and the zucchini once had its annual population explosion, there are now orderly rows of old-fashioned things like zinnias, scabiosas, larkspur, sunflowers, and, above all, cosmos, which my wife professes is the mainstay of anyone who likes to arrange flowers in a loose and informal way, simply fixing them so they look right in a vase. Over the years, I'd come to forget how striking zinnias can be. It's good to see them again.

Hydrangeas? Never!

Show me a person without prejudice of any kind on any subject and I'll show you someone who may be admirably virtuous but is surely no gardener. Prejudice against people is reprehensible, but a healthy set of prejudices is a gardener's best friend. Gardening is complicated, and prejudice simplifies it enormously.

Plants can be divided into three basic sorts. There are those that only a madman could love. These include poison ivy (though it's pretty in the autumn), chickweed, crabgrass, wild onions, sticker burrs, and bull nettle—weeds that tempt most normal people to declare chemical war, no matter how deeply they may feel that Rachel Carson was on to something. Then there are those plants that only the perverse could dislike. Among garden flowers, these include bleeding heart, clematis, lilies, roses, and tulips. Among wildflowers, add butterfly weed, gentian, shooting stars, sunflowers, and, despite its name, toadflax.

But in between there are hundreds of flowering plants about which some controversy is possible. No gardener, not even those few who still have lots of land and hosts of workers to do their bidding, can plant them all. Here, a little dose of prejudice comes to the rescue.

I have a friend who can't bear the sight of any flower whose stamens show. It may sound Victorian and quaint, but this antipathy makes her gardening exquisitely simple. At a blow, it excludes single peonies, daylilies, daisies, and dozens and dozens of other species from her consideration.

My own prejudices include celosias, purple alyssum, fancy-leafed caladiums, annual salvias, gladiolas, and a surprisingly large number of other plants. Since my wife has a list that only partially overlaps mine, ordering seeds is for us much simpler than it might otherwise be.

But let me dwell for a moment on one plant I especially detest—the hydrangea, by which I mean the bushy ornamental sorts, not the tree and climbing kinds, which I admire. Where I live, a great many people adore hydrangeas. These folks are as inexplicable, to me, as those who enjoy eating haggis. There is a Hydrangea Trail that stretches more miles than I like to think about. People compete to win prizes for the best hydrangea. They call in photographers to have their pictures taken in front of their prized shrubs. They talk lovingly to total strangers about the hydrangeas they've got, the way some people talk about their grandchildren.

Not me. I just don't like them. I think they're a major mistake on the part of the evolutionary process. They seem best suited for the terraces of the fashionable spas of bygone days, not for home gardens. (I did like the hydrangeas that appeared on the terraces of the Lido hotel where Von Aschenbach stayed in the film *Death in Venice*. They added to the overall mood of decadence and obsession.)

Hydrangeas look artificial. I'd be hard put to tell the difference between a plastic one and a real one. And they are far too accommodating to people who have color schemes in mind for their gardens as well as their living rooms. Add lime to the soil, and the blossoms turn pink. Add aluminum sulphate, and they go cobalt-blue. Add both, and they look confused. I like plants that have firm convictions about what color their flowers will be. Off with their heads!

I can imagine now a hundred devoted hydrangeaphiles advancing in protest, shouting, "Sir! Your negative feelings toward these plants are ill-considered and irrational. Unfair! Unfair!"

They would be absolutely correct, of course. I give reasons for not liking hydrangeas, but the dislike came first and the reasons afterward. Perhaps one day I'll decide that I like hydrangeas, after all, just as not long ago, after a lifetime of disaffection toward them, I decided that I really liked hostas. If and when that comes to pass with hydrangeas, I'll find new reasons to support my changed opinion.

Elephant Ears

My wife and I have an agreement about what goes into our garden. Each of us holds absolute veto over the plants that are allowed to grow there, except for the weeds, which ignore our wishes. This isn't to say that there's no room for persuasion or for reopening the case of something that one of us has black-balled in the past. Right now, I have a hankering to grow some elephant ears, but I know it will be tough going to overcome her conviction that elephant ears are high on the list of plants the Lacys don't grow.

She says they're tacky. I'm not so sure, but she's certainly right that elephant ears sometimes occur in surroundings that no one could possibly call classy. There's a house not far away that is the epitome of tacky—tacky-died-and-gone-to-heaven, as my Aunt Faye used to say. The lawn is perfect, the closest thing I've seen hereabouts to the bent grass lawns of England, thanks to the constant application of every chemical made by Scotts and to the thrice-weekly mowing and edging it gets during the summer. Every shrub is ringed with impatiens and wax begonias. One bed spells out the owners' last name in letters of dusty miller against a mulch of pine chips. Since the house sits on a corner lot, almost everything in the garden is visible to passersby, and there's a lot to see besides the grass and all that impatiens. There's a darling little bridge arching an imaginary stream and leading nowhere, for no reason. A plaster Madonna stands next to a fake wishing well, gazing benevolently in the general direc- tion of a hugely swollen concrete toad. There are several blue-mirrored glass globes atop vinyl birdbaths. But the pièce de résistance is a phony flamingo, cunningly placed just to one side of a whitewashed tractor tire planted entirely in elephant ears. I know the elephant ears are beloved of the people who inhabit that house, for they alone, of all the attractions in their garden, are floodlit at night. Tacky is the right and proper word for that place. I know tacky when I see it. I've been to the Smoky Mountains and seen those chenille bedspreads with peacocks on them.

My wife may be right. She may also fear that if I permit myself to grow some elephant ears, the next step will be to buy a plaster burro pulling a sweet little cart filled with pink geraniums.

Nevertheless, I'm growing to like them, probably for the same reason that lately I've been looking at castor beans and cleome with a fond heart. They're big and splashy and unmistakable for any other plant. They make a statement. No one could possibly overlook them. If I wanted to write about plants the same way some critics write about wines, I'd say that elephant ears "have an assertive resonance in the home landscape." Also, they bring back some good childhood memories of neighbors who grew them—always, for some reason, right by their front stoops, and often in washtubs. They sprout up quickly every spring and rapidly reach their ultimate size, as much as six feet high with leaves two feet long, each on its private stem from the base of the bulb. And I love what they're called. Whoever dreamed up their common name deserves to be memorialized by the Association for the Promotion of Literalmindedness, for the metaphorical distance between the ears of a pachyderm and the leaves of this plant goes only as far as their color. (I am puzzled, however, at having learned not long ago that in Costa Rica, where they grow wild in pastures, they're called *ojo de pata*—"duck's eye.")

For now, I'm content merely to think about elephant ears and to read about them, without popping the question, "Dear spouse, might I please plant some elephant ears in our garden?" In some recent research, reading the entry on *Colocasia* (their scientific name) in T. H. Everett's *Illustrated Encyclopedia of Horticulture*, I'm inspired by the thought that maybe I could smuggle elephant ears onto our premises by presenting them as a vegetable, since the tubers of some species are also known as taro or dasheen, a common food crop in the tropics. The leaves are also eaten, boiled, in Hawaii, where they are one of the essential ingredients of poi. Everett warns, however, that both tubers and leaves absolutely must be cooked, and cooked a long time, to destroy the crystals of calcium oxylate they contain, which are like "tiny slivers of glass" capable of causing "intense and lasting pain" in anyone unlucky enough to ingest them.

Cooked, they're edible. (What I hear from people who have tried poi is not encouraging, but I've got one friend at least who assures me that cooked dasheen is very good.) Raw, they're a fitting means of torture. It sounds to me as if elephant ears would have been perfect for some of the great and noble art patrons and poisoners of Florence to have grown in terra-cotta tubs on their piazzas. No one ever accused the Borgias of being tacky.

That Aster

Ever since St. Augustine wrote conclusively on the matter in his *Confessions*, Western philosophers have had no excuse for ignoring the fact that human memory is a tricky thing. We forget a great many things that happen in our lives, perhaps most of them. What's more, we are perfectly capable of remembering things that never really happened at all, at least not in the way we tell ourselves they did.

So it is with that aster. In my version of its history, firmly reinforced by having been told so many times, I found it growing in an odd corner of the garden the first fall after we bought our house, a former farmhouse now surrounded by the typical houses of the New Jersey suburb that have filled what were its fields a century ago. Although we had some splendid trees and a fine lilac hedge on our property, the only perennials were a bank of *Hemerocallis fulva*, the hateful tawny daylily—and that aster, which was a wonderful dark purple, although the shade it grew in gave it weak stems. The next spring I planted it in an open, sunny spot in a new perennial bed. That fall I was rewarded by a truly glorious sight, an aster clump of eminent virtue.

It grew almost four feet high and as many feet across. Its woody stems were so sturdy that it required no staking, unlike most of the other perennial asters (some call them Michaelmas daisies) in my experience. For almost three weeks it was covered with many hundreds of small single purple blossoms, which, seen from a distance in early-morning light, shimmered like a mountain haze. It withstood a coastal storm that wrecked the chry-

That Aster

santhemums and played havoc with the tall marigolds. Best of all, it was irresistible to the monarch butterflies that gather in the marshes nearby on their flyway, awaiting favorable conditions to cross the Delaware Bay en route to their winter homes in the jungles of Mexico and Central America.

If Van Gogh had ever seen that aster on a bright September day, with the bright host of monarchs hovering about it and resting on its blossoms, I told myself, he would have forgotten all about cornfields and sunflowers and set up his easel in my front yard. It would surely have tempted Claude Monet away from water lilies, Georgia O'Keeffe from black irises and jack-in-the-pulpit. And it brought out the saint in me. With utter unselfishness, I wanted to share this treasure with others, starting with my neighbor Ed Plantan across the way. Ed is a formidable man when it comes to growing tomatoes. All during August and September he had kept us well supplied, leaving a small basket of ripe Big Boys and Beefsteaks on our side stoop every three or four days. I repaid him by giving him a small portion of the aster. It wasn't entirely an unselfish act, of course; since his garden is visible from my own, there would be more asters in my sight.

I divided the aster into many small clumps, sticking them anywhere in my garden that I thought might benefit from a purple September shimmer. I took a great many photographs of the aster at its height, but was disappointed when the slides came back and showed them pale blue. Some trick of emulsions and dyes, I suppose, but whatever it was, the beauty of that aster entirely eluded the ingenuity of chemistry and Kodak.

I wanted to spread that aster around the world. With the thought that gardeners everywhere ought to be growing it, I sat down one winter day at the typewriter to compose a letter to Amos Pettingill, the nom de plume of Eliot Wadsworth II, the current owner of White Flower Farm, a nursery in Litchfield, Connecticut, known for its rich list of perennials and other plants and for the extreme intelligence and wit of the prose in its catalog. Would White Flower Farm be interested, I wrote, in trying out a genuinely superior perennial aster and offering it to its customers if it lived up to my praise?

The answer was yes, and the following spring I delivered about half my stock to Wadsworth's chief propagator.

I wasn't at all surprised late that fall when the first reports came in. The aster had performed as well in Litchfield as it had in my garden in New Jersey. It would be increased to build up stock. It seemed very likely that in a couple of years it would be offered to the public in White Flower Farm's catalog. For several months, letters flew back and forth between Wadsworth and me about the plant we'd been calling simply Old Purple.

Then a new thought occurred to me. I hadn't dreamed of asking any payment for Old Purple. The thought that it would be growing in a myriad gardens all over the country was enough compensation. Well, almost enough. I've always liked the idea of naming a plant for someone. So I wrote Wadsworth again to say that, as names go, Old Purple lacked panache. Why not call it Hella Lacy, for my wife? She was less thrilled at being immortalized than I had imagined, but Wadsworth was agreeable. The Hella Lacy aster it would be. I sent small clumps of Hella Lacy to as many gardening friends as I could think of—even to Susan Leach, the head gardener at The Cloisters museum in New York, who promised to plant it in a prominent spot in the Cuxa Cloister.

The blow came in late winter, a year after it seemed a cinch that Hella Lacy would burst upon the garden world and create a sensation. Wadsworth wrote me a letter than can only be called a rejection notice—something I was quite familiar with as a writer but wholly unprepared to get as a would-be garden benefactor and wife immortalizer. Wadsworth was sorry, but a British visitor to White Flower Farm had seen my aster and declared it to be completely indistinguishable from Treasurer, an English cultivar already on the market.

I was forlorn, but Hella Lacy—the woman, not the plant—didn't mind at all, and I kept sending occasional plants to friends I'd missed, stubbornly telling them to call it Hella. And my disappointment has dimmed over the years as my original clump increased into dozens of clumps in my yard and Ed's, each a billowing cloud of glorious purple every fall.

There's only one trouble with the beginning of this story, the part about how I rescued the aster from its shady spot and turned it into a thing of beauty. I remember it all distinctly, including taking a clump over to Ed to repay him for the tomatoes. But that isn't true. The last time I trotted out my story about how I found the aster that almost got named for the mother of my children and told it to someone in her presence, the mother of my children hesitated slightly and then informed me that I had gotten it from Ed, not the other way around.

"That can't be," I said.

"But it is," she said. "Just look at Ed's yard. He's got five times as many of those asters as we do. Can you explain how that happened if you gave him his start? Besides, I remember the day he brought you your first clump."

I thought she was wrong. The explanation was simple. I had fewer clumps because I'd been dividing my own and sending them to friends, museum gardens, even an editor or two. Nevertheless, the first chance I had, I confronted Ed with a question: Did he happen to know where the asters we both grew came from?

"Sure," he said. "From Pennsylvania, an old garden on a farm that had belonged to a relative. We brought them here when we bought this place a couple of years before you moved into the neighborhood. They're real old-fashioned, but I still think they're pretty."

I've sheepishly stopped telling my version of the story. And sometimes when I'm browsing through a plant catalog and come across an aster called Treasurer I'm tempted to order it, to find out if the Englishman who banished my aster and my spouse from the White Flower Farm list had his spectacles on right.

[1991: This story has a happy ending: that Englishman was wrong. I sent Hella Lacy—the plant, not the woman—to several nurserymen besides Eliot Wadsworth, including Andre Viette, Allen Bush, and Nancy Goodwin. They all said that it wasn't Treasurer, but that it was very beautiful indeed. They propagated it until they had sufficient quantity to sell under the name I had proposed. Retail mail-order perennial catalogs all over the country now offer aster Hella Lacy, and wholesale growers are propagating it by the hundreds of thousands for sale in garden centers. Our son Paul just reported that he had found his mother in a nursery a few blocks from his house, growing in a one-gallon pot.]

Jaundiced View:
Yellow Geraniums

For anyone who writes on gardening, winter is the season for a great blizzard of promotional press kits and news releases from seed companies with their annual crop of breakthroughs, exciting innovations, great new departures, and historical firsts to announce. I have in front of me, for example, a fat folder from the Pan-American Seed Company, a wholesale house in West Chicago, Illinois. The covering letter, addressed "Dear Garden Communicator," informs me that it now offers the gardening public its Sweetheart strawberry, a perennial, everbearing sort it describes as "tasty," "colorful," and "bountiful." Its particular novelty is that it grows directly from seed, rather than from plants purchased from a mail-order nursery.

Pan-American Seed obviously hopes to persuade home gardeners to raise from seed plants that they used to grow in other ways. In 1982 the firm introduced its Explorer potato, also grown from seed, rather than from sections of tubers culled out of the previous crop.

Having grown neither this new strawberry nor this potato, I cannot speak to their merits except to observe that they should reduce the profits of the U.S. postal service and UPS.

Another recent horticultural press release has come to me from Thompson and Morgan, Inc., of Farmingdale, New Jersey, the recently established American scion of a venerable British seed company that has been in existence since 1855. The flier was disguised as a personal letter from Bruce J. Sangster, president, who not only misspelled my name but also managed to give me

Jaundiced View: Yellow Geraniums

a title I do not possess, garden editor of *The Wall Street Journal.*

I'm not complaining. Genealogical destiny gave me a last name that can be spelled in two ways, and my parents christened me with a first name that can be spelled in three. Besides, like most human beings, I don't mind if others take me to be more than I am, elevating me from writer to editor.

In addition, the president of Thompson and Morgan had big news to pass on—the achievement not only of a breakthrough and a historical first but of "a unique historical first," the breeding of a yellow-blossomed geranium. "This color," Mr. Sangster wrote, "has eluded gardeners since time began and so it became an increasingly more attractive goal to seed houses and plant breeders throughout the world to attain, always with the knowledge that this would become the most sought-after windowsill plant of the century."

Even the greatest of breakthroughs do sometimes run into problems. This particular breakthrough, for example, which did its original breaking through in England, encountered difficulties "associated with shipping large volumes of live plants across the Atlantic and satisfying the endless requirements of the U.S.D.A."

A catastrophic blow, it would seem. I pictured gardeners in this country panting for yellow geraniums, for this elusive, unique historical first that was, alas, forbidden them by the persnickety strictures of the Department of Agriculture.

But there's a happy ending. Insurmountable problems were surmounted when Plant Genetics, a California firm, heard of Thompson and Morgan's plight and offered a solution: fly in a few specimens of these plants to be multiplied by tissue culture in laboratories under sterile conditions with "surgeon-like precision cutting." "The end result," I have learned, "will be that this historical breakthrough will be available to garden fanatics in Europe, and, thanks to American technological expertise, in the United States simultaneously." But there's a hitch: every American household is limited to two plants, available at $24 the pair by mail order.

As for me, no thanks. The absence of yellow geraniums in this world has never bothered me especially, and I'm a little surprised to hear what an attractive goal such flowers have been for the plant breeders of our century. I can live contentedly without this particular historical breakthrough, and a good many others besides. I wouldn't be happier if there were white day-lilies (another elusive dream) out in my garden, or sky-blue zinnias, or marigolds the color of amethyst. I've heard tell of yellow delphiniums, and maybe red ones, but I wouldn't lift a finger to add them to my perennial border.

This year, when all danger of frost is past, I'll go out again to buy some geraniums for the old whiskey barrels I use as planters on our back yard deck. Red ones for sure, unless we decide on pink for a change. Maybe a few whites. And if there's someone who wants to have four of these yellow-bloomed historical breakthroughs instead of two, please, Mr. Sangster, let him have my allotted share.

Eminent Victorians:
Odd Practices on Lily Pads

Several garden books in my library make the same claim: The large, floating leaves of *Victoria amazonica*, the water lily named for Queen Victoria early in her long reign, will easily support the weight of a child, provided a little caution is used. And Alice Morse Earle's classic *Old Time Gardens* (1903) provides evidence that our Victorian ancestors were indeed overcome from time to time by the strange urge to emplace children on these lily pads, which can reach 10 feet in diameter and have upturned rims, like those on quiche pans. About her own experience, Miss Morse wrote, "I have never forgotten it, nor how afraid of it I was, for someone wanted to lift me upon the great leaf to see whether it would hold me above the water . . . I objected to this experiment with vehemence."

But I have some evidence of even more peculiar behavior on the part of grownups of that bygone day. Unsatisfied with merely lifting children onto lily pads, they occasionally stood on water lilies themselves and sometimes hired photographers to catch them in the act. A photograph from the archives of the Missouri Botanical Garden, dated 1900 or so, records one instance of this strange practice. Using a makeshift bridge of three wide planks resting on the leaf margins, a young couple stand on adjacent pads of *V. amazonica*. Dressed in their Sunday finery—he in a dark suit and starched shirt, holding a straw hat in his hand, she in a long skirt and a frilly blouse with a high collar, her waist cinched in sharply, a feathered bonnet clutched to her side—neither betrays the slightest hint of the thought that standing on a water-lily leaf is possibly dangerous and certainly odd. (And a closer look shows that they've cheated a bit, covering the leaves with boards to distribute their weight and avoid a sudden and embarrassing dunking.)

From its discovery in Bolivia in 1803, when the Czech botanist Thaddaeus Haehnke fell to his knees in wonder on the banks of the sluggish and muddy river where he saw it growing, the Victoria water lily has excited the imagination of many. The French naturalist Aimé Bonpland is said to have almost fallen off his raft when he spotted it in a stream in Brazil and to have talked excitedly to himself about nothing else for a solid month afterward. Robert Schomburgk, who came upon V. *amazonica* in Guyana in 1837 and sent seeds to the Royal Botanic Gardens at Kew, wrote this account: "It was impossible to form any idea of what it could be, and animating the crew to increase their rate of paddling, we were shortly afterwards opposite the object which had aroused my curiosity—a vegetable wonder. All calamities were forgotten."

This water lily is indeed a vegetable wonder, one of the prodigies of nature. Its leaves, before they unfold into the giant platters they swiftly become, at a rate said to occur at a square inch a minute, have something of the look of an imaginary plant on Venus or Mars, resembling a baseball catcher's mitt of an intense green all covered with prickles and sharp thorns. Once they have unfolded and reached their full immensity, the leaves owe their extraordinary buoyancy and great strength—they can support up to 300 pounds evenly distributed—to the elaborate system of radiating veins and ribs on their undersides and to the fact that these structures are hollow. The nocturnal blossoms, which open white and change to pink or red in a day or two, can reach eighteen inches across and have a fragrance like ripe pineapple.

The first seeds that Robert Schomburgk sent to Kew failed to germinate, and it wasn't realized until some years later that they must be stored in water, allowed to ripen properly, and then spurred into growth by raising the temperature of the water to almost 90 degrees F. But by 1849 V. *amazonica* was successfully grown and flowered at Chatsworth in England. At this point it became something more than a prodigy of nature, for it made architectural history when the botanical-minded architect

Joseph Paxton was inspired by its system of ribs and veins in designing a building to house the Great Exhibition of All Nations, which opened in London in 1851. The plant named for Queen Victoria thus led directly to the most powerful symbol of the Victorian Age and its pervasive optimism and faith in technology—the Crystal Palace.

Few of us who garden on a modest scale have very much use for *V. amazonica*, any more than we can stand a few elephants in the back yard. But a number of large gardens open to the public—the New York Botanical Garden in the Bronx, the Missouri Botanical Garden in St. Louis, and Longwood Gardens in Kennett Square, Pennsylvania, to name three—have it on display every summer, as well as a somewhat smaller species, *V. cruziana*, and also a hybrid between the two.

There's just one hitch. These days, thanks to fear of lawsuits, standing on the lily pads is strictly forbidden, no matter how much fun it may sound.

The Miseries
of an August Garden

T. S. Eliot was dead wrong about April being "the cruellest month." If he'd been more of a gardener and if he hadn't moved to England, where the late-summer climate is angelically kind both to blossoming things and to poets, he'd have known better than to say what he said about April. For Americans who garden, August is the cruelest month by far.

Having grown up in Texas in the 1940s, I know this as an absolute fact, something as certain as algebra. Except for those who could afford elaborate sprinkling systems and for country ladies who grew portulaca, August was a month rich in distress and poor in flowers. Even in the best of years, a Texas August is hotter than the hinges of hell. It's a time to hunker down and wait for a cooler month. The newspapers report, with a hint of what may be the last remnants of pioneer endurance tinged with a little modern masochism, yesterday's record temperature: 104, 109, even 115 degrees Fahrenheit.

Bermuda grass goes dormant and brown in August in the American Southwest, although it's a very tough critter indeed. Fields that were covered with a dazzling array of wildflowers in the spring go dry and sere. Only the sunflower blooms by the roadside, and its very name seems to drive the thermometer up another notch. Sandy soils blow in the wind with the fuzz from cottonwood trees. Clay soils crack into pentagonal pieces, like fragments of a puzzle. The children who set up lemonade stands by the curbs of city streets find few customers. It is no time for a sane grownup to be outside.

The Miseries of an August Garden

I keep an abiding affection for some of the things of the place where I grew up. I still draw my water from a spigot, not a faucet or a tap. I've taught my German-born wife and our sons the joys of chicken-fried steak with cream gravy, enchiladas and chile con queso, and pepper on cantaloupe. But as a gardener I was delighted many years ago to escape to the Northeast.

For a time I thought that by moving I had escaped August. There was some ground for this belief. It's been about twenty years since I've seen an asphalt pavement melt at 8 a.m. I manage to live without air conditioning, thanks to some sea breeze in the vicinity of my house, and I've almost forgotten what it was like, in the days before air conditioning appeared in Texas homes, not to be able to sleep until after midnight because of the sweltering heat radiating from the walls and ceiling. Up North, my lawn stays fairly green in August with only occasional deep watering. Something or other is usually blooming.

Nevertheless, August is still the cruelest month, North or South, East or West. It's the month of the horticultural blahs. Every year when August rolls around again, I know precisely what Alice Morse Earle meant when she wrote in *Old Time Gardens* of the "scanty unkemptness and dire disrepute" of the late-summer garden.

In August, I long for an untimely killing frost to put an end to the misery in my yard. Crabgrass has spread like a vicious rumor into every corner of the lawn and flower beds. The maple leaves are dull with summer dust. The lilac hedge is covered with mildew. The perennial border, so spectacular in May with peonies and late tulips, so lovely well into July with daylilies and phlox, lies in an ugly August funk. To be sure, the heleniums are in bloom. Nurseries call them "bridge plants" and assert that they are fine for filling the season between the last of the phlox and the first of the chrysanthemums and perennial asters. I assert that they are ugly and gangling and that I mean one of these years to yank them up and consign them to the compost heap.

There is no comfort in annuals, except for the white impatiens in a shaded bed and some volunteer Madagascar periwinkles, white with a pink eye, which have sprung up on the south side of the house and which thrive on heat and drought. But the petunias sprawl, pooped from the miseries of August, and mildew is afoot among the zinnias. And why is it that most of the flowering plants that take August in their stride come in garish colors that neither soothe the eye nor calm the soul? It may not be nice to hate an innocent plant, but in these dog days I come to loathe torrid red salvias and splashy orange and yellow zinnias. As for marigolds—well, I think that Henry Mitchell had the last word on marigolds in *The Essential Earthman* when he recommended that they should be used "as sparingly as ultimatums."

I wish that it would snow.

But there are remedies for August, and the first of these is to make good resolutions for next year, to ensure that the next time August rolls around, the garden will look cooler, even if it really isn't. Early next spring I must remember to think blue, and especially white, to make more use of blue lobelia and ageratum and of cool white impatiens, begonias, alyssum, and periwinkle.

The second remedy is flight, a strategy followed by most of my friends in Philadelphia, who generally arrange to spend the eighth month of the year at the Jersey Shore. This strategy unfortunately won't work for me, since I already live here, but I am seriously pondering following Mr. Eliot's example and expatriating myself, this one month of the year, to England, where the climate, the lawns, and the perennial borders are all at their best—and the envy of all in America who dare to call ourselves gardeners.

[1991: I would retract this essay if I could, but I allow it to stand as evidence of the fallibility of the garden writer who doesn't always know what he is talking about. I was ignorant of what I eventually learned: that August, when the Joe Pye weed starts to bloom, is the vestibule of the very best season for gardening in America—autumn. In *The Garden in Autumn* (1990), I made my amends to August once I learned that it was a month of new beginnings, not of endings.]

All Decked Out

I had my doubts about whether it would be finished on time, but it made it, just under the wire, on August 28, 1980. It's been there ever since. It will be there for a good long time to come. It has changed—*improved*—the way we experience our garden. It's an enduring and deeply treasured gift to the family from our older son, Paul. It's a California invention, with Oriental roots, that finally made its way across the nation to coastal New Jersey. It is, of course, a garden deck.

Having a deck was entirely Paul's idea. For several years he'd pointed out from time to time that there really wasn't a decent place outside to sit or to read or to sunbathe, and also that the rear of our house was awfully bleak and boring. He suggested a deck as the solution to both problems. Then, in the late summer of 1980, he found himself with three weeks on his hands between the end of a summer job and the beginning of the fall semester at college. So one evening, he got out some graph paper and a mechanical pencil, and doodled up plans for the deck, which he thought he would build unaided in precisely twenty-one days. It was a simple, attractive design, a rectangle twenty by twenty-four feet running from one corner of the back of the house toward the maple tree and covering over a patch of scrappy lawn that had never been particularly appealing. At the corner farthest from the back door, a pair of wide steps came together, offering enough room for about eighteen people to sit drinking gin-and-tonic on a hot July evening, side by side like doves perched on a telephone wire. Another, much narrower flight of steps led down from the deck to the side yard where the clothesline lives. The floor of the deck was designed to stand about eighteen inches, on the average, above ground level. There were no railings to obscure the view of the garden from the deck—or to keep those who had exceeded their capacity for gin-and-tonic from plunging into the shrubbery and ground covers Paul had suggested we plant in a semicircular bed abutting one edge of the deck.

I had reservations about so ambitious a project, partly because I am ungifted when it comes to even the minima of carpentry. In junior high I made D's in woodshop. It surprises no one to hear that in a high-school psychology course I once took a test measuring eye-hand coordination and placed in the last percentile. What if Paul ran into snags along the way? All my inadequacies would be revealed, my fatherly flaws exposed. My wife said not to worry, that since they were two years old both my sons had known better than to ask me to fix something of theirs that was broken. She asked if I hadn't noticed that as a result both boys were extremely able handymen, perfectly able to put up shelves, replace broken windows, even deal with problems in automobile carburetors.

"Nature abhors a vacuum," I mumbled.

It was agreed. There would be a deck.

The deck building got underway the next morning. Paul translated his simple drawing into a set of working blueprints and calculated the amount of wood and hardware and concrete he would need. A truck arrived from the lumberyard and dumped a load of planks and beams beneath the maple tree. Paul demolished the existing back stoop with a sledgehammer, and discovered that it concealed an abandoned well, four feet across and walled with handsome old brick to a depth of over twenty feet. I regretted that we couldn't retrieve the brick and use it for a walkway, but time was short. Paul covered over the well with a thick metal plate and six inches of concrete. Sixteen holes were dug at regular intervals, and forms were built to hold the concrete for the pillars supporting the deck. Problems inevitably arose, especially in making the top of the pillars an even height, so the deck would be level and true. The schedule fell badly behind. Just five days before my son had to leave for school, the deck consisted of a lot of lumber under tarpaulins, sixteen concrete pillars, and a high level of anxiety on all sides.

At this point, the guardian angel of carpentry stepped in, in the form of Ed Plantan, the neighbor I frequently consult on such vexing questions as what to do when the tire on the wheelbarrow goes flat. ("Fill it up with air.") Ed is a man of vast and channeled energies who is usually putting me to shame by building things in his garage, taking down his shutters and then getting them right back up after giving them their annual coat of paint, or working in his garden at dawn, doing whatever it is he does to his tomatoes that makes them luscious, red-ripe things the size of grapefruits. By profession, Ed has spent most of his life as a precision tool-and-die maker, which means that he not only makes things but also makes things that other people make things with. I suspect that he's omnicompetent.

Ed was on vacation until the end of the month. For a couple of days he walked back and forth on the sidewalk by our driveway, peering in to watch the slow progress of the deck. Finally, he wandered over to ask Paul if he could lend a hand, proceeding to take over as supervisor, master carpenter, and above all *teacher*, not only to Paul, but to the four friends who joined him the last two days. At eleven on the eve of Paul's departure, the last plank of decking was nailed into place, in the midst of a grand celebration involving much of the neighborhood, a keg or two of beer, and some thirty friends who had assembled to launch the deck.

There was much to celebrate. First, thanks to Ed's patient teaching, my son and the friends who had helped him learned things about working with wood that will serve them all their lives and that they can pass on to their own children when the time comes. Second, the deck turned out marvelously well. It's a deck that will outlast the century and then some. The wood was pressure-treated against rot and decay; but as an extra measure of precaution we painted it with additional preservatives. The ground beneath was treated with chlordane to keep termites away. (Yes, I know about chlordane and somewhat regret using it. But I also know about termites.) The framework is bolted solidly together, not nailed, and every last bolt was sprayed with a rustproofing compound.

The deck is clearly one of the best things that's ever happened to our garden. When all is almost perfect there, on those rare occasions when the lawn is newly mowed and there's scarcely a weed in sight in the flower beds, it makes a kind of viewing platform from which we can contemplate good and proper order. When, as is more usually the case, there's much that needs doing, the deck separates us from the garden, elevating us above its blemishes. Furthermore, it extends the garden year, enabling us to get outside sooner in the spring and to remain outside later in the fall. When it's sunny but cold, the steps down to the side yard make a good, wind-protected place to sit.

The deck has brought about some changes in our style of gardening, for there's something about it that invites setting out plants in containers, of which we have a miscellaneous and eclectic lot. At the moment, there's an old cast-iron pig trough, rescued from a rotting barn in upstate New York, sitting at one edge of the deck, brightly planted in wax begonias. Next to it sit three redwood containers filled with the enormous hibiscus plants we bring outside every spring. There's a strawberry jar filled with enough strawberries to give us at least a dozen fruits, plus a little ageratum. Terra-cotta urns display geraniums in several colors, and in other pots we grow agapanthus and plumbago. An old whiskey barrel spills over with cascading petunias and vinca, and hanging baskets of asparagus fern and Boston fern adorn the eaves above the back door.

We can't always use the deck, alas. In our part of the world a parade of especially annoying insects appears, each in its order, to plague local humanity. In May, a few days after a heavy rain, clouds of mosquitos and gnats and no-see-ums arise from the nearby marshes and head right for our yard. In late June we get the small, triangular, fiercely biting flies that locals call strawberry flies, and for two weeks every July the greenhead flies come, horrible creatures whose need for blood matches that of the American Red Cross. On the days when the insects are out there lying in wait for our hemoglobin, we sit in the living room, turn on the stereo, pretend we're reading, and mope, waiting till it's safe to return to the deck that turned out even better than Paul thought it would.

Something Must Be Done
about This Shed

No doubt they are all right. My wife and one of my next-door
neighbors agree in their judgment, though their reasons differ.
So does Bob Buganski, my young sculptor friend. He supports
his ravenous appetite for scrap metal, bales of compressed excelsior, and other materials of his art by freelancing as a carpenter. The three of them say the same thing: Something simply
must be done, and soon, about the garden shed out back.

My wife predicts that it will probably fall down in the next
good windstorm and that the horde of spiders it harbors will head
right for the house. My neighbor who owns the gas station next
door points out every chance he gets that the building leans dan-
gerously toward the ancient Mercedes-Benz stored in its lee,
which his son means to restore. And my sculptor friend sees it
as another carpentry project that will help him buy several more
tons of the offal of industrial society, which he wants to elevate
into art. He advises me that no wall is attached to any other or
to the floor, a six-inch-thick concrete slab that has cracked into
a dozen pieces, none of them even remotely horizontal, thanks
to the maple tree that someone planted too close to the shed
some years ago. He reckons that he would put up a really fine
new shed for a few thousand dollars or so. If I want to go higher,
he can even attach a small greenhouse on one end.

I have had until now only the flimsiest of reasons to resist
all this good counsel about the shed. To support my procrastination I could only call on the quirky homeowner's insurance laws
of my state. They classify that ramshackle and derelict piece of

architecture as an "additional structure," and require enough coverage on it, in case of catastrophe, to pay for a month in Martinique, as well as replacing the shed. There's got to be some small print somewhere, but still I've daydreamed a little: the shed might be struck by lightning and burn down, and then I could be admiring frangipani and feasting on conch.

But some recent reading has persuaded me to keep the shed a little longer, despite all the good advice to the contrary. Browsing in Joseph Wood Krutch's 1959 anthology, *The Gardener's World*, I found an excerpt from "Observations on Modern Gardening," written in 1770 by J. Whately, an Englishman. Whately reminded me that the British and European poets of the Romantic movement were deeply attracted to ruins of all sorts—dilapidated abbeys, tumbledown chapels with ancient stands of ivy clambering over ruined choirs, the remnants of castle keeps and moldering cloisters.

Whately put the matter neatly: "Whatever building we see in decay, we naturally contrast its present to its former state, and delight to ruminate on the comparison." Being a sensible soul who realized that many persons were not so fortunate as to have on their premises a bona fide ruin, he went on to offer the opinion that a "fictitious" one would do almost as well in inspiring melancholy rumination about decay and decline.

By Romantic standards, then, my shed is no painful eyesore but a spiritual asset. It isn't exactly Tintern Abbey, but it's unarguably a ruin—and a genuine one, not some fictitious contrivance concocted according to Whately's recipe. Generations ago it was built by someone whose name I don't know, whose mortal remains may well now rest in the old churchyard down by the salt marsh. He appears to have used lumber rescued from some former building, maybe a barn torn down back when the farms hereabouts were turning into a suburban town. Later owners added their own touches—several successive layers of paint (I still detect traces of magenta, persimmon, and turquoise), a layer of tarpaper, and a final covering of imitation-brick asphalt siding, vintage 1948 or so.

The interior of my shed is as gloomy as any Gothic crypt. Once my eyes adjust to its dimness, I find ample testimony to the passage of time. Under the dust and the cobwebs there's many an artifact of years gone by. These treasures include: six metal lawn chairs whose tattered webbing and corroded frames call forth a melancholy worthy of Byron or Shelley; a croquet set bought on impulse eight years ago, never used because it turned out that no one in the family, myself included, enjoyed croquet; a rusted pump sprayer that never worked anyway; a sack of concrete mix, now turned hard and solid after long storage under a leaky roof; a spare tire for the VW Beetle we no longer own; and a great many boxes of rusty nails.

Then there are a dozen old cans of paint and twice that many brushes, useless because I forgot to clean them; a mosaic tabletop I made the year I got married, depicting something vaguely Byzantine that might just be a fish; a crab trap I picked up at a garage sale for reasons my wife failed to understand and which I no longer can explain to my own satisfaction; two lawn-mowers, one of which works; two complete bicycles and the pieces of several others; and a basketball hoop taken down in 1974, the year my sons forsook the game for soccer and I ex-propriated their back-yard court for a vegetable patch.

Gloomy as it is, my shed nevertheless abounds with life. Besides the aforementioned spiders my wife believes will join us if the shed should go, there are all the insects they feed upon. Most years there's a wasp nest above the broken window or up in the rafters. Sometimes toads squat in the doorway. Last summer I found a praying mantis perched on a shelf, munching on a grasshopper. The cracks in the floor are home to sow bugs, ants, and snails. This spring sparrows nested above an old shovel with a broken handle hung on a wall. Every fall the shed sings with the crisp din of a host of crickets.

But ruins can't hold out forever against the press of life. It won't be long before I have to give my friend Bob a call and ask him to drive over with new lumber and all his tools. I just discovered new inhabitants of my shed. Some termites are making a fine and hearty meal out of the north wall.

Ukruman, Askoot-Asquash, and Fembaby

Something funny has been going on of late with the people who name vegetables, whoever they are. I don't mean the people who decided that the red and squishy things that attract slugs when they ripen in August should be called "tomatoes," and that we should use the word "potato" to refer to a tuber that tastes terrible raw, smells vile when rotten, and makes a splendid feast boiled and mashed with butter and cream and a little salt. This basic kind of naming was done long ago by people who will remain anonymous until the crack of doom. Any dictionary tells the tale. The handful of people in this country who can stand okra call it that because in West Africa, where it originated, it was called *ukruman*. Among the Nahuatl-speaking peoples of Mexico at the time of Cortez, the *tomatl* was eaten, so we eat "tomatoes." (We also drink chocolate because they drank *chocolatl*. It would be mistaken, however, to infer that we eat potatoes, under that name, because the Aztecs ate something they called *potatl*. Potatoes came from Peru, not Mexico, and the name derives from *patata*, a Haitian word originally used for sweet potatoes and then applied, by extension, to the vegetable that in the course of time oddly took on an Irish identity.) "Squash" comes from the Algonquian *askoot-asquash*, meaning "eaten raw," and although "squash" isn't one of the more melodious words in the English language, I'm grateful not to have to eat askoots.

No, the people I'm taking to task are those who dream up the names by which we distinguish one tomato or one cucumber from another, the names on the packages of seeds that we order from catalogs or pick out from the local hardware store.

Once upon a time, and not so long ago, these people were sober and serious. They didn't take their responsibilities lightly, and for good reason. Vegetable eating, after all, is a weighty matter, no cause for levity. When I was a child—and I believe my experience is typical—much of the dinner-table conversation directed at me by my parents concerned my duty toward the vegetables on my plate. "Honey, if you don't *start* on your okra, there's no way on God's earth that you're going to *finish* it." "Life isn't just meat and potatoes, boy; it's also turnip greens." "Allen, you still haven't cleaned your plate, and there are millions of starving children who would give their eyeteeth for those nice beets I boiled." I imagine that my parents heard precisely such things at their own tables when they were children, and I know that I went through all these litanies about vegetable eating with my own children, except that I instituted a firm policy against okra in any form early in my marriage and my wife has unswervingly vetoed beets.

If vegetable eating is a serious thing, then naming the vegetables we eat ought to be serious, too. A generation ago, it was. Good, sturdy vegetables had good, sturdy names: Blue Lake beans, Kentucky Wonder beans, Fordhook limas, Detroit beets, Long Island Improved Brussels sprouts, Country Gentleman corn, Lincoln and Thomas Laxton peas, Rutgers and Marglobe tomatoes. These were serious names, as grave and solemn as the lists of ships and heroes in epic poetry. A seed catalog from the year 1945 had dignity and weight.

But something has gone astray. Looking through recent vegetable seed catalogs, I discover that dignity and weight are rapidly departing. To start with, there is an awful lot of bragging going on. If someone offers a Big Boy tomato, someone else follows with a Better Boy and even an Ultra Boy. There are tomatoes, peanuts, squash, peppers, and cucumbers all called Whopper. Here, braggadocio combines with a striking lack of originality.·

Whoever decided to call a cucumber by the name of Burpless lacked an element of good taste. But another cucumber is truly alarming, and not just for its name; called Fembaby, its

most prominent feature is that its blossoms, entirely female, produce a full crop of fruit by parthenogenesis, without benefit of
pollen. (How the seeds of Fembaby come into being I leave to
mystery fans to ponder.)

Who decided that it was okay to call a pumpkin Lady
Godiva, and why? Is it really necessary to celebrate organized
crime by introducing a tomato named The Godfather? How come
a new corn is burdened with the moniker BiQueen, and is this
name a by-product of the so-called sexual revolution, now trick-
ling into seed catalogs and other family publications? Why is a
melon called Resistant Joy, a broccoli named Focus, a winter
askoot-asquash called Sweet Mama?

It is high time that we turn the rascals out and put in a
brand-new set of vegetable namers who have some sense of
dignity and high purpose. In the meantime, I refuse to eat a
Whopper of any sort, and you won't find any Fembabies on my
premises.

The Narrow Escape
of Jenny Lind

Two summers ago Jenny Lind disappeared, seemingly forever. I don't mean the nineteenth-century Swedish soprano, but a muskmelon named for her in her heyday. My Jenny Lind was an "heirloom vegetable," a cultivar whose survival depends on ordinary home gardeners saving its seeds each year, since it isn't produced commercially or listed in any standard seed catalog that I know of. Until last year, a handful of farmers in my area did save the seed so they could sell this exceptionally flavorful melon at their roadside stands during its fleeting season of perfection, the first two weeks of August.

Jenny Lind was no beauty. Its fruit bordered on the grotesque, considering the misshapen turban—a large, lumpish protuberance—on the blossom end. My private name for it was Quasimodo, for it brought to mind Charles Laughton in *The Hunchback of Notre Dame* far more than the Swedish Nightingale. But the trip into the country to buy a bushel was always worthwhile, and a bushel never lasted very long. The spicy sweetness of its luscious pale-green flesh was unmatched by any other melon. (A real old-timer, Jenny Lind is listed in the 1870 edition of A. J. Downing's *The Fruits and Fruit-Trees of America*, which praises it for its abundant crop of fruit especially notable for its "rich, delicious sweet flavor.")

But last summer I couldn't find Jenny Lind. At one roadside stand after another someone pointed out some new hybrid variety as its replacement. The farmers in my area have been badly misinformed. The melons they offer now are so flavorless that they might as well have been picked unripe and shipped here from thousands of miles away. I wished, too late, that I had saved seeds from Jenny Lind. I wondered if on a back road somewhere some hold-out farmer or other was still growing it. But I knew that even if Jenny Lind hadn't completely vanished, its survival was precarious. And its disappearance in my own area was something more than a personal disappointment.

Jenny Lind's fate is merely one instance of a far-reaching problem that some critics of present practices and tendencies in the world's agriculture find alarming and dangerous—the loss of genetic diversity in our major food crops.

The problem is fairly recent. As late as the end of World War II, the production of seed for food was decentralized and richly varied. In the United States, as in many other countries, hundreds of private firms sold seed, much of it produced on their own farms, of cultivated strains they had developed. Most of these firms were owned by families (Burpee, Harris, and so on) who handed down control from one generation to the next, according to the fortunes of time and mortality.

All these houses offered a great variety of vegetable seeds. Most were purebred strains rather than F_1 hybrids, meaning that gardeners could save seed one year and plant it the next with little difference in the crop. Furthermore, many small growers saved their own, purely local varieties as treasures— "heirlooms"—to be passed down from parents to children. As a result, the pool of genetic material for such staple crops as beans, corn, and squash was broad and deep.

Today a good many plant scientists are getting edgy about the probability that the gene pool on which we ultimately depend for our sustenance is endangered. The old stereotype of botanists as carefree, gentle, untroubled souls with a passion for collecting plants for storage in a herbarium doesn't hold these days. A lot of botanists have worried looks, feel a sense of urgency about their profession, and speak in the tones of Jeremiah.

They point with alarm to the increasing uniformity and homogeneity of agriculture—to, for example, the fact that a few varieties of hybrid corn are now grown worldwide. Some speak of a possible cataclysm to come, of "genetic wipeout." Many are troubled by the fact that the world depends on a surprisingly small number of grains and other vegetables, a dependence which is all the worse as a limited number of hybrids of each kind come to have unprecedented dominance everywhere. (Dr. Peter Raven, who holds the Engelmann chair of botany at Washington University in St. Louis and is the director of the Missouri Botanical Garden, estimates that 85 percent of all food consumed by humans, either directly or through animal produce, comes from only twenty species of plants.)

Dr. Hugh Iltis, a professor at the University of Wisconsin internationally known for his research in Mexico with *Teosinthe*, a wild relative of maize (which occurs in one perennial form that must be enough to cause troubled dreams on the part of seed companies whose business rests on the need to replant grains annually), is among these worried botanists. Alarmed by the destruction of the original New World habitats of potatoes and maize and other important domesticated food crops, he urges that if we continue to allow their wild ancestors and relatives to be lost, we will lose for all time genes we may desperately need. According to Iltis, "We ought to take whatever immediate steps we can to freeze the genetic landscape—to stop exporting our hybrids to every corner of the world, to preserve potentially important plants such as *Teosinthe* in the wild, and to encourage agricultural diversity worldwide. Otherwise, we may be very sorry, and very soon."

But freezing the genetic landscape is much more easily said than done: the pressures against it are immense. There are fewer and fewer farmers, and many of those families that once saved local varieties of vegetables and passed them down from father to son have moved from the farm to the city, replaced by agribusiness. The number of seed houses has declined sharply. Of those that remain, many that still bear the old and reassuring names of their founding families are actually owned by conglomerates whose interest in plants is purely a matter of short-range profits.

The public has become conditioned to the very questionable notion that "hybrid" is synonymous with "better"; thus, hybrids (which, it must be said, sometimes *are* better in uniformity and yield) have increasingly replaced older, purebred strains of vegetables. The number of cultivars on the market keeps declining, and this drop is perilous for a simple reason: if a very limited number of cultivars of some particular food crop are widely grown, and if a new disease or insect suddenly appears with a special affinity for those cultivars, then high yield may turn out to be low yield, or even no yield. The disastrous potato blight and consequent potato famine in Ireland in the past century are, after all, a sobering part of the historical record, not theoretical speculation by an armchair alarmist.

Pondering all these matters and lamenting the seeming demise of Jenny Lind, I decided to get in touch with a serious young man named Kent Whealy, just in case I might be wrong, that there still might be a few seeds of my favorite melon left on this earth. Whealy would know if anyone would, I thought. And he was obviously a man with a mission, the mission of making it possible for ordinary home gardeners to offer some resistance to the pressures of the marketplace that encourage agricultural homogeneity and work against genetic diversity. In 1976 Whealy founded the Seed Savers Exchange, which has 250 members dedicated to seeking out and preserving heirloom and endangered vegetable cultivars, like Jenny Lind. I had gotten a mimeographed sheet from him describing the purposes and services of his exchange, a sheet he gladly sends out to anyone who mails a self-addressed, stamped envelope to Route 2, Princeton, Missouri 64673. I knew from this sheet that I didn't meet the qualifications for membership. Members must agree to grow and offer seeds of one or more heirloom vegetables, such as the Brandywine tomato, the Turkey Craw pole bean, and the Black Turtle bush bean, which they grow under carefully controlled conditions to assure that their purity is maintained, that they are kept free of contamination by other cultivars nearby. My vegetable garden was far too small, and far too many bees buzzed into it each morning loaded with pollen from the vegetable patches of my neighbors. But I knew that some of the members of the Seed Savers Exchange, who are identified each year in a list that sells for $3, sometimes offered small quantities of seed to non-members for a modest price.

Perhaps there was hope for Jenny Lind. Perhaps I could locate a few seeds. I wasn't sure what I would do with them. Maybe plant them in a tub on the deck. Maybe press them into the hands of a local farmer, tell him how precious they were, and urge him to do his duty for genetic diversity.

But when I telephoned Kent Whealy, I gave up hope. None

of the members of his exchange grew it. There were no seeds. Jenny was gone, just one more example of the good things known to my ancestors which my own generation has allowed to disappear from the face of this earth.

POSTSCRIPT

In slightly different form, the above essay was published on the Leisure and Arts page of *The Wall Street Journal*. It produced an enormous volume of mail for an article about gardening. Garden writers seldom raise much ruckus or controversy or cause anyone's hackles to rise by even a millimeter, but my lament for Jenny Lind did all of these. There were a few letters from readers who expressed general satisfaction with my point of view and my layman's limited understanding of some of the issues that are bothering botanical experts lately about the loss of genetic diversity in food crops. The rest of the letters came from readers who were either irate, to varying degrees, or who wanted to remedy my obvious and gross ignorance. Oddly, these letters of protest could be subdivided into two categories: those who thought I hadn't gone nearly far enough, and those who thought everything I said was either patently false or else wildly exaggerated.

Those who thought I hadn't gone far enough wrote to say that since I sometimes wrote for *The Wall Street Journal* I was obviously under the sway of the conglomerates who do, in fact, own many American seed companies. Some of these conglomerates, I was informed, were primarily involved in petrochemicals, a point that is obviously true and a matter of record. But then I was accused of covering up a conspiracy. Petrochemical companies manufacture a variety of substances used in agriculture, including fertilizers and pesticides. Why, I was asked, had I failed to inform readers that the plant breeders who work for Seed Company X were developing strains of corn and other vegetables that would utterly fail unless they were fertilized and pesticided with chemicals produced by companies owned by the same conglomerate that owned Seed Company X? Didn't I realize that the world was about to see a vast scheme of agricultural blackmail perpetrated by utterly nefarious and unscrupulous men? Or had I been paid to shut up?

Everyone has a right to his own point of view or his own paranoid scenario, but I wasn't much impressed. No doubt there are conspiracies in this world, but most of the damage that gets done takes place because people of good will and noble intentions don't really anticipate the consequences of their actions. Sometime around 1870 a man in Massachusetts named Leopold Trouvelot deliberately brought the gypsy moth to this country from Europe. He wanted to hybridize it with the silk moth. His action proved in time to be a tremendous boon to those who manufacture Sevin and other insecticides, but no conspiracy was involved. Just well-meant ignorance.

The other letters came from people in the seed trade—hybridizers of corn and soybeans, lobbyists for agribusinesss, representatives of farmers' cooperatives in the Midwest. To put it succinctly, they all thought I was Chicken Little, needlessly worrying people that the sky was about to fall when the fact was that it was just fine and full of pie. Didn't I know about the Green Revolution? Didn't I trust the well-trained plant scientists who work for seed companies and know precisely what they are doing, especially now that they have learned a few tricks about genetic engineering? Wasn't I just a hopeless nostalgic? As far as poor old Jenny Lind was concerned, wasn't my mind playing tricks on me? Didn't it taste far better in my memory than it ever had in reality? And didn't I know that when Jenny disappeared, it was really the fault of consumers like myself, since we hadn't assured its survival by "contracting for production at a price that rewarded the producer"? Again, people have every right to their opinions, but I stick by my own about the superiority of Jenny Lind and about botanists like Dr. Iltis being on the track of something important when they worry about the loss of genetic diversity.

There's also good news about Jenny Lind. She has been rescued, she's in good hands now, and I'm proud to say that I did my part, with a lot of help along the way.

After the essay was written but before it appeared in *The Wall Street Journal*, I stopped by a nursery and garden store a couple of counties away, where there were some unusual perennials on display. On a seed rack way in the back of the store, I found a small, plain envelope marked "Jenny Lind Melon—30¢." The store's owner told me that the pack had been there for several years and that I could have it free since the seeds probably weren't viable. He used to get a few packs a year from an old farmer nearby who saved the seed. But the farmer had died, and there really wasn't much demand anymore for the melon. There were sixteen seeds in the packet. It was late summer, too late to plant them in New Jersey, so I mailed them off to Claude Hope, a plant breeder I much admire, who raises a goodly portion of the world's flower seeds on his *finca* outside Cartago, Costa Rica, where the even climate permits him to get in four crops in twelve months. I asked him to try Jenny Lind, let me know what he thought, and perhaps send me back some of the seeds.

Four months later he wrote. Jenny Lind was indeed, in his professional opinion, an exceptionally tasty melon. It was also, because of its strange appearance (Quasimodo, again!), unsuitable for commerce. He enclosed a packet containing 2,000 seeds. I held back 100, which I pressed into the hands of a local farmer in the hope that henceforth he will be able to supply me and a few other souls who don't mind green melons with strange protuberances with our annual share of Jenny Linds. The rest went to Kent Whealy for distribution to those members of his Seed Savers Exchange who will do their bit to see that Jenny escapes her demise.

[1991: Another, later, word is in order. I also sent fifty seeds to Dick Meiners, of Pinetree Garden Seeds in Maine. He planted them, thought that Jenny Lind was extraordinarily delicious, and replanted the seeds the next year to build up enough supply to offer them in his spring catalog, where Jenny now turns up reliably every spring.]

Weighty Matters

From time to time after they had learned to drive, one of my sons would stop off at the grocery store in the middle of winter and bring home a watermelon for dessert. It would sit among the cartons of milk on the top shelf of the refrigerator, a round, mean-looking, dark-green object about the size of a soccer ball and weighing in at twelve pounds or so. It had reached its final destination in a journey that began too long ago and too far away, over a month ago in a field somewhere in Mexico, Arizona, or Southern California.

After supper someone would retrieve the alleged melon for us to eat at the dinner table, where I would grumble over the persistent and pervasive ignorance of my household in the matter of watermelons. I could not, however, blame my sons for their ignorance. They had spent most of their lives in New Jersey. About watermelons, I had a decided edge on them. Born and raised a Texan, I came from a long, proud line of watermelon eaters, watermelon experts, watermelon thieves.

Whenever I consider the watermelon, I soon find myself thinking about my grandfather Roscoe Lee Surles, who once preached to me in his back yard in Wichita Falls an impromptu sermon about the place of the watermelon in God's Plan of Creation.

I remember him in August 1945, huddled over his old Emerson table radio with its cracked Bakelite case, listening as Gabriel Heatter told about the atomic bomb an American plane had just dropped on the city of Hiroshima. Grandmother Surles was out in the kitchen fixing supper and my Aunt Betty Joy was there talking to her and shelling black-eyed peas while she waited for her new husband, a sailor soon to ship out to the Pacific, to get back from a visit to his parents' house on the other side of town. As the nuclear age dawned in the living room, I remember a song playing on another radio in another part of the house—the Andrews Sisters singing "Three Little Fishes."

After supper, Grandfather Surles went off to the icehouse and returned with a watermelon—a thirty-pounder of a kind called Rattlesnake, one of his favorites—in the back seat of his 1936 Plymouth, wrapped in a blanket to protect the upholstery and keep in the cold. He would buy as many as ten watermelons at a time off some farmer's truck from Weatherford (a town known mainly for Mary Martin and the best watermelons in Texas and therefore, of course, the universe) and take them down to the icehouse. He carved his initials in each and left them there, going back to get them one at a time. At his house on McGregor Street, the fireflies flickered tentatively near the shrubbery, not yet daring to take full possession of the night. As the sky faded into its final purple, Grandmother Surles sat on the back stoop, still in her kitchen apron, a cup towel in her hands. She called for Betty Joy and her husband, James, to come outside for watermelon, and she went inside to fetch forks and a large salt shaker. (Everyone in Texas knows that a little salt improves the flavor of even the sweetest melon on earth.)

Grandfather Surles set the melon down on newspapers on the white-enameled wooden table next to the crape myrtle tree, whose blossoms exactly matched the red flesh of the fruit. After wiping off his hunting knife, he cut the melon lengthwise into eight pieces. Betty Joy and her husband retreated with theirs, laughing, bending over slightly with each bite so the juice wouldn't dribble down their clothes.

I sat at my grandmother's feet, my shirt off, since I knew that I'd have to be hosed off in the driveway before bedtime, while she listened to my grandfather explain what little he knew about the atomic bomb.

The night air was beginning to cool. A breeze stirred the slender, feathery branches of the salt cedar tree by the garage. But it was still warm enough that the watermelon tasted delicious in its crisp, sweet coldness. There was nothing I liked better than watermelon. Suddenly a question popped into my head about my family's firmly held dogmas about watermelon. If we could have chili or barbecue whenever my father felt like walking to the Pig Stand, and salmon croquettes more often than I liked, thanks to my mother's tidy ways with rationing stamps, then why couldn't we have watermelon except in "watermelon season"?

Among my people, watermelon season was something as fixed as Christmas. Watermelons were sold from May to October, but we bought them only during the season, which lasted from the Fourth of July (when watermelons cost about three cents a pound) until Labor Day (when the price had usually dropped to a penny a pound). Watermelon eating at any other time was a transgression. The doctrine that there was something downright sinful about melons out of season was as little questioned in my family as the truth of the Christian faith.

But I trespassed into heresy. Once the question popped into my head, it popped right out of my mouth.

"Granddaddy," I asked, "I love watermelon so much that I wonder—why can't we eat it *all year round?*"

Grandfather Surles must have thought it was an important question, because he looked down at me, spit a couple of seeds to the ground, and thought a minute or two. When he answered, he called on all the wisdom and authority of Almighty God, Maker of the Texas earth he loved so deeply. He chose his words carefully, so that I would understand, get everything right once and for all.

"We have watermelons," he said, "because the Good Lord saw fit to give us watermelons. It was one of the better things He did, and special things need special times and seasons. Think, boy—would you like to have to eat watermelon on Thanksgiving? It takes a whole lot of heat to make a watermelon sweet and good. God gave Texas a little more heat than most places just so that the watermelons that grow down in Parker County around Weatherford would be the best on this earth. It's a blessing, but the last thing in the world we need here in Texas is a few more months of heat, just for the sake of a little more watermelon."

My Grandfather Surles was not a talkative man. He was often monosyllabic. That sermon about watermelons and their place in the God-given order of things, delivered to me on a late-summer evening not quite two years before he collapsed on the steps of the courthouse in Henrietta, was one of his longer and more eloquent utterances. I remembered it whenever one of my sons brought home a midwinter melon from the grocery store. My sons were wrong. Roscoe Surles was correct. There is a right and proper season to eat watermelon. Watermelon in December is as wrongheaded as eggnog in July. The reasons are simple. Watermelons taste best, have their special watermelon crispness, only when they ripen thoroughly on the vine, out in a field under a blazing sky in Texas, or possibly Georgia. A fully ripe—*vine-ripe*—melon is a poor traveler. It must go quickly to market. It must be promptly chilled and promptly eaten. If a melon is picked before its time, so that people a continent away can eat it in December, it goes mushy, it develops bruises in its flesh, it tastes of cucumber, and even a dash of salt cannot redeem it from its sin against right and proper order.

Granddaddy's sermon on watermelons elaborated no doctrine about what size a watermelon ought to be, for one good reason: he, like every other Texan back in the 1940s, had never seen a tiny melon, except for unripe ones early on the vine, before the hot sun began to spur them on toward immensity. He assumed that by nature and almost by definition any watermelon worth, quite literally, its salt must be of a considerable size. Thirty pounds was the minimum, a very modest melon. Fifty pounds was common. All the watermelons my people knew in Texas years ago—ones like Rattlesnake, Charleston Gray, and Dixie Queen—were very large indeed. Black Diamond, it was commonly known, sometimes reached 125 pounds.

If he were alive today, my granddaddy would probably not believe me if I told him that that green soccer ball in my New Jersey refrigerator was a watermelon. If he believed me, he would ridicule the thing. A melon that fits easily into a modest-sized refrigerator and weighs only twelve pounds, he would say, was never meant to be. All things have their proper sizes—a cantaloupe should not aspire to the size of a watermelon; a watermelon should not be reduced to the size of a cantaloupe. It's as simple as that.

But watermelons have not escaped the attention of plant breeders. The old respectable melons like Charleston Gray and Rattlesnake now have their tiny parvenu rivals, with cute little names, minimal aspirations, and modest claims on space in the refrigerator. Sugar Baby (eight pounds), You Sweet Thing (thirteen pounds), Golden Midget (five pounds)—all are now among us, in our seed catalogs and our grocery stores. One cultivar, Red Lollipop, calls it quits at a ludicrous three pounds.

The diminishment of the noble watermelon, though contemptible, is understandable. In its natural state, a watermelon is a challenge. It must be chilled before it's fit to eat, and it's no mean thing to chill a watermelon, the only fruit on earth—before the hybridizers set to work—incapable of fitting into the average refrigerator. A thirty-pound melon can be cooled in a metal washtub with fifty pounds of ice and a bath towel on top for insulation. Four or five melons can be chilled at a time by putting them in a bathtub for a couple of days with three hundred pounds of ice and a little rock salt to hasten things along.

But then a question arises: Who will eat the watermelon? A fairly small boy can polish off ten pounds of melon at a sitting, though he will be awash for several hours thereafter. I have known people who could put away fifteen pounds, given a little time to walk around now and then. But larger quantities are beyond the capacities of most. The fact is that a watermelon of noble and respectable dimension requires help to eat. Implicit in its very being is an entire society of like-minded folk. It bespeaks a large and extended family whose members live near one another, kin to ask in for a picnic. It promotes hospitality to neighbors, who may be invited over for a slice or two as the sun is going down.

Such was true of the old, traditional watermelon. But shrink the melon and the need of people for one another is correspondingly diminished. A couple can manage a ten-pound melon all by themselves, with no children. A man with a steady supply of Red Lollipop may live alone and have his melon, too. It is a solipsistic fruit, appropriate to a narcissistic day. Those old Black Diamond watermelons capable of reaching 125 pounds were testimony to a large network of persons tightly bound by mutual ties and affections. No less than bread and wine, they were the food of holy communion.

Now that they are grown, I would hope that my sons think on these things.

Status Quo Ante

Thomas Wolfe was only half right: you can go home again, but much will have changed since you left.

My two sons have twice tried to find that house on Chestnut Street in Harrisonburg, Virginia, hitchhiking their way down into the Shenandoah Valley after they had backpacked along the Appalachian Trail. They wanted to find the place they once called home, a desire that I suspect is universal to the human race, except perhaps among true nomads.

We moved there in 1962, when Paul was not quite three and Michael not quite born, an event he saved up for November 26, his brother's birthday. We lived there for four years, in that small, white frame house with dormer windows upstairs and a fine view from the breakfast room out back, which overlooked a patch of lawn, a clothesline, and an apple orchard. Lower in the valley we could see the red tile roofs and blue limestone walls of the buildings on the campus of Madison College, the small and rather backward state school where I came fairly close to making a living by professing philosophy to a handful of students. Further to the east was the dark and somber ridge of Massanutten Mountain, and beyond it the foothills and high peaks of the Blue Ridge.

My sons often speak fondly of that house and of the orchard where they roamed, picking wild asparagus in the spring, native strawberries in the summer, and wormy apples in the autumn. It is firmly in their memories.

Mine too, though not all the memories are good ones.

I remember the sober gathering of friends who camped out in our living room to watch the shattering succession of events that began three days before my sons' common birthday, when J.F.K. was killed at the Triple Overpass where Elm, Main, and Commerce Streets come together in my old hometown. I remember my last year at the college, which began with a promotion and praise from my departmental chairman and ended with my dismissal, after someone maliciously spread the rumor that I was the head of a Communist cell—a fallacy that took us away from many good friends, people I loved then and still love now.

But I also remember the garden I made on Chestnut Street, my first real garden as a family man. There was no garden there when we moved in, except for the lawn, a small maple tree out front, a Red Radiance rosebush, and a clump of iris by the water faucet next to the steep driveway. We were renters, not owners, but we had illusions of permanence in Harrisonburg, expecting one day to buy a house to whose yard we could move the bulbs and perennials we collected in the meantime. Anyway, whoever said that renters couldn't also be gardeners? If I hewed to that principle, my years of gardening would have been reduced by half.

Our first summer, I dug a long, wide bed at the back of the yard and enriched the already rich soil with weathered cow chips picked up one by one from a colleague's pasture. I planted Shasta daisies and delphiniums raised from seed and a great many daylilies bought from the Benziger Nursery beyond the Blue Ridge, in Ruckersville.

My friend John Wood gave me irises, phlox, and red bee balm from his garden that fall, and I planted them along with a couple of peonies and some spring bulbs from the local garden center. Early the next year my wife planted cosmos, Gloriosa daisies, baby's breath, and marigolds for cutting, and I ordered some bedding dahlias from Park's. When the second summer rolled around, our garden was thriving and lovely, a wonderful addition to the already spectacular view from the breakfast-room windows. I planted moonvines on a trellis by the entrance to the basement garage and petunias in a large planter box at the bottom of the back stairs, which I concealed behind a double row of large river rocks carted three at a time from a stream in the foothills of the Alleghenies. Our neighbors Durwood and Ruby Garber, whose daughter, Jane, often served as our babysitter, said that everything was a great improvement over the former bleakness of the yard, that they were glad that renters had finally come along who were also gardeners.

My sons never found that house on their two pilgrimages to Chestnut Street, possibly because in the 900 block of Chestnut Street there are quite a few small white frame houses with dormer windows upstairs and a fine view out back.

This summer I returned to the Shenandoah Valley, attending a meeting in Staunton (a horticultural society meeting, not a convention of Marxists). Afterward, I drove up to Harrisonburg, to stay with friends and to see how Madison College had survived without my services.

Madison, I discovered, had done quite well. Now fully coed and integrated, it had become James Madison University, with a student body of 10,000, an increase of 8,800. Very depressing. When my friend Robin McNallie, a member of the English Department (who was also falsely alleged to have a pipeline to the Kremlin but for some reason got tenure instead of the sack), suggested that we drive about Harrisonburg, I almost decided not to drive up to Chestnut Street, look for that house, take pictures to show our sons, and see what had happened to my garden. The college had done so well without me that I suspected that my old back yard by now probably resembled Sissinghurst or Longwood Gardens.

But I went, snapped a picture of the front yard, rang the bell, and asked the owner if he would mind if I wandered into the back to take a couple of pictures. He agreed.

The garden wasn't there. There was only grass and a clothesline out back. Next to the driveway there was a Red Radiance rosebush and a clump of iris by the water faucet. Nothing else. I had no more made a lasting impression on that piece of earth than a swimmer can alter the ocean by moving through its waters. Everything was as it had been before I came.

Almost everything. I asked a man who was weeding a patch of marigolds at the house next door where Durwood had moved. He had died of cancer, fairly young, a couple of years ago. A month later, Ruby was killed when an automobile struck her. Their daughter, Jane, now owns the house.

I was sorry that she wasn't there. I would have liked to have said hello, told her I was sorry about her folks, and asked her when and how the garden I left behind so many years ago went out of existence, without a trace.

Jasmines of Memory

As Marcel Proust knew quite well, there comes in middle life a subtle change in the balance of the senses. Hearing and vision weaken, sometimes only slightly, sometimes dramatically. But taste and smell gain a new significance as the senses most closely connected with memory. Thus, for Proust, a steaming cup of tea and the delicate almond scent of madeleine cookies provided a way back into the days of his boyhood and youth, into his remembrance of things past.

I know nothing of madeleines and take my tea only on hot summer days, heavily iced. But certain fragrances do have their power of evocation, calling up for me the days when the world was larger and I much smaller. On Christmas Day, when we tuck the turkey in the oven, lightly stuffed with cornbread dressing made from my grandmother's recipe, I wait an hour for the aroma of cornmeal mingled with onions, celery, thyme, and the first rich juices of the turkey. I close my eyes and dream myself back into my boyhood. It is 1943, and I am eight again. The Christmas gifts have been opened, the mess of boxes and wrapping paper has been hauled out to the alley, I have made my first exploratory efforts behind the house to master the BB gun I didn't really want, and my parents and I have made the brief drive through the bright, cool crispness of a Texas December day to the house of my grandparents, Big Dave and Pauline Lacy. The turkey, an enormous tom large enough to feed their four children, a growing brood of grandchildren, and several distant and childless cousins, has been cooking since dawn. The whole house smells of the feast that is about to begin—roast turkey and giblet gravy and dressing and biscuits and sweet potatoes cooked with marshmallows and three kinds of pie—apple, pumpkin, and mince.

When I was growing up, we never had Christmas dinner at home. My mother, to put it plainly, was not much of a cook. The rich smells of good Southern-style cooking evoke my grandmother's house, not hers. But Mother was a gardener, and I believe, though it's now past proving, that she harbored an active resentment against any flower that didn't smell good. She was contemptuous of zinnias for their construction-paper stiffness and their utter lack of scent. She resented morning glories. They were early risers and she was not, and they had no perfume. Moonflowers were much more to her taste. She planted them every May, when the soil had warmed, and on August evenings, after the dishes were done, she would sit on the back stoop, sipping bourbon whiskey, smoking Camels, watching the last swallows swoop through the air, and waiting for the moonflowers to open slowly in the fading light. As each blossom unfurled its creamy white chalice, it delicately scented the air for her delight and for the evident pleasure of the night moths that hovered about the glossy green vines.

In one of my father's more prosperous years, he gave my mother a brick patio, surrounding the large mimosa tree she had planted the first year they bought the house. She planted the raised beds separating it from the house thick with fragrant things: sweet William, nasturtium, nicotiana, mignonette, and heliotrope. She sometimes cursed the mimosa tree in the early fall, when it came time to sweep up the thousands of seed pods— but never on a June night when the air was sharp with its deep spice. She often complained about the wisteria and honeysuckle vines that covered the garage and protected several nests of wasps that turned mean as autumn approached. But she refused to root them out or even to prune them back—for what is spring without the strong scent of wisteria, or a summer day without the pervasive odor of honeysuckle?

But of all the fragrances of my childhood, it is jasmine I remember best. One of my earliest memories—a bitter one—is of a bouquet of jasmine floating away on the shallow waters of the Rio Grande. We lived briefly in San Antonio in 1938, when I was three. My parents and I had driven for the day to some small, dusty town across the Mexican border. My mother bought a bag of oranges and a small nosegay of white jasmine while we were there, but at the border a U.S. Customs official spotted both, confiscated them, and threw them over the bridge rail. My mother wept. My father, who had a marvelous talent for obscenity, tongue-lashed the official. I wondered about this strange place called a "border," where some people assumed the right to steal other people's flowers and fruit.

When my parents bought the house in Dallas where I lived from the time I was eleven, there were always jasmines. Every spring my mother bought a dozen or so rooted cuttings of sambac jasmine (*Jasminum sambac*), the cultivar known as Maid of Orleans, which is notable for its generous number of snow-white semi-double blossoms that fade to wine-red as they age and for its strong, sweet, clove-like odor. She set them out in the raised brick beds, along with other fragrant plants and some blue plumago and red hibiscus. (Neither the plumbago nor the hibiscus offered any fragrance, but their clear, bright colors were compensation for that deficiency.)

There were other jasmines as well, starting in late January when the yellow winter jasmine (*J. nudiflorum*) burst into golden bloom, weeks before its foliage appeared. In the spring, one of the glories of the patio was the Carolina jasmine, whose fragrant golden trumpets almost covered from sight the glossy, evergreen leaves of this attractive vine, which clambered up a trellis. Our yard was separated from the alley by a solid hedge of gardenias— Cape jasmine—that bloomed most deliciously in June. The blossoms could be gathered (very carefully, since touching their petals would cause them to turn brown) and brought inside, to be floated in a bowl as a spicy centerpiece for the dining table. One year, at a time of adolescent romanticism, a girlfriend discovered that the blossoms of the Cape jasmine could be eaten, apparently without harm. To be honest, they tasted of rubber dipped in dime-store perfume, but it was a time for a little experimentation on my part, of several different sorts.

My mother was a gardener, not a botanist. I suppose she never knew that her Carolina jasmine's proper name was *Gelsemium sempervirens*, that Cape jasmine was really *Gardenia jasminoides* and Confederate jasmine was *Trachelospermum jasminoides*, and that none of these was truly a jasmine, a species within the genus *Jasminum*. She probably wouldn't have cared a bit about such niceties of taxonomy. Whatever they were, they were something special.

For many years strangers have lived in that Dallas house with its patio out back. When we moved in, there were few trees. The house faced west, and on summer afternoons it sat in a cruel and painful glare. Now it's almost hidden in the cool, green shade of three ash trees and two oaks I planted when they were saplings. The trees tower over the house, measuring the distance of my days.

But I still have jasmines, as house plants, several sorts, but especially the sambac. Whenever it blooms, it is Texas for me, and summer, and I can almost call back the smell of honeysuckle, mimosa, gardenias, and moonflowers. The sun has finally gone down. The pavements are starting to cool off. The air is filled with the quiet noises of lawn sprinklers up and down the block. The grownups are sitting in canvas chairs on the patio, sipping whiskey. I lie on my back on the warm brick, looking up through the delicate sculpture of the mimosa tree, and wonder who I will be when I grow up.

A Plea for Alleys

Every Wednesday, when I must haul four heavy plastic garbage cans from their berth behind the compost heap and put them back after the trash truck has visited our block, I sorely miss having an alley. My regret is entirely practical, a feeling that the citizens of my town, where there are no alleys, would save a great deal of work without making things any harder for the garbage men if we could just take the trash out to the cans and leave it at that. But I also sometimes feel sorely remiss toward my sons, who are grown now. I never once gave them an alley to play in. They may not know what they missed, but they did miss something.

When I was growing up, except during our brief interlude of country living, all the houses I lived in had their alleys out back. An alley was indispensable.

For the grownups, the alley was something purely utilitarian, a place for garbage cans, a place to enter quickly and leave just as quickly. My parents and their neighbors carted out their kitchen scraps, empty cans and bottles, and stale newspapers almost furtively, as if afraid that someone would see how much trash they were producing. The people in the neighborhood feigned indifference to one another's garbage for one simple, obvious reason: garbage is symptomatic. It can be read and diagnosed. It offers clues to the lives we lead. Both good cooks and terrible ones give themselves away in their kitchen scraps. There's something awry in a marriage when both partners throw away the letters they received from each other in courtship. Empty pill bottles and gin bottles, in sufficient quantity, have their meaning.

But what the grownups so quietly secreted in the galvanized metal cans behind their houses in those days of my childhood was picked up two or three times a week with much unceremonious commotion by the garbage crews, loud and laughing men who worked stripped to the waist in the summer and drank bottles of Pearl or Lone Star as they banged and clattered their way up the block. From each house they collected the untidy evidence of a sober truth: humans sometimes create poems and symphonies and systems of morality, but our chief contribution to the surface of the planet is an awesome pile of trash. All earth is our midden.

The garbage men, of course, never removed quite everything. They left tin cans behind, flattened and rusting. They overlooked stray scraps of newspaper, crumpled-up bills from the electric company, silver-foil gum wrappers, wads of Kleenex stained crimson with lipstick—things to be lifted in a breeze and deposited in tall weeds or against the slats of a tumbledown wooden fence.

Those alleys were really for us, the children of the neighborhood. We knew them intimately. There we rode our tricycles, our shiny red scooters, our first wobbly bicycles. We pulled our baby brothers and sisters back and forth in metal wagons, and we knelt in the grimy dust of the narrow concrete pavement to shoot marbles and play jacks. At dusk, when the last swallows were dipping in the air in pursuit of the day's last morsel of insect, we played hide-and-seek and piggy-wants-a-signal as darkness gathered and bats replaced the swallows against the violet evening sky.

We knew, of course, all the characteristic smells of the alley. Yellowing piles of lawn clippings, warm to the touch, gave off a faint, sweet scent. From the garbage cans, the odors of rancid grease, moldering grapefruit and cantaloupe rinds, soured milk, fermenting potato peels, all taught another sober human truth: the universality of rot.

In our private yards, we lived among rosebushes, privet hedges, gardenias, and zinnias—whatever our parents planted to make a garden, a place that was tamed and orderly, homey and reassuring. But in our common alley we lived among the spontaneous and the uninvited, in the midst of things that just grew somehow, of their own accord, unplanted. On the alley's sides grew chinaberry and hackberry trees, their branches meeting overhead to form a cool green tunnel. In sunny patches Johnson grass and three kinds of sticker burrs flourished. Clumps of hollyhock, tall sunflowers, and four-o'clocks sprang up behind garages. Occasionally there would be a dense stand of the deadly jimsonweed, with its blue-white musky blossoms, its seed pods armed with sharply pointed hooks.

The alley had its native fauna as well as flora. Stray cats prowled among the garbage cans, calling no one block their home. We had tarantulas—huge, hairy, terrifying. There were wild rabbits and squirrels, chipmunks, and sometimes prairie dogs. We found, in discomforting abundance, things that stung: red ants with venom so potent that the painful swollen knots it produced in the armpits lasted for days, yellow jackets that turned nasty as autumn drew near, dirt daubers of an odd shade of purplish-black, red wasps, and scorpions.

The alley had its dangers and its surprises. A copperhead or a rattlesnake was always possible. Possums thrived, and the children knew: Let sleeping possums lie. One year a monkey escaped from its cage at the house next door and took to the alley. He chattered his defiance at us from garage roofs up and down the alley for a week before vanishing into the wooded grounds of a nearby country club, never to appear again. Another year a mad dog appeared one July day, lurching and stumbling about the alley, until the town warden came and shot him.

I miss alleys, but I do not mean to romanticize them. Our play was never entirely peaceful, for there were always a few bullies who believed that they owned the alley and that the rest of us who used it owed them homage. And when night fell, the alley claimed itself, becoming like a cemetery, a place to fear. On a moonless night, it was a river of darkness, broken only by pools of dim light beneath the infrequent lamp posts. I hated it when it was dark and my parents asked me to take out the garbage, for I was afraid and didn't want them to know.

My father sees my hesitation and asks if I am still afraid of the dark. I tell him and myself that I am not, but my hands shake as I pick up the paper bag and walk out the back door, feigning courage. I have told a primal lie. I am still afraid of the dark and of what it might conceal. The alley is black. The other children on my block are all safe inside their houses. *Somewhere down the alley, the lid of a garbage can falls to the pavement with a great din and clatter. Only a cat prowling for food, I tell myself. But deep in my bones, I know otherwise. The alley is now haunted by horrible beings. It is almost too late. I need only a second to open the gate and slam it behind me. Turning, I run toward the brightness of my house, toward the home that offers safety for the night.*

Mystery and fear give comfort and safety their meaning. Thus, I regret that my sons never had an alley to play in, an unordered spot, a place not like a garden at all. When they were small, they never tired of hearing me read Maurice Sendak's *Where the Wild Things Are* just before their bedtime. I think I know why.

Memories of
Old-Fashioned Bonfires

Now is the time for raking leaves. Summer has departed, as has that bright season that began when the first tupelo and sumac and Virginia creeper along the roadsides flamed into crimson. The splendid display is over, the bright yellow, gold, and red that botanists tell us are caused when chlorophyll disappears, revealing xanthophyll and carotene, the other pigments that have been hidden in the leaves all along. When photosynthesis slowed down dramatically, complicated chemical reactions produced tannins and anthocyanins to improve the show.

The leaves are falling from the trees, more of them every day, moving before the wind, swirling along the sidewalk, catching in fences, gathering in heaps beneath the shrubbery. And they must be raked. Otherwise they will ruin the lawn and tell the neighbors that we let winter arrive with our fall chores undone.

My wife cajoles me by her example and by a couple of firm hints to put on a sweater against the morning chill and join her in the task. By noon, we are in shirt-sleeves and I have made umpteen trips with the wheelbarrow to the compost heap so that the nutrients and organic matter in this last harvest of the year will in time return to our piece of earth.

It is unquestionably autumn, a Saturday afternoon in November. Two blocks away we can hear the sounds of a high-school football game—the cheering of the crowd at a touchdown, the voice of the announcer, the brassy blare and quick drumbeat of the marching band at halftime. Above us we hear geese honking as they make their way south toward the Delaware Bay, in flight to their winter feeding grounds.

We pause for cigarettes and a cup of hot chocolate, laced with a splash of rum and topped with marshmallows. The air is warm and the sun is bright, but something about the intensity of the cloudless blue sky promises that tonight we will get our first hard freeze.

All seems well, but at this time of year I always feel a deep autumnal sadness, a longing for the good days before there were black plastic bags and laws to give us cleaner air. I want to pile all our leaves in the street gutter and light a proper bonfire.

It really isn't much fun to rake leaves, despite my wife's assurances that it's good exercise and that if I didn't rake them I would be just another armchair gardener, not to mention a lousy husband. It used to be different, back when I raked leaves at my mother's insistence that I stop reading and make myself useful. I didn't really like raking leaves even then, but from time to time I would stop and rest, lying on my back on the growing pile of oak and sweet gum leaves, listening to their dry crackle as I watched the clouds race across the sky. All up and down the block other children, and sometimes grownups, piled their own leaves in their own gutters.

If the air was calm, when evening was on its way and the day's quota of raking was done, I'd go to the kitchen for wooden matches and then set fire to the pile. Smoldering briefly, it would then roar into flame, warming my face from a dozen feet away. All over the neighborhood other fires burned, sending bright sparks upward against the darkening sky. The leaves were quickly gone, but the smoke lingered in the air for hours. The odor was wonderful, one of those distinctive smells that is some-how both sharp and sweet—like lemon peel, perhaps, or witch hazel, or magnolia blossoms, or bay rum, or a marsh at low tide. For hours I could still smell the odor of burning leaves on my skin, in my clothing, in the blue haze of the air itself.

We know better now than to burn our autumn leaves. We are more sensible. We are more responsible toward the environment. We no longer find the word "ecology" difficult or odd. We have laws to punish those whose nostalgia might move them to set old-fashioned bonfires in the street. The fall air is clearer and fresher now. We have also lost something uncommonly delicious, an autumnal aroma that once gave the season a special delight.

Gardening and Expertise

Our friends Carol and Leonard have been city people for some time. One day they invited us up to see the weekend place they had just bought in New Rochelle. The old house they had refurbished sat on a considerable piece of land overlooking Long Island Sound. Some time around the turn of the century the grounds had been thoughtfully planted with trees that had now reached their handsome maturity. It was a cold December day when we visited, but not so cold that we couldn't all venture outside to inspect the property.

Carol and Leonard said that they were novice gardeners, but they meant to learn, to care for what they had, to add new trees and shrubs, to put in a vegetable garden next summer, perhaps a modest border of perennials that might in time become something grand. Meanwhile, they found their property a bit mysterious. They had trees, but they didn't know what kind.

"Easy enough," I said. "Let's go see what you've got." We walked around the grounds, I identifying things as we went along and Carol writing the names down in a small spiral notebook. In fifteen minutes I'd identified almost everything except for a strange clump of trees down by the water's edge. I pointed out the oaks, the sweet gum trees, the Japanese maples, and to tell the truth, I allowed myself to bask in my friends' gratitude that I'd come avisiting with what they thought was a vast store of botanical and horticultural information.

But to tell the truth a little more, the task wasn't difficult at all. A couple of characteristic five-pointed, star-shaped leaves re-

mained on the sweet gum tree, and the ground below was covered with its prickly seed pods, so I didn't have to go by the bark,
where I might well have misguessed. Anyone who's ever seen a
Japanese maple can identify it any time of year. Oaks are easy;
anything with acorns on it is an oak. I didn't get into risky territory with my friends by going further than identifying their
oaks as oaks—I didn't tell them about white oaks, scarlet oaks,
chestnut oaks, northern pin oaks, blackjack oaks, and so on.

I suspect that for most people one of the darker joys of gardening is that once you get started it's not at all hard to find
someone who knows a little bit less than you, and then it's very
difficult to resist the urge to strut your stuff. Gardeners are
natural-born show-offs, and once you learn the merest basics,
stuff-strutting comes easy. A person who knows which end of a
tulip bulb goes up and which goes down is possessed of information that a surprising number of people in America don't have.
(It's probably much different in Great Britain, which is vastly
more qualified to call itself a nation of gardeners.) I confess it:
I've taken perverse pleasure in the ignorance of some of my closest
friends, the non-gardeners among them. I loved it when a dear
friend lamented that the cattleya orchid I gave her in full bloom
one May was dead by the following spring, and I discovered that
she had taken it out of the fir-bark mix in its pot and planted it
in dirt in her Manhattan garden, where it couldn't possibly survive the soil, much less the winter. But of course we all must
start somewhere when it comes to gardening; no one is born
knowing the difference between a zinnia and a ragweed seedling.

But there are a couple of other things about horticulture
that are much more humbling than the ease with which gardeners can find people who know less than they. First, it's terribly
simple to know things that happen not to be true. (I'd say one
simple case in point is people who believe that house plants love
Mozart and detest domestic squabbles within their earshot.)
Second, no matter how much you know, there are always a lot
of people who know a great deal more. I've got a terrifying book
in my library which humbles if not humiliates me every time I
go near it. Called *Hortus Third: A Concise Dictionary of Plants
Cultivated in the United States and Canada* and written by the
staff of the L. H. Bailey Hortorium at Cornell University, it is

an absolutely essential reference book for anyone who needs for some reason to have the botanical name for the turkey oak (it's *Quercus cerris*). And whoever dreamed up the word "concise" in its subtitle was a master of droll understatement, considering that it runs to 1,290 pages. And it's written in a language I comprehend but very little, tossing around words like "nucellus" and "pergamentaceous" and "zygomorphic" as easily as most of us say "nice" and "pretty" and "zilch." The thought that there are people alive on this planet today who actually read every word of *Hortus Third* and understand what they're reading is a very large slice of humble pie.

It's also humbling to realize that in matters horticultural there's always the possibility of seeing something without realizing what it is you're seeing. A personal example concerns a pleasant excursion I made to Costa Rica—a gloriously beautiful country that ought to be Mecca for every plant lover in North America. Almost everything grows there superbly, except plants like daffodils and tulips, which require winter cold, and plants like perennial asters, which require sharp differentials in day length in order to bloom. The smallest courtyard garden of a modest house in a Costa Rican village is likely to be crammed with gorgeous plants of every sort—jasmines and allamandas and cannas and daturas and crotons and gardenias and oleanders, almost anything most gardeners could name and a few things they can't. And it's a place where *house plants grow wild*, where you can have the quite peculiar experience of looking at an immense tree, seventy or eighty feet high, with a vast and spreading crown, and then suddenly realizing that it's a *Ficus benjamina*, just like the one in your living room, except for its quite considerable size. And one of the things I admired most in Costa Rica was the profusion of lantanas growing everywhere along the roadside, absolutely covered with bloom.

I came back envying the Costa Ricans their lantanas and looking at my own three specimens with disdain, wondering why I bothered to grow them. They're plagued by white flies. I never seem to get them pruned right at the right time. Sometimes I cart them downstairs from their winter habitat in a bedroom and put them on the deck too early or too late, and they retaliate by dropping most of their leaves. If I forget to water them two hours past schedule, they wilt. Until just recently, I thought how lucky lantana lovers are in Costa Rica, where the lantanas love them back.

But the fact is that I had seen those lantanas in Central America with no idea at all what I was really seeing. The sad story is told in *Plant Extinction: A Global Crisis* by Harold Koopowitz and Hilary Kaye, an important book that deserves the widest public attention possible for the alarm it sounds about the astronomical loss of many species of plants currently taking place, especially in the tropics. Here's what the authors say about lantana:

Lantana was created using a complex of West Indian and South American species taken to Europe at the end of the 1600s. The species were hybridized (mainly in France) to make attractive summer bedding plants. More than six hundred different hybrids were made. The colorful flowers are like verbenas and made delightful mounds of showy spikes in the summer. Being tender, *Lantana* were carefully grown and protected in greenhouses during winter. . . .

Enterprising gardeners soon realized that since *Lantana* hybrids provided summer color in temperate areas, they would be fantastic garden plants in the tropics. . . . By 1860, colorful *Lantanas* were displayed in private and public gardens from Calcutta to Cape Town, from the Gold Coast to Tahiti. The plants reveled in the warm sunshine, producing colorful layers of flowers as they clambered and grew luxuriantly. Butterflies pollinated the plants and soon blackberry fruits glistened among the bright colorful blossoms. Birds who came to feast on the berries flew off to spread the seeds.

Man unwittingly had created, and then let loose upon the world, a green plague.

Now, according to Koopowitz and Kaye, lantana is a superweed, a terrible menace that has spread everywhere in the tropics of the Southern Hemisphere, poisoning the livestock that feed on its toxic leaves, threatening agriculture, and competing with native species so successfully that it threatens the very existence of many of them.

Koopowitz and Kaye have convinced me how wrong I was. Instead of envying the Costa Ricans their lantana, I should have given them my sympathies. I didn't truly see what I was seeing, for I was ignorant. Now I know better, of course, but I also know that this isn't the last time I will have to unlearn what I "know" and be taught better by someone more expert than myself.

What Do You Say
to a Friend Who's Afflicted
by Peach Borers?

Every gardener who likes to be thought expert in the craft needs a friend like my friend Joe Walsh. Once a priest, he's now a family man with a house and a garden, which like most gardens offers its share of vexations as well as pleasures. Joe knows I envy him the enormous fig tree in his back yard. It survives every winter without dying back, even though he gives it none of the recommended protections. It bears a magnificent crop of luscious, red-brown fruit every August, and although I also have a fig tree, I have to rely on Joe for the figs that come to my table.

I've tried wrapping my own fig tree some years, as the books suggest. I've moved it from one location to another in the hope that somewhere in my yard it will find an agreeable microclimate. I've left it to the elements occasionally, and sometimes I've weighed down its branches with bricks and covered them with dirt. The result is always the same: disappointment. It dies back to the ground in winter, remains dormant until late May, ignoring the springtime all around the garden, and then bursts into luxuriant growth, producing only a few small fruits, which are blasted by the first killing frost before they ripen.

But despite the evidence of our two fig trees, Joe believes I know a great deal about gardening, so he turns to me whenever something in his yard seems doomed. Today it was his peach tree. The phone rang and Joe's voice said, "Allen, my peach tree may be dying."

When I commented philosophically that peach trees were

often short-lived, he groaned. To distract him from his pain and grief, I asked what the specific problem was.

"Orange gunk," he replied. "There's a lot of sticky orange gunk dribbling from the trunk near the ground. And holes. I can see some holes."

"Hmmm," I mumbled, suggesting that I was pondering the matter. Meanwhile, I had grabbed from the shelf one of those handy-dandy, fully illustrated, complete gardening guides that most bookstores carry, usually on the remainder table of publishers' overstocks. This particular one I privately call "The Pessimist's Garden Book" because of its relentless attention to the catastrophes that can overtake plants.

After a slight pause while I checked the index and found the two pages devoted to the woes of peaches, I was able to tell Joe that the chances were strong that his tree was suffering damage from the voracious larvae of the peach borer (*Aegenia exitiosa*), that he should kill as many as possible by inserting thin, flexible wire into their tunnels, clean out the wounded areas with cotton swabs, and then spray the trunk with carbaryl or lindane immediately and then again in three weeks. In the fall he should dig in some mothballs around the tree to kill any eggs laid by the adult moths as they hatched.

"Then my peach tree will live?" he asked.

"We can't be absolutely sure," I said, "but we have a chance, if we follow the treatment scientifically."

I felt a warm glow after he hung up, probably to rush out for swabs and chemical means of destruction. A friend with faith in my knowledge had consulted me, and I had given him judicious advice—diagnosis, prescription, and prognosis. I felt for a moment that I was the Michael De Bakey of the fruit-tree world. The fact is, however, that I've never seen a peach borer in my life. If I had a peach tree in my own garden and found orange gunk oozing from its trunk, I wouldn't go to that book on my shelf. Instead, I'd place an immediate long-distance call to a friend in Boston and ask his advice. He *really* knows almost all there is to know about gardening.

Thinking over my conversation with Joe, I felt a bit shabby and foolish: shabby because I had pretended to a wisdom not my own, not even mentioning to him that my advice came straight from the pages of a book; foolish because Joe might not have borers at all, since for all I knew there might be dozens of things that could cause orange gunk and holes. It's comforting to think that every problem has its solution, if we only take care to proceed in a scientific way and follow the experts. Gardening, however, teaches another, quite different, lesson about problems and solutions. To a certain extent, horticulture is a science, and like every science it rests on a few simple necessary assumptions: that every effect has its cause; that if the cause is known, the effect may be altered; that observation of regular patterns in nature, deftness in framing hypotheses of explanation, and patient experimentation may lead to remedies that will keep borers from destroying peach trees, chickweed from taking over the perennial border, and onion maggots from getting the onions. There may even be some rational way to make my fig tree bear. For the scientific gardener there may be things we don't know yet, but there are no mysteries, only problems to work on with pluck, good cheer, and confidence.

I admire those who approach gardening scientifically. I have learned many beneficial things from them. But I also know that gardening is an art and that as an art it has its mysteries, its inexplicable transactions between ourselves and the earth we inhabit. A garden is a living place where strange and sometimes unnameable forces meet and intersect, where outcomes are never fully predictable. It is a place where we are often surprised and taken unawares by sudden disappointments and by equally sudden delights.

Though I sometimes succumb to the temptation to play the scientific expert with friends like Joe, deep in my bones I'm a hopeless mystic who is often overcome by a sense of nameless wonder over the things I find in gardens. The beauty of daffodils in April, when they are momentarily lit by the last golden light of afternoon, the stark loveliness of the reddish branches of blueberry bushes in midwinter, the sudden hint of honeysuckle in the air on a June evening—any of these things is enough to woo me and win me from my Cartesian pretenses to science and method. But there is mourning as well as celebration, lament as well as praise, when some plant I loved and thought safe unexpectedly sickens and then dies, and although I know better, I cannot think of gypsy-moth caterpillars as being anything other than the incarnation of evil.

Science, although it is the activity of persons who individually can never achieve the full measure of the objectivity they claim, works because it is a collective endeavor that excludes everything personal. It operates by refusing to admit purpose in the matters it studies, because it tries to understand processes in the simple faith that they must finally be capable of being understood, and because it refuses to attribute will to anything in nature, except for human beings.

I take a different view. The world is a place with foes and friends. My crabgrass is out to get me, and my chickweed and I are engaged in a mutual vendetta. My tomato plants appreciate the care they get, and they say thanks with ripe red fruit. My fig tree stands pat, refusing to produce fruit because it has doubts, probably valid, about me.

Science tells us what to do about borers, but it doesn't have the final word. Gardening involves the feelings and the affections we have for things, not just the techniques we have learned, the information we happen to know. Gardening is my friend Joe Walsh loving his peach tree, asking advice from others, and then tending its wounds with cotton swabs and strong medicines, in the perhaps vain hope that it will live for many a year to come.

Navy-Blue Tulips and
"Early Stardrift," Indeed!

Why should I be upset when on the very day that the last petal has dropped from the last tulip out in the garden the postman comes up the walk and hands me, absolutely free, a 60-page booklet, lavishly illustrated in full color, with eighteen magnificent tulips on the front cover and a great many savings and great bargains on spring bulbs from Holland, if only I order early from an American firm whose name is well known to most gardeners? And when the booklet itself is obviously a bargain, inasmuch as the price printed on the cover tells me it ought to be costing me $2? And how can I possibly justify feeling peckish when the back cover addresses me personally (Mr. Allen Lacy or—a touch of fickleness here—"current resident") and refers to my very own garden in Atlantic County, New Jersey? The computer knows my name and spells it right. The catalog demonstrates the company's faith in my credit rating by offering me instant credit ("send no money") and shows good intentions by giving me the right to inspect what I order when it arrives and to refuse it if I wish. Why should I complain about this nice company that wants me to have the special values and great savings and top-of-the-crop merchandise and low-cost sampler collections of the finest Dutch bulbs?

Well, I am complaining, and I'm so irritated that I won't even mention the name of the firm here, just in case that theory, much believed by all hucksters and public-relations counselors, that there's no such thing as bad publicity turns out to be correct.

Navy-Blue Tulips and "Early Stardrift," Indeed!

Even if the bulbs happen to be of the best possible quality, which I have no grounds for doubting, and even if the prices represent fantastic savings (which I doubt: $8.99 for 40 crocus bulbs strikes me as a trifle pricey), I wouldn't want to give this company a penny's worth of free publicity by excoriating it in print. I have my reasons.

First of all, there's the matter of the navy-blue tulips. Tulips aren't blue. Period. Never have been, probably never will be. The text of the catalog doesn't lie in describing a tulip called Insurpassable, which appears on page 6, as "orchid lavender," a claim I can accept. But the adjacent picture shows a tulip blossom that's supersaturated with a color I can only call navy blue, and the same color appears in one blossom of a tulip mixture on the next page. Doesn't this company get proofs of its catalog from the printer before publishing it? Doesn't it have an art director capable of raising a little hell with the printing company, saying, "Look here, the color on the tulips in these two pictures is off by a good country mile. Fix it—we don't want to disappoint our customers by giving them orchid lavender after a misleading picture has made them think they'll have navy blue next spring." But farther on in the catalog, both text and picture are misleading, where a parrot tulip is shown in a rich sapphire blue and described as "clear amethyst blue." (Here I'm a little confused: aren't amethysts purple? Or simply amethyst?)

Second, there's the matter of the star-of-Bethlehem bulbs, offered at $2.99 per 16, and described as "carefree" plants that "multiply quickly" and are "excellent for naturalizing." Whoever wrote this particular bit of prose is a master of snake oil and could probably write glowingly about the virtues of crabgrass for a fine summer lawn. Translating "multiply quickly" and "excellent for naturalizing" into plain English, what these words mean is that star-of-Bethlehem (*Ornithogalum umbellatum*) is a horrendous pest and that anyone who plants it deliberately will early rue the day. Here I defer to the stern advice of the eminently sensible Eleanor Perényi in *Green Thoughts: A Writer in the Garden*:

Don't touch it. It will invade every part of the garden, choking out everything in its path, and like many undesirables is cunningly constructed to thwart easy extraction—the slippery foliage when tugged instantly separates from the bulblets, leaving them snugly far below ground.

I agree wholeheartedly, having to contend every spring with the thick tufts of this unspeakable weed (though the white flower clusters *are* pretty), which has spread by self-sowing all over the garden. I cannot believe that the proprietors of a company specializing in spring bulbs are ignorant of its bad habits, which they gloss over so easily by talk of easy naturalization. Shame on them! Besides, every part of the thing is poisonous.

But what really gets my dander up and sticks in my craw and elevates my dudgeon about this firm and its catalog is its loose and easy way with names, its daring feats of imagination in rebaptizing plants with appellations hitherto unknown or undreamed of. Now, I know that some people who garden are sometimes intimidated by botanical or scientific nomenclature. I'm often among them, being happy to speak of snowdrops rather than *Galanthus nivalis*. It doesn't especially bother me that this offending catalog resolutely omits all botanical names, though I don't think including them would do any harm or put off a single customer. The nub of the matter is that it makes up new common names, not only for bulbs that don't have them, but also for bulbs that have perfectly fine common names they've been known by for generations of English-speaking gardeners.

Overlooking the case of Golden Charm tulips, which I take to be the species tulip *Tulipa dasystemon*, let us proceed to alliums. Halfway through the catalog there is an offer of the Giant Persian Blue Allium, described in the text as purple-blue (but depicted in the illustration in ink the color of sapphires). So far so good, though I'd really like to know which of several possible large alliums it might be. A couple of pages over, however, other alliums are offered, without the slightest hint that they are alliums, and thus smaller cousins to Giant Persian Blue. One is called Sunny Twinkles, another Cascade Bells, a third Alpine Rosy Bells, and, rather confusingly, the lot of them seem to be known collectively as Mountain Bells. I shudder to think that if this catalog were my first encounter with horticulture and if I bought some alliums, I might report to friends next June that the twinkles and the bells were blooming in my garden.

Navy-Blue Tulips and "Early Stardrift," Indeed!

Then there are Pink Buttercups, actually no such thing at all but some species or other of oxalis. A minor matter, however, compared with the atrocities lying in wait on page 36, the same page that offers star-of-Bethlehem to the unwary. First, there's something called Early Snow Glories, whose scientific name is *Chionodoxa luciliae*. Usually it's called glory-of-the-snow, and I don't quite see the need to turn "snow" into an adjective here. Then we arrive at *Scilla siberica*, a pleasant Russian native well worth celebration for its deep-blue flowers in late March and early April. It, too, has a common name long accepted—Siberian squill. The name isn't especially attractive, I'll grant, but then I've heard of people named Otha and Brandy Kay. Siberian squill in my catalog has been altered to Star of Holland, a major geographical shift, and no more justified than deciding that Texas bluebonnets should be renamed Pride of Moscow. And finally there is *Puschkinia scilloides* var. *libanotica*. Admittedly, the scientific name's a mouthful (but no more so than the name of the eighteenth-century Russian naturalist who named it, Appolos Appolosovich Mussin-Puschkin), and the established common name, striped squill, lacks both poetry and precision, since it's not a member of the genus *Scilla* at all, though it's close kin. But there's no reason at all that some pretty plants can't have ugly names. And here this catalog brought by the postman to me or "current resident" in my house in Atlantic County, New Jersey, utterly outreaches all its other flights of fancy in nomenclature. *Puschkinia scilloides*, hitherto stuck with its ugly-duckling name of striped squill, becomes—Early Stardrift! The description suggests what the person who renamed it had in mind. "Create a Milky Way drift with these early spring beauties." I am dazzled, but I am also puzzled. Is there a Late Stardrift as well? And what is a stardrift, anyway? My dictionary lists star chamber, star apple, stardom, stardust, starfish, starflower, stargazer, starlight, star-nosed mole, star-spangled, star thistle, but nothing does it say of stardrifts. The word sounds pretty, but it's as insubstantial as cotton candy. Again, I shudder to think that if I had only this catalog to go on I might embarrass myself by walking into the garden of some more experienced horticultural friend when the *P. scilloides* was at its best and exclaiming, "Mighty fine mass of early stardrifts you've got there, Angus!"

My son Michael tells me I'm overreacting, just a little. I think not. Seed companies and bulb houses and nurseries are businesses, not charitable institutions. If their wares are good, they have every reason and every right to advertise their merits in as attractive a way as possible. But they owe it to their customers to educate them a bit as they sell their merchandise. Ultimately, it's in their own interests to do so, for better-educated gardeners make better customers, who are apt to be more adventurous than just sticking in a couple of dozen daffodils one fall and then leaving it at that forever after. I can think of several businesses in horticulture, both large and small, whose catalogs do manage to engage in a little education along the way. Wayside Gardens is one. White Flower Farm and Thompson and Morgan are admirably thorough and uncondescending. Among bulb firms, I can mention the catalogs of Messelaar and De Jager as admirable, especially the latter. Neither stoops to phonying up spring with Early Stardrifts and similar offenses to both language and gardening, and I thank them for that.

It's a Bug-Eat-Bug World Out There, or Revenge among the House Plants

I sympathize with people who refuse to grow house plants on the moral grounds that the things generally perish under their care, leaving them feeling guilty about what happened to the African violet or Swedish ivy they brought home from the supermarket. There's a lot of grief in watching anything you love turn sick and die.

A couple of Junes ago, it looked as if our ancient and beloved hoya vine wouldn't make it until Labor Day. My wife bought it in Virginia in 1962 as a rooted cutting, just before the birth of our second son. It has moved with us several times. We have treasured it for its handsome waxy foliage all year long and for its fragrant, long-lasting clusters of velvety pink blossoms in summer. Now grown enormous, it covered two windows in our entranceway, giving us privacy from the street.

But for some time it had suffered sorely, being as afflicted by mealybugs as Job was with boils and other woes. An exploding population of these wretched creatures was enjoying our hoya as much as we. Feeding on the sap, these lethargic, cottony-gray insects were sucking away its life. In what seemed to be its last days, it was a sorry sight indeed. The insects' sticky secretions attracted ants and caused an unsightly, sooty, black mold on most of the leaves, already yellowed from the mealybugs' constant feeding.

The bugs were out of control. They resisted our best efforts to exterminate them by both hand combat (cotton swabs dipped in rubbing alcohol) and chemical warfare (systemic poisons and a variety of nasty-smelling sprays).

We got a few of the bugs along the way, but they were winning the war. The hoya seemed doomed, but my wife suggested that I call our friend Roger in Boston. A Harvard-trained biologist who wrote his dissertation on methods of seed dispersal by Costa Rican ants, or some such thing, he's seldom stumped for an answer when it comes to the things that can go wrong with plants. Sometimes he has no remedy to offer, but he can usually give a name to my distress, like a dentist with some very bad news.

But this time he had a remedy. "Call Rincon-Vitova Insectaries in Oak View, California," he instructed, "and tell them you want an order of 100 *Cryptolaemus montrouzieri.*"

After some silence from my end of the wire, he went on to explain. Rincon-Vitova is one of several firms that specialize in biological control of harmful insects in house or garden. In other words, it sells bug-eating bugs—lacewings and ladybugs and predatory wasps to gobble up pests like whiteflies, aphids, and scale insects. *Cryptolaemus montrouzieri* is a small beetle from Australia whose gruesome diet consists entirely of mealybugs. Even its larvae, which look alarmingly like mealybugs themselves, eat mealybugs. A scientific journal had recently reported that the Des Moines Botanical Center had used these little wonders—affectionately known as "Crypts," for reasons painfully apparent to anyone who attempts to call them by their full Latin name after a highball or two—to cure a bad epidemic of mealybugs in its greenhouses after every other means had failed.

It sounded as if these little beetles were bugs after my own heart, so I called California and ordered 100 Crypts—under $10 worth, including airmail delivery. While I was at it, I asked the pleasant-voiced woman who was taking my order and who told me her name was Sue if she had any weapons in her arsenal for the brown-scale insects that were attacking the asparagus fern in our living room, and she said yes, for a few more dollars she'd send along 100 *Metaphycus helvolus,* a parasitic wasp whose earthly pleasures seem limited to copulation, except for the females, who have the added pleasure of depositing their eggs in scale insects, assuring them a grisly death when the eggs hatch and begin their voracious feeding. I told Sue to add the *Metaphycus* to my order and send the bill.

While I waited for my purchase to arrive in the mail, I

horrified friends and relatives by telling them what I'd done. Our friend Phyllis, who detests anything that stings, said on hearing about the wasps that she wouldn't be dropping by the house very much from then on. I assured her that the wasps didn't sting. Still, I felt a little uneasy. I hadn't really asked Rincon-Vitova about the matter, nor had I thought to inquire about the size of the wasps. If they were the size of most of the wasps I've experienced, they'd be awfully unnerving, stings or not, flitting about the house and perhaps alighting on my pillow at night when they were bored with copulation and assuring the destruction of brown-scale insects. From Dallas, one of my brothers offered the opinion that the beetles probably ate sport coats. The word spread fast in my family. Soon another brother called from San Marcos to suggest that if the beetles should cross-breed with the wasps the progeny would probably end up drinking my whiskey and maybe my blood. My youngest brother sent a postal card from Tulsa saying that he was shocked and embarrassed that one of his kin would introduce the law of the jungle into his own house, considering our Southern Baptist and Methodist origins.

The package arrived. The wasps, considering my unadmitted apprehensions, were almost disappointing, being barely visible to the naked eye, far, far smaller than fleas. I opened their container, some tiny flecks floated out, and they were gone. Within weeks, the scale was also gone. I take satisfaction in the result, but there was no pleasure in observing the process, since it was unobservable.

The Crypts, on the other hand, were wonderfully voracious, and they attacked the mealybugs with an impressive ferocity. As soon as I opened the small ice-cream carton in which they had been packed with a bit of excelsior to cling to during their journey from California, they flew right to the hoya and busily began marching up and down its stems and leaves on their mission of search and destroy. I watched the bloodthirsty destruction of their prey with undisguised joy. The next morning, my wife reported that she had just observed two beetles devour an especially fat victim, one at either end.

In two weeks, the battle was over. There wasn't a single mealybug in sight. I opened the window so my Crypts could look for food in the larger world outdoors.

The hoya not only made it to Labor Day, it also burst into vigorous growth. The leaves lost their yellow pallor and turned a rich, glossy green. It bloomed spectacularly, putting out almost seventy-five clusters of blossoms during a six-week period.

Nevertheless, a battle won does not necessarily mean the war is over. Although the brown scale has never returned to our asparagus ferns, I can't report the same solid and lasting success with our hoya and its mealybugs. It turned out that the Crypts had missed a few, and six months after the hoya bloomed I discovered a new, but milder, infestation. Furthermore, a great many mealybugs turned up on a clivia in our living room. Again I called Rincon-Vitova and placed an order for 100 *Cryptolaemus montrouzieri*.

When they arrived, I dumped half of them on the hoya and the other half on the clivia. For the second time, they did fine work with the hoya. The result was less happy with the clivia, whose leaves seemed to repel them. Refusing to stay on the plant, they took to the window screens. I fashioned a kind of cage of cheesecloth surrounding the plant, gently picked what Crypts I could find from the screens, and set them loose inside the improvised cage, hoping that the confinement would encourage them to do their duty. It didn't work. They simply clung to the cheesecloth, apparently preferring to starve rather than approach the clivia, no matter how many tender morsels of mealybug it was home to. The clivia now gets the alcohol-and-swab treatment from time to time to keep its mealybug population in check.

The Crypts aren't perfect. In my experience, at least, they *control* mealybugs rather than eradicating them forever. At intervals of six months or so I must order a new batch of beetles. But they do keep our hoya reasonably healthy, without my having to resort to chemical pesticides I'd just as soon not have around the house.

They also answer one of life's more puzzling riddles: *What good are mealybugs?* The answer is simple. They make a fine meal for *Cryptolaemus*.

Orchid Cactus

The three monsters in hanging baskets at the east end of our living room take up so much space that I'm tempted to refer to them as hog plants rather than house plants. Furthermore, when they're not in bloom, from the middle of June until late April, they border on the grotesque. With their round, spiky stems jutting outward and upward above their pots and their thick, fleshy leaves (technically not leaves at all but flattened stems), they look like something H. G. Wells might have dreamed up for a Martian landscape. On seeing them during their off-season, several outspoken guests have asked what on earth they were, in tones they might have used had there been, say, voodoo dolls hanging in the window. But visitors who come when they're in bloom usually ask about them with a touch of awe and even reverence in their voices—and properly so, I think.

Botanists used to call them phyllocactus, meaning leaf cactus, but the preferred term now is epiphyllum, meaning that they've sometimes got something, namely flowers, on their leaves. I won't quibble here about the oddity of the name, given the technicality already mentioned parenthetically. Their common names include pond lilies and forest cactus, although the latter term also refers to Christmas cactus and Easter cactus, to which they are closely related. Most people who grow them call them orchid cactus, unless they affectionately shorten their botanical names and call them eppies. Orchid cactus is certainly an appropriate name: first, because they are hybrids among several genera within the cactus family (all natives of tropical America, where they grow as epiphytes on trees); second, because their blossoms are as spectacular and opulent as any orchid.

I got started with orchid cactuses about ten years ago, when on impulse I ordered three unlabeled rooted cuttings, all minuscule in comparison with their eventual size, from a mail-order nursery in California. It was three years before the first plant bloomed, producing two small greenish-pink flowers at nodes near the bottom of one of the trailing stems. I wasn't much impressed, especially considering that the plant which bore them had already reached a troublesome size. But over the next three weeks the flowers intensified in color and swelled larger until they were very toothsome indeed—a deep and glowing pink, three inches across, with something of the form of lotos blossoms. Two years later the second joined it in blooming, this one with much smaller but more abundant trumpet-shaped blossoms of fuchsia red. The following year the third one finally bloomed. The most beautiful of the three, it produced cigar-shaped buds which grew fatter and fatter before opening one evening into a flower so lovely I had to pick up the telephone and call some friends in to bear witness. Perhaps four inches across, its petals, a clear shade of reddish-orange with a fine silken sheen, swept back sharply at their tips with an uncommon grace and elegance.

Epiphyllums are not for the impatient. People who mind long waits and want flowers instantly if not sooner are better advised to forgo them, to plant petunias or marigolds from their nearest garden centers instead. But their care is simple and undemanding, their problems are few, and the beauty of their flowers makes them entirely worth the wait.

We've never repotted our orchid cactuses, having read somewhere that they like to be potbound, as do clivia and agapanthus. And over the years my wife has worked out a regimen which seems to suit them well. In the summer, after they've finished blooming, they usually go outside, spending the hot months in the shade of a maple tree from whose branches we hang them to keep them away from slugs, which have an ardent relish for their stems. In the autumn, after the night temperatures have dropped into the forties, they come back inside. Their home in the living room is usually kept at 50 degrees F. They are given a period of rest until early March, watered sparingly about once a month, and not fertilized at all. Then they're given a good soaking with 20–20–20 liquid fertilizer, the thermostat in the living room is turned up to 68 degrees F., and the first buds appear about six weeks later.

Just recently I was overtaken by a sudden desire to know more about epiphyllums, which aren't covered very fully or satisfactorily in any of the garden books in my library. Spotting an ad in *Pacific Horticulture*—an excellent garden magazine, although people in the East and the Midwest who read it will find their pleasure accompanied by deep pangs of envy for gardeners who can grow acacias and leptospernum in their own back yards—I called Rainbow Gardens, a nursery specializing in orchid cactuses, and found myself talking to Jerry Williams, one of the firm's two owners.

I had a few questions for Mr. Williams.

First, I outlined the regimen we follow with our own three orchid cactuses. He said it was basically okay, with a couple of exceptions. The fertilizer we used is far too rich in nitrogen, which only encourages the foliage to become more and more rampant. He recommended using 0–10–10 (or 2–10–10, since the leaner mix can be hard to find), from the end of dormancy in March at monthly intervals until bloom stops in June. Then, once a month until September, he advocated fertilizing with liquid fish emulsion (5–10–10, or half as much nitrogen as phosphates and potash).

Second, *please*, have any hybridizers succeeded in cutting orchid cactuses down to more manageable size? I was thinking that if someone had produced cultivars that called it quits when they reached, say, one-sixth the size of the Gargantuas in my living room, I could start over and have eighteen of the lovely things instead of three. I knew it was hopeless when he sighed the kind of sigh parents do when they learn that their kleptomaniac teenager, presumed in remission after eighteen months of expensive psychotherapy, is at it again. "No," he said. "There's been some interesting breeding of orchid cactus with miniature flowers, but no one has been able to crack the genes to produce compact growth. It's just their nature to sprawl, but they can be controlled by keeping them potbound and by pruning here and there."

Third, orchid cactuses were all pink or fuchsia red or reddish-orange, weren't they? I said a silent prayer that the answer would be yes, so I wouldn't be struck down by color lust that would in a few years' time turn our dining room as well as our living room into a jungle of eppies gone wild. The answer was no, and each successive color that he named was like a hammer blow to my heart. "*White*: Calisto and President F.D.R. are both fine whites. *Yellow*: Jennifer Ann is hard to beat. *Purple*: Malcho's Beauty is a dandy purple. *Red*: As for reds, I'd have a hard time picking between John F. Kennedy and Clara Ann." The only good news he had was that so far no orchid cactus is available in blue, black, or brown. Meanwhile, I was wondering if we couldn't get rid of one schefflera, seven large begonias, a dieffenbachia, an immense pot of papyrus, seventeen African violets, three asparagus ferns, a hefty *Ficus benjamina*, several hanging baskets of Swedish ivy and wandering Jew, and a few more items in the vegetable menagerie inhabiting the windows of our house to accommodate John F. Kennedy, the unbeatable Jennifer Ann, and company.

Fourth, what did orchid cactuses cost these days? I was hoping to hear upward of $500 each, to quench my lust with the waters of thrift. But the answer was anywhere between $2.50 and $10.00, for plants large enough to bloom in two or three years.

I asked no more questions before saying my polite goodbye, but Mr. Williams, obviously an eppie aficionado who sensed that he had a potential convert on the other end of the wire, continued to ply me with information. I could join the Epiphyllum Society of America for just $5, an act that would unite me with some 700 other members of the faith. He knew I would enjoy the catalog he would send, and also the photocopy of the recent article his partner, Chuck Everson, had published in *Flower and Garden*. And if Rainbow Gardens didn't suit me as a source for orchid cactuses, I could try the California Epiphyllum Center in Vista, California, or Greenlife Greenhouses in Georgia, both of them fine places. (Obviously, Mr. Williams isn't monopoly-minded about epiphyllums, and he's charitable toward his competitors.)

The catalog from Rainbow Gardens—in full color, damnit! —hasn't arrived yet. But I know it's on the way. I have a day or to to think. Is it time for us to buy a larger house? With more windows that face east? Or with, perhaps, a small greenhouse?

Passion Flower

Not believing it a good policy to court frustration, I decided a few years ago that one plant I would never try to raise inside the house would be the night-blooming cereus, whose blossoms open in late evening and close the next morning. This transitory indoor show doesn't appeal to me. Besides, I have heard that after the flower of the night-blooming cereus folds up, it looks much like the head of a dead goose hanging in a slaughterhouse. It would probably be my luck to catch the goose head often, but never the glorious blossom that preceded it.

I was terribly surprised, therefore, as may be imagined, to discover not long ago that among the house plants in hanging baskets in our living room there is one of these cereuses, identified to me as such by a good friend who is a cactus freak. It had been given to me as a rooted cutting by one of my students, who thought it was a Christmas cactus. I knew that couldn't be right, since it didn't look like any other Christmas cactus I'd seen, but I never suspected what it really was. So far, the frustration that I wanted to avoid by excluding night-blooming cereus from this household hasn't materialized—our plant grows well enough, putting out new shoots every summer, but it also shows a striking disinclination to bloom. My policy still seems to be a good one, though: house plants that are raised for their bloom ought to stay in bloom long enough to be appreciated. (But not *too* long; I much preferred poinsettias back in the old days when their "flowers"—actually colored bracts—fell off the day after Christmas. Now, after hybridizers have worked their magic, the damned things stay in what seems to be bloom, though it really isn't, long into the daffodil season, when they look as silly in the living room as a Christmas tree still standing in full decoration.) Right next to the night-blooming cereus that sneaked into our midst, posing as a Christmas cactus, is another plant—a passion-flower vine—that violates my policy, though I didn't know it when I bought it at a greenhouse in Connecticut. The mother plant from which it was taken covered one whole wall and was almost smothered with strange and compelling blossoms—all over three inches across and spectacular for their ten petals and sepals, their wispy fringe of odd rays coming from the center, their blue color, which turns out on close inspection to be a mixture of blue, violet, purple, green, and greenish-white. Discovering from the label that it was *Passiflora alato-caerulea*, a hybrid of two species native to tropical America, I bought it on the spot, along with a red-flowered counterpart, *P. coccinea*, which died en route home. I consoled myself that the survivor would be a pleasant reminder of the purple passion-flower vines (*P. incarnata*) or maypops I have admired growing wild along the roadsides in Texas and Tennessee.

I've always liked the thought of passion vines in the vicinity, ever since puberty at least, for I thought the name had something to do with the urgings of the flesh that appear then, along with acne and a tendency to hog the telephone and dream of car keys. I was of course wildly off the etymological mark; the passion flower is called what it is not in celebration of human randiness but in commemoration of the suffering of Christ. As T. H. Everett tells it in his description of the 400 species of *Passiflora* in his *Illustrated Encyclopedia of Horticulture*, it received its name because Spanish priests and other explorers soon after the discovery and colonization of the New World

professed to see in the curious and wonderful blooms and other parts of these plants symbols of the crucifixion, which they accepted as Divine assurance of success for their enthusiastic, but unfortunately often fatal efforts to convert the heathen Indians. The five petals and five sepals were thought to represent the ten apostles present at Christ's death, Peter and Judas being absent. The conspicuous fringed corona was considered emblematic of the crown of thorns or of the halo, and the five stamens of the five wounds or of the hammers employed to drive the nails. The latter, three in number, were symbolized for the devout Christians by the stigmas. Recalling the scourges or the cords were the tendrils of the passion flower and the fingered leaves of some kinds suggested the persecutor's hands or the head of the lance that pierced the Savior's side.

I can think of no other flower so burdened down with theology, not even the Judas tree!

I wish I could say that our passion-flower vine is a great success as a house plant. It isn't. It grows fine, competing lustily with the nearby epiphyllums to achieve dominance at the windowpane. Several times a year it puts out six or seven buds, which are large but still quite inconspicuous, thanks to their light-green color, which fades into the foliage. The flowers can't be missed, of course, but they open with little warning and last less than a day. Much more often than not, I discover, a few hours too late, that the plant has sneaked in and out of bloom on me, wasting its strange loveliness on an unpopulated living room. Only once has it managed to bloom when there were visitors here to admire it, but that occasion made it entirely worthwhile. A painter friend, David Ahlsted, had dropped by the house for a couple of drinks. He wandered from the dining room into the living room and discovered that, once again, the passion flower was blooming behind my back. When he saw it, he shouted out, in great astonishment at the sight, "Jesus Christ, Allen! What is this?" It seemed a good response.

Randy and Ma'am
and Mr. Tallat-Kelpsa

Not far from my house there is a discount garden center. The name doesn't matter, as there are thousands of places like it all over the country. Call it Randy's, but keep in mind that it is a symbol and a symptom as well as an actual commercial establishment. A very busy place, its parking lot usually stands thick with station wagons, vans, and tiny Japanese automobiles whose owners shake their heads while pondering the logistics of getting home with the two bales of peat moss, six rosebushes, and four dozen bedding plants they just bought.

Randy's sells a great variety of merchandise. It sells feeders to entice birds and red-and-yellow whirligigs to scare them away. It specializes twelve months out of the year in what it calls "garden accessories," including birdbaths in the form of giant clam shells, a choir of Permastone putti, and an entire herd of painted plaster deer, each with meltingly soft brown eyes and a price tag dangling from the antlers.

Much as some churches follow the liturgical year, Randy's follows a cycle of merchandise seasons. In early spring, the consignments of vegetable and flower seeds arrive from Burpee and Ferry Morse and Mandeville. Trucks from distant growers pull up in the parking lot, and the improvised nursery out back fills with prepackaged tea roses and floribundas and a limited, ho-hum assortment of yew, euonymus, ornamental fruit trees, and pyracantha. Randy celebrates the advent of another garden year, another year of ringing cash registers and sturdy profits, by taking out full-page ads in the local press. The ads often achieve marvelous feats of spelling: customers who remember to clip the special coupons will get a 30 percent discount on "Wigilla," "Mogo Pine," "Crapapple," "Fercythea," and "Annoymous."

A few weeks later the front sidewalk is covered with market packs of annual bedding plants: alyssums, impatiens, petunias, salvias, but mostly marigolds. Business slacks off in June. The bedraggled market packs are dumped in the alley. The remaining shrubbery, looking pretty peaked, is sold at deep discount to customers who will soon wish that they'd thought to ask for a guarantee. To keep up his trade, Randy sets up a summer produce stand, selling last fall's apples from cold storage, and local lettuce, blueberries, and tomatoes during their seasons.

In July, the unsold seeds go back to the consignment houses, usually just before local gardeners remember that they need to buy a couple of packs of lettuce seed to keep their salad gardens producing during the fall. Come August, the crocuses, daffodils, and tulips arrive from Holland. Randy's offers a poor selection of inferior-grade bulbs, prices them dearly, and ensures their mediocre performance next spring by storing them in the hottest corner of the store, where the temperature often reaches 90 degrees F. October is the month for cider and pumpkins, replaced in late November by evergreen "grave blankets" (an interesting local custom) for the dead, and Christmas trees—real, flocked, or plastic—for the living.

Randy's, I must grudgingly admit, performs some useful services. It meets the needs of the plaster-donkey crowd very well indeed. It's also a handy place to buy bird food, lawn seed, peat moss, and tomato stakes. I'm a regular customer. Nevertheless, I have increasingly severe reservations about what Randy's and its myriad counterparts across the country are doing to lower the quality of American horticulture and to bring about a bland, boring, homogenized suburban landscape.

Probably there are some garden centers whose personnel know what they are doing; but starting with the proper way to spell forsythia, the evidence suggests that no one who works at Randy's knows very much about gardening.

I am an inveterate and practiced eavesdropper, and I have heard Randy himself, as well as his clerks, give customers astonishingly misinformed advice. One day, while I was in the store weighing the relative merits of two pocket pruners, a distressed woman approached Randy, removed a handkerchief from her pocket, and with a look of disgust unfolded it before him. It contained a well-nourished bagworm in its silk-and-juniper cocoon. "I've got this juniper tree," she said, "just covered with these horrible things. What can I do?"

"You got nothing to worry about, lady," Randy explained. "Those are pinecones, but baby ones."

In an act of vigilantism, I waited until Randy was out of earshot, explained about bagworms, and suggested a cure—find a child not given to squeamishness, hand him or her a tin can, and pay two cents apiece to pick the bugs off the juniper before the eggs inside can hatch and the infestation spread.

Another time, I heard a woman complain that $10 a dozen was too much to charge for grape hyacinths. Randy said it was the going price that year for hyacinths. His customer, sensing that Randy was confused, tried to explain that grape hyacinths, *Muscari*, are minor bulbs and never as expensive as proper hyacinths.

"I don't know nothing about this muscari stuff, lady," he replied, "but none of the bulbs I sell are minor. And hyacinths is hyacinths. Grape hyacinths, pink hyacinths, white hyacinths, I got all kinds of hyacinths and they're all $10 a dozen."

It need not be thus. One can imagine a world in which the salesclerks who wait on gardeners in a garden store are both courteous and well informed. I can, because my first job, at age ten, was working as a clerk and porter every Saturday at a seed store in the Dallas suburb of Highland Park.

I don't remember the name of my boss. Like everyone else who worked there, I called her what the British call their queen —"Ma'am." Ma'am had a pleasant smile, but she was formidable. Every Friday she went to the beauty shop next door and renewed the purple tint on her hair. She carried herself within a rigid system of corsets, like my notion of an opera star or an Austrian countess. She wore sensible shoes and tailored purple dresses almost matching the shade of her coiffure.

She gave me a no-nonsense introduction to the workaday

world. I would have to get a social security card. My wages would be $3.25 a week. I must arrive promptly every Saturday morning at 7:30 to help open the shop, and I would work until 6:15 p.m. I had one hour for lunch, but Ma'am would show me how to spend it in a profitable way.

Ma'am had a rigid philosophy of merchandising. Everyone who worked under her must know what we sold. At our first interview, she concluded by handing me a copy of the store's catalog and commanding me to memorize it. Before I actually started to work, I should come into the shop every afternoon after school and read the cultural information on the seed packets that lined one wall and the instructions on all the bottles and boxes of insecticide.

Two weeks later I began my career in the gardening trade, terrorized by Ma'am into some understanding of its barest rudiments. From the bright pictures on the printed seed packets I knew what lobelia and salpiglossis looked like, though I'd never seen any. If a customer asked, I could explain the differences in color among the several kinds of caladium we sold. I knew that poppies and larkspur should be sown in the fall and that they bitterly resented transplanting, that zinnias mustn't be planted until all danger of frost was past, and that the large seeds of moonflower vines should be nicked slightly or soaked before planting to help them germinate.

I still know all these things indelibly, even though it's been many years since I was in Dallas and many more years since that particular shop was closed; the look, the feeling, and the aroma of that place are still with me. It was small and dark and narrow, and it smelled of lemon oil. (My first chore each Saturday was to polish the long wooden counter.) The scent of burlap and the stronger pungencies of cottonseed meal, bone meal, and blood meal, of rabbit manure and cow manure and sheep manure in their paper sacks, pervaded the warehouse out back and sometimes reached the shop itself.

Ma'am had a dark cubbyhole of an office at the back of the shop. There was a rolltop desk and a swivel chair. The only decoration was a reproduction of an oil painting of a Texas landscape in spring—some distant hills, a great many mesquite trees, a haze of bluebonnets on the ground. Garden magazines, nursery catalogs, and books on horticulture filled a shelf. On my first real day of work, Ma'am invited me into her office at lunchtime.

"There's no reason to waste time just eating," she said. "Bring your lunch pail in here and you can read at the same time. Learn something every chance you get." For starters she handed me *The Garden Encyclopedia: A Complete, Practical, and Convenient Guide to Every Detail of Gardening.* (For sentimental reasons, I bought my own copy of the 1936 edition a few years ago in a used-book store.) It was four pounds of book in gray cloth binding; 1,300 pages, starting with Aaron's Beard and proceeding systematically through the alphabet. (I was only halfway to Zygopetalum some 150 Saturdays later when I retired to start a new career in the cherry-phosphate trade at a pharmacy much visited by girls my age.)

At Ma'am's we sold no shrubbery, no trees, no perennials, and only a few bedding plants each spring, from a sidewalk table under our green front awning. But Ma'am took a special interest in those customers who came in for advice about what to grow in their gardens. We kept a list of the best local nurseries, those with the healthiest and most varied stock. We had on hand the catalogs of the best mail-order nurseries. Ma'am was firmly of the opinion that gardeners should use a little imagination when considering what to plant, and that they should be discouraged from imitating each other.

To be frank, Ma'am was often a little short with those customers, horticultural novices, who would come into the shop asking where they could buy bushes or trees.

"What kind of bushes? What kind of trees?" she would demand.

If the customer stammered out Chinese elm or nandina or anything else that everyone in Dallas was planting in the mid-1940s, Ma'am would express her disdain unmistakably: "Nandina? *Nandina?* Whatever for?"

Sometimes she would recommend planting something native to our region, such as mesquite. "I know," she would say, "the ranchers in West Texas hate them, but have you ever noticed how pretty they are? There's no reason your garden shouldn't look as if it's in Texas."

Randy and Ma'am and Mr. Tallat-Kelpsa

In New Jersey, the weeping mulberry was much planted early in the century. I never drive by the house of someone fortunate enough to have a mature specimen on his lawn without feeling a pang of envy, for the weeping mulberry is one of the handsomest of all moderate-sized ornamental trees. In the spring and summer it is lovely for its large, glossy, green leaves. In the winter its cascade of pendulous branches descending in steps, like a frozen waterfall, is truly spectacular.

Few people these days sell weeping mulberries. Certainly Randy's doesn't. It sells euonymus, pyracantha, and yew.

The woods to the west of my coastal community abound with beautiful native trees, though no mesquite. Besides the oaks and the pines that dominate the forest succession, there are sourwood trees (*Oxydendrum arboreum*), sweet gums (*Liquidambar*), and sweet bay magnolias (*Magnolia virginiana*). Sourwood makes a handsome lawn specimen—shapely, stunning for its fall foliage and for the sprays of flowers and seed pods that hang gracefully from its branches like outstretched fingers. The leaves of the sweet gum are spectacular green stars in summer, even more spectacular purple-red ones in autumn, and the seed pods make wonderful accents in a Christmas wreath. The sweet bay in bloom has a delicious lemony scent, and in the fall the red seeds evoke thoughts of bay rum.

Randy's sells no sourwood, sweet gum, or sweet bay. It sells euonymus, pyracantha, and yew.

To the east, the sandy marshes are rimmed by thickets of bayberry. Bayberry makes a good informal hedge attractive to birds. Its soft gray delights the eye that has grown weary of green. Its waxy, fragrant berries, collected in sufficient quantity and added to paraffin or tallow, make holiday candles with a fine, subtle perfume.

Randy's sells no bayberry, or beach plum either.

Sometimes when a customer came in for advice about trees and shrubbery, Ma'am said not a word about mesquite. Instead, she would fetch some mail-order catalogs from her bookshelf, and perhaps turning first to the one from Wayside Gardens, then in Ohio, she would point out some viburnum or hawthorn or new variety of crab apple, something she hadn't seen anyone grow in Dallas. "Why don't you try something different," she would suggest.

The newer houses in my town have an architectural sameness that is reinforced by the identical sorts of landscaping at each. Pink dogwood. Purple-leafed plum. Pyracantha, yes, and euonymus, and the everlasting yew. All from Randy's, I'm afraid. It's increasingly a suburban landscape that could be anywhere, just as our main commercial artery, with its McDonald's and its Wendy's and its Bonanza Steak House, could be anywhere. There are no surprises and nothing rare to see when we turn a corner, except in the older parts of town, which were planted in a more complicated time, before Randy made everything simple with what his ads call "one-stop garden shopping."

Randy must be resisted. But how? The answer lies in the determination to seek out those few nurserymen scattered across the land who do have a feeling for plants and whose ambitions transcend turning a profit on pyracantha and euonymus and the everlasting yew. Such people do exist. My own best example is Teddy Tallat-Kelpsa, the owner of Cream Ridge Gardens, a nursery just outside Robbinsville, New Jersey.

I must have passed Cream Ridge Gardens a hundred times or more as I drove the eighty-odd miles from my house to the Firestone Library at Princeton University, but I was always in too much of a hurry to stop, until one day last summer when a sudden hunch made me pull into the driveway. When I got out of the car, I felt that I was about to fulfill an ancient longing. There wasn't a single yew in sight in the lathhouse adjacent to the driveway, and no tacky conversation pieces for the front lawn. But there were many fine dwarf evergreens, and I was encouraged to see that this nursery sold in five-gallon containers a number of the excellent native plants that too many gardeners overlook, such as bayberry and clethra.

I was greeted politely by Mr. Tallat-Kelpsa, who introduced himself to me in a soft accent that proclaimed his Baltic origins. I got right down to business, asking him if he had any weeping mulberries, and wasn't at all surprised when he nodded yes.

He led me back to the nursery field behind his house, stopping along the way to point out an ancient and magnificent beech tree growing on a steep hillside leading down to a stream. "Isn't he a fine old tree?" he asked. I liked the man. Not only did he have a mulberry for me, he also thought of trees as personal presences, not objective things.

We found the mulberries, two of them, some three feet high. Without asking the price, I said I'd take both.

"No," he answered. "I've only got two, which I grafted two years ago. If I sell you both of them, then someone else may come by asking if I have this mulberry, and I would have to give a disappointment by saying no. I will sell you one of them, except not now. If I dig him up, he might die during the winter."

We shook hands in agreement, and now, months later, a weeping mulberry grows in my garden. At the moment, it's hardly prepossessing. It's not likely to reach its maturity during my lifetime. But a generation from now, thanks to Mr. Tallat-Kelpsa, someone will turn my corner one winter day, see the cascading branches of a splendid weeping mulberry, and feel his spirits brighten at the sight.

Appendix:
Sources and Resources

To be a dedicated gardener means to be constantly on the prowl, seeking reliable information about plants and also searching out good sources of plant material beyond what is available at local garden centers such as Randy's. Good gardeners tend also to be avid readers about gardening; the longer they have pursued the horticultural life, the greater the likely accumulation of printed matter on the subject on their library shelves. They also tend to join organizations that promote the cause of gardening in general or that serve people who are interested in particular sorts of plants. And they often travel beyond the confines of their own back yards, searching for new ideas and superior plants to try for themselves. It goes without saying that their mailboxes fill up every January with catalogs for seeds, perennials, shrubs, and trees. Here follow some of my own, doubtlessly idiosyncratic suggestions about horticultural reading and related activities.

REFERENCE WORKS

One of the most useful tools for any gardener is a general book of practical information on horticulture. Donald Wyman's *Wyman's Gardening Encyclopedia* (New York: Macmillan Publishing Company, rev. ed., 1977) is the one I happen to own, but I can also recommend Norman Taylor's similar *Encyclopedia of Gardening* (Boston: Houghton Mifflin Company, rev. ed., 1961). *The Reader's Digest Illustrated Guide to Gardening* (Pleasantville, N.Y.: The Reader's Digest Association, Inc., 1978) is handy, fairly complete in its cultural information, and attractively illustrated. Originally published in England in 1975, it has been scrupulously revised to suit North American conditions, something that unfortunately does not always take place with British imports.

For botanical reference, the hefty *Hortus Third: A Concise Dictionary of Plants Cultivated in the United States and Canada*, written by the staff of the Liberty Hyde Bailey Hortorium of Cornell University (New York: Macmillan Publishing Company, 1976), is indispensable, although it contains no practical information about gardening per se.

I frequently consult Barbara Ellis, ed., *North American Horticulture: A Reference Guide* (New York: Charles Scribner's Sons, 1982), an annotated list of horticultural organizations, publications, and much more, compiled by the staff of the American Horticultural Society. Some other gardeners may find that they will make insufficient use of it to warrant spending the $50 it costs; they should, however, insist that their local public library keep a copy in its reference collection.

Among other general works about horticulture, T. H. Everett's *The New York Botanical Garden Illustrated Encyclopedia of Horticulture* (New York: Garland Publishing Company, 1981–82) stands in a class by itself. Lively and witty as well as absolutely authoritative, it contains over 16,000 black-and-white photographs and color plates, most of them taken by the author, who also wrote every word of the 3,600-page text in ten volumes, a task undertaken at the age of sixty-five, which occupied the first fifteen years of his retirement from The New York Botanical Garden. The current price for the set is $600. It is worth every penny, for it is virtually a complete horticultural library in itself.

PERIODICALS

I don't know why, but the bibliographies of most garden books are oddly silent about horticultural magazines, of which there are several in the United States that deserve the support and attention of gardeners, not only for the articles and essays they publish, but also for their classified advertisements for small, discriminating nurseries that specialize in particular kinds of plants such as clematis, jasmine, sedums, and wildflowers. Here are several I recommend:

American Horticulturist
American Horticultural Society
Box 0105
Mt. Vernon, Va. 22121

Flower and Garden
4251 Pennsylvania
Kansas City, Mo. 64111

Garden
The New York Botanical Society
Bronx, N.Y. 10458

Appendix: Sources and Resources

The Green Scene
The Pennsylvania Horticultural Society
325 Walnut Street
Philadelphia, Pa. 19106

Horticulture
300 Massachusetts Ave.
Boston, Ma. 02115

Organic Gardening
33 East Minor Street
Emmaus, Pa. 18049

Pacific Horticulture
Hall of Flowers
Box 22609
San Francisco, Ca. 94122

Plants and Gardens
Brooklyn Botanical Garden
1000 Washington Avenue
Brooklyn, N.Y. 11225

ORGANIZATIONS AND SOCIETIES

Although gardening is often an individual and even solitary pursuit, it can be
the occasion of forming social bonds with like-minded people. It is hardly surprising that organizations exist that promote the cause of gardening in general
or of particular kinds of plants. Here are several of both sorts. In revising this
list I have borrowed freely from the third edition of Barbara J. Barton's *Gardening by Mail* (1990), about which I will say more at the end of the nursery
list, also revised.

American Horticultural Society
7931 E. Boulevard Drive
Alexandria, VA 22308

Massachusetts Horticultural Society
300 Massachusetts Avenue
Boston, MA 02115

Appendix: Sources and Resources

Pennsylvania Horticultural Society
325 Walnut Street
Philadelphia, PA 19106

American Daffodil Society
1686 Grey Fox Trails
Milford, OH 45150

American Dahlia Society
159 Pine Street
New Hyde Park, NY 11040

American Hemerocallis Society
1454 Rebel Drive
Jackson, MS 39211

American Hibiscus Society
P.O. Box 321540
Cocoa Beach, FL 32932-1540

American Hosta Society
5300 Whiting Avenue
Edina, MN 55435

American Orchid Society
6000 S. Olive Avenue
West Palm Beach, FL 33405

American Rock Garden Society
15 Fairmead Road
Darien, CT 06820

Perennial Plant Association
3383 Schirtzinger Rd.
Columbus, OH 43026

Appendix: Sources and Resources

PUBLIC GARDENS

Some of the most useful information a gardener can have is obtained not by reading but by visiting the great number of botanical gardens, parks, arboreta, and former estates that are open to the public and that maintain plantings of flowers, shrubs, and trees that may be the source of many new ideas for home gardeners. Among these are the Arnold Arboretum of Jamaica Plain, Massachusetts; the Missouri Botanical Garden in St. Louis; the Brooklyn Botanic Garden; the New York Botanical Garden in the Bronx; Longwood Gardens in Kennett Square, Pennsylvania; the Fairchild Tropical Garden in Miami; the Huntington Botanical Gardens in San Marino, California; and the Morton Arboretum in Lisle, Illinois. Again, *North American Horticulture* (whose sponsor, the American Horticultural Society, maintains attractive test gardens of daylilies, dahlias, roses, and other ornamentals at its headquarters at River Farm in Mt. Vernon, Virginia) prints a list of hundreds of these gardens, large and small, and describes in some detail the plantings on display.

SELECTED MAIL-ORDER NURSERIES

B & D Lilies, 330 P Street, Port Townsend, WA 98368. Catalog $4. Excellent source for alstroemerias as well as lilies.

Bluestone Perennials, 7211 Middle Ridge Road, Madison, OH 44057. Catalog free. Offers good value in many perennials as small rooted cuttings.

Canyon Creek Nursery, 3527 Dry Creek Road, Oroville, CA 95965. Catalog $2. Discriminating list of unusual perennials.

The Cook's Garden, P.O. Box 65, Londonderry, VT 05148. Catalog $1. Vegetable seeds of unusual varieties, including European and Oriental kinds.

Crownsville Nursery, P.O. Box 797, Crownsville, MD 21032. Catalog $2. Has a very wide selection of perennials.

The Daffodil Mart, Rte. 3, Box 794, Gloucester, VA 23061. Catalog $1. All sorts of Dutch bulbs as well as daffodils.

Forestfarm, 990 Tetherow, Williams, OR 95744. Catalog $3. Woody plants in small sizes to be grown on to size.

Gossler Farms Nursery, 1200 Weaver Road, Springfield, OR 97478. Catalog $1. Magnolias and witch hazels are specialties.

Greenlife Gardens, 101 County Line Road, Griffin, GA 30223. Catalog $2. Orchid cactus and Christmas cactus.

Heaths & Heathers, P.O. Box 850, Elma, WA 98541. Send long SASE for catalog. Hundreds of cultivars of these ericaceous small shrubs.

Heronswood Nursery, 7530-288th Street N.E., Kingston, WA 98346. Catalog $2. Many rare vines, perennials, and woody plants.

Appendix: Sources and Resources

Hildenbrandt's Iris Gardens, HC 84, Box 4, Lexington, NE 68850. Catalog $2. Offers peonies and Oriental poppies as well as irises.

Holbrook Farm and Nursery, 115 Lance Road, Box 368, Fletcher, NC 28732. Catalog $2. Charming, chatty, friendly catalog; fine perennials and woody plants.

Kelly's Plant World, 10266 E. Princeton, Sanger, CA 93657. Catalog $1. A good source for cannas in particular.

Klehm Nursery, Rte. 5, Box 197, South Barrington, IL 60010. Catalog $4. Iris, peonies, daylilies, hostas, many other perennials.

Lamb Nurseries, E. 101 Sharp Avenue, Spokane, WA 99202. Catalog free. Perennials and rock garden plants.

Logee's Greenhouses, 141 North Street, Danielson, CT 06239. Catalog $3. Excellent source for tropical plants and house plants.

Grant Mitsch Novelty Daffodils (formerly Daffodil Haven), P.O. Box 218, Hubbard, OR 97032. Carries on the breeding of Mitsch hybrid narcissus.

Montrose Nursery, P.O. Box 957, Hillsborough, NC 27278. Catalog $2. The only source for seed-grown hardy cyclamens, many species and forms. Extensive catalog of rare and uncommon perennials that can take summer heat.

Niche Gardens, 1111 Dawson Road, Chapel Hill, NC 27516. Catalog $3. Offers nursery-grown wildflowers and other native North American plants.

Park Seed Company, P.O. Box 46, Greenwood, SC 29648. Catalog free.

Pinetree Garden Seeds, Rte. 100, New Gloucester, ME 04260. Catalog free. Seeds for flower and vegetable gardens, including melon 'Jenny Lind'.

Rainbow Gardens, 1444 E. Taylor Street, Vista, CA 92084. Catalog $2. Orchid cactus.

Rincon-Vitova Insectaries, Box 95, Oak View, CA 93022. Free list of beneficial insects.

Sandy Mush Herb Nursery, Rte. 2, Surret Cove Rd., Leicester, NC 28748. Catalog $4. Great for salvias, scented geraniums, many herbs.

Seed Savers Exchange, Rural Rte. 3, Box 239, Decorah, IA 52101. Annual dues, $15.

Shady Oaks Nursery, 700-19th Avenue N.E., Waseca, MN 56093. Catalog $1. Hostas and other shade-tolerant or shade-loving perennials.

Shepherd's Garden Seeds, 6116 Highway 9, Felton, CA 95018. Catalog $1. Gourmet vegetable seeds, terrific recipes in catalog.

Siskiyou Rare Plant Nursery, 2825 Cummings Road, Medford, OR 97501. Catalog $2. Excellent for both exotic and native woody plants.

Sunlight Gardens, Rte. 1, Box 600-A, Andersonville, TN 37705. Catalog $2. Native American wildflowers, nursery-grown, not collected in the wild.

Thompson & Morgan, P.O. Box 1308, Jackson, NJ 08527. Catalog free. Huge list of seeds at high prices. Order early, as many items are scarce.

Andre Viette Farm & Nursery, Rte 1, Box 16, State Route 608, Fishersville,

VA 22939. Catalog $2. Wonderful place to visit, terrific list of perennials, although specialties are iris, ferns, grasses, peonies, and daylilies.

Wayside Gardens, P.O. Box 1, Hodges, SC 29695. Catalog $1.

We-Du Nurseries, Rte. 5, Box 724, Marion, NC 28752. Catalog $1. Many rare and unusual plants.

White Flower Farm, Rte. 63, Litchfield, CT 06759. Catalog $5.

Woodlanders, 1128 Colleton Avenue, Aiken, SC 29801. Send long SASE for catalog. Especially good for native and exotic woody plants and perennials.

Note: Nurseries come into existence, each year bringing new ones, and they also pass from the scene. For the 1992 reprinting of this book I have revised the list, including only those mail-order nurseries I currently depend on, but there are many others. A much more exhaustive list of mail-order nurseries, with fuller descriptions of their offerings, is found in Barbara J. Barton's *Gardening by Mail: A Source Book*, 3rd edition, Houghton Mifflin, 1990, which is probably the most often consulted reference book in my library.

FOR FURTHER READING

Browne, Roland A. *The Rose-Lover's Guide: A Practical Handbook on Rose Growing.* New York: Atheneum, 1983.

Coon, Nelson. *The Dictionary of Useful Plants.* Emmaus, Pa.: Rodale Press, 1974.

Creasy, Rosalind. *The Complete Book of Edible Landscaping.* San Francisco: Sierra Club Books, 1982.

Cruso, Thalassa. *To Everything There Is a Season.* New York: Alfred A. Knopf, 1973.

Dillard, Annie. *Teaching a Stone to Talk.* New York: Harper & Row, 1982.

Earle, Alice Morse. *Old Time Gardens.* New York: Macmillan, 1901. Detroit: Singing Tree Press, 1968.

Gould, Stephen Jay. *Ever Since Darwin.* New York: W. W. Norton and Company, 1977.

Hunt, William Lanier. *Southern Gardens, Southern Gardening.* Durham, N.C.: Duke University Press, 1982.

Johnson, Hugh. *The Principles of Gardening: A Guide to the Art, History, Science, and Practice of Gardening.* New York: Simon & Schuster, 1979.

Koopowitz, Harold, & Hilary Kaye. *Plant Extinction: A Global Crisis.* Washington, D.C.: Stone Wall Press, 1983.

Krutch, Joseph Wood. *The Gardener's World.* New York: G. P. Putnam's Sons, 1959.

Lust, John. *The Herb Book.* New York: Bantam, 1974.

Appendix: Sources and Resources

Mitchell, Henry. *The Essential Earthman.* New York: Farrar, Straus & Giroux, 1983. (Paperback ed.)

Perényi, Eleanor. *Green Thoughts: A Writer in the Garden.* New York: Random House, 1981.

Rou021ché, Berton. *The Medical Detectives.* New York: Times Books, 1980.

Sackville-West, Vita. V. *Sackville-West's Garden Book.* New York: Atheneum, 1979.

Stone, Doris. *The Lives of Plants.* New York: Charles Scribner's Sons, 1983.

Swain, Roger. *Earthly Pleasures.* New York: Charles Scribner's Sons, 1981.

———. *Field Days.* New York: Charles Scribner's Sons, 1983.

White, Katharine S. *Onward and Upward in the Garden.* New York: Farrar, Straus & Giroux, 1979.

Yang, Linda. *The Terrace Gardener's Handbook.* Beaverton, Oregon: Timber Press, 1982.

Index

Index

Index

Index

Index

Hope, Claude, 189
horticulture, as science, 216
Hortus Third, 33, 65–66, 99, 210–11
hostas, 132, 156
house plants, 227*ff.*, 231*ff.*
hoya vine, 223, 224, 225, 226
hydrangea, 89, 156
Hyperion (daylily), 59

*Illustrated Encyclopedia of
Horticulture* (Everett), 158, 232
Iltis, Hugh, 185, 188
impatiens, 153, 157, 171, 172
Impresario (daffodil), 13–14, 15, 8
Inca lilies (alstroemerias), 71–73
insect control, biological, 224–26
Insurpassable (tulip), 219
International Carnivorous Plant
Society, 137
Iris brevicaulis, 48
Iris danfordiae, 30
Iris fulva, 48
Iris giganticaerulea, 48
Iris reticulata, 30
irises: American, 48; bearded,
46–47, 49; Cambridge, 47;
Carnival Glass, 49; Dresden
Frills, 49; Frosted Crystal, 49;
Happy Days, 46; Louisiana, 48;
Plum Creek, 49; Siberian, 47–48;
Tealwood, 47; White Swirl, 47

Japanese maples, 110, 129, 142, 209
jasmines, 200, 201–2
Jasminum nudiflorum, 201
Jasminum sambac, 201, 202
Jenny Lind (muskmelon), 183, 184,
186, 187, 188, 189
Jetfire (daffodil), 16, 18, 24
jimsonweed, 70, 205
Job's tears (grass), 79
Johnson grass, 205
jonquils, 12
journal, garden, keeping, 142–44
junipers, 100

Kaye, Hilary, 212
Kendall, John, 23
Kerr, William, 65
King Alfred (daffodil), 11, 17, 18,
23
Koopowitz, Harold, 212
Krutch, Joseph Wood, 178
kudzu, 36

lacewings, 224
ladybugs, 224
lady's slippers, 132
Lagerstroemeria indica (crape
myrtle), 104, 105, 106
lantanas, 211–13
larkspur, 152, 154, 237
Lauder, Harry, 125
lawnmower, and Edwin Budding,
149, 150
lawns, 149, 150, 151, 157
Leach, Susan, 87, 88, 162
leaf burning, 207–8
Leeds, Edward, 23, 25
Lent lily (*Narcissus
pseudonarcissus*), 22
Leptospermum scoparium, 101–2,
103
Liebig, Justus, 149, 151
Ligtu Hybrid (alstroemeria), 73
Ligustrum vulgare (privet), 118,
119, 120–21
lilacs, white, 99
lilies, 95; Aurelian hybrid, 74, 80;
Black Dragon, 74; Crimson
Beauty, 75; Empress of Japan, 75;
Enchantment, 74; Harlequin, 74;
Imperial Gold, 75; Madonna, 96;
martagon, 131; Moonlight, 74;
Oriental hybrid, 74–77; Parfait,
74; Pink Perfection, 74; tiger, 41,
89; trumpet, 96, 97
Lilium auratum, 74
Lilium longiflorum, 26
Lilium speciosum, 74
lily of the valley, 99
Linnáeus, Carolus, 50, 71, 85
Liquidambar (sweet gum), 239
lobelia, 172, 237
lobster claw heliconia, 52
Logee's Greenhouses, 45
Lona Eaton Miller (daylily), 59
Longwood Gardens, 80, 169, 197,
246
Lonicera japonica (honeysuckle),
65–67, 200, 216
Louisiana iris, 48
Lubenow, Bill, 112, 117
lunaria, 40
Lust, John, 88
Lyrebird (daffodil), 14, 15
lythrum, 40, 88

McAdoo, Dama Adeline and
Joseph, 4–5
McKana Giant (columbine), 41

Index

Index

Pacific Horticulture (pub.), 229, 244
painted daisies, 87
pampas grass, 79
Pan-American Seed Company, 164
Parfait (lily), 74
Park Seed Co., Geo. W., 48, 51, 73, 196
Passiflora alato-caerulea, 232
Passiflora coccinea, 232
Passiflora incarnata, 232
passion flower, 231–32
Paxton, Joseph, 169
peach borer (*Aegenia exitiosa*), 215, 216
Peck, Virginia, 57
Pennsylvania Horticultural Society, 244
peonies, 56, 131, 142, 171, 196
perennials, 40, 41, 46, 51, 57, 79, 83, 85, 86, 88, 130, 131, 160, 171, 185, 211
Perényi, Eleanor, 76, 219
periodicals, 243–44
periwinkles, 171, 172
Peruvian lilies (alstroemerias), 71–73
pesticides, 145, 187
Petrel (daffodil), 24
petunias, 153, 171, 176, 196, 228
Philadelphia Flower Show, 101
phlox, 48, 59, 88, 131, 171, 196
Phlox subulata, 98
photosynthesis, 207
Phyllostachys bambusoides, 93
pine, bristlecone, 93
Pink Perfection (lily), 74
Pixwell (gooseberry), 116, 117
Plant Extinction: A Global Crisis (Koopowitz and Kaye), 212
Plant Genetics (firm), 165
Plantan, Ed, 161, 162, 163, 175
Plato, 135
plum, purple-leafed, 240
Plumbago auriculata, 44–45, 201
Plumbago capensis, 44–45
Plum Creek (iris), 49
poinciana, 52
poinsettia, 231
poppies, 152, 237
portulacas (moss roses), 91–92, 94, 170
potentillas, 108, 153
Pride's Crossing (daylily), 60
primroses, 132
privet (*Ligustrum vulgare*), 118, 119, 120–21

Puschkinia scilloides (striped squill), 29, 221
pyracantha, 239, 240

Queen of the Night (datura), 69
quince tree, 129

Rainbow Gardens, 229, 230, 247
Ramona (clematis), 96, 143
Rattlesnake (watermelon), 191, 193
Raven, Peter, 185
Reader's Digest Illustrated Guide to Gardening, 63
record-keeping, 142–44
Red Lollipop (watermelon), 194
Red Radiance (rose), 62
reference works, 242–43
Rex Bulb Farms, 76
rhododendrons, 56
Rincon-Vitova Insectaries, 224, 225, 226
Root, Grace, 132, 133, 134
Rosa multiflora, 61, 119
Rosa rugosa, 63
Rosa wichuriana, 63
Rose Beauty (cyclamen), 32
Rose-Lover's Guide, The (Browne), 63
roses, 61–64, 95, 96, 97, 142
Rossetti, Dante Gabriel, 27
Roueché, Berton, 70
Royal Botanic Gardens, 168
Royal Horticultural Society, 14, 22, 23
Rudbeckia fulgida, 85
Rudbeckia hirta, 85
Rudbeckia purpurea, 85
rudbeckias, 84–86
rugosa rose, 63–64, 96, 142
Ruskin, John, 29

Sackville-West, Vita, 106
salpiglossis, 237
salt cedar (*Tamarix ramosissima*), 102
salvias, red, 153, 172
Sangster, Bruce J., 164, 165, 166
scabiosas, 152, 154
scale insects, 224, 225
Schomburgk, Robert, 168
Scilla campanulata, 30
Scilla hispanica, 30
Scilla siberica, 26, 29, 221
Scotch broom (*Cytisus scoparius*), 35–36, 37–38, 39

Index

Scotch thistle (*Onopordum acanthium*), 82, 83
Seabrook, Janet E. A., 24, 25
Seed Savers Exchange, 186, 189
Semper Augustus (tulip), 26
Sendak, Maurice, 206
Shasta daisies, 41, 74, 87, 89, 90, 196
shooting stars, 155
Siberian irises, 47–48
Siberian squill (*Scilla siberica*), 26, 29, 221
Silken Sails (daffodil), 14
Sissinghurst, 106, 197
snowdrop (*Galanthus nivalis*), 27, 220
Snow Queen (columbine), 43
societies and organizations, 136–38, 244–46
sourwood tree (*Oxydendrum arboreum*), 239
Spanish wood hyacinth (*Endymion hispanicus*), 30
Spaulding, Edna, 57
Spirea cantoniensis, 99
Spirea trilobata, 99
Spirea x vanhouttei, 99
Spring Song (columbine), 43
spruce, Colorado blue, 110, 119
star-of-Bethlehem (*Ornithogalum umbellatum*), 89, 99, 219, 221
Steichen, Edward, 41
Stella D'Oro (daylily), 58
Stout, A. B., 57
striped squill (*Puschkinia scilloides*), 29, 221
Sugar Baby (watermelon), 194
sumac, 207
sunflowers, 152, 154, 170, 205
Surles, Mollie Adeline, 3–4
Surles, Roscoe Lee, 190, 191, 192, 193
swamp maple, 122–24
sweet bay magnolia (*Magnolia virginiana*), 239
sweet gum (*Liquidambar*), 239
Sweetheart strawberry, 164
Sweet William, 200
synchroneity, 93

Tallat-Kelpsa, Teddy, 240, 241
tamarisks, 102–3
Tamarix parviflora, 102–3
Tamarix ramosissima, 102
tannins, 207

Teaching a Stone to Talk (Dillard), 92
Tealwood (iris), 47
Tenby daffodil (*Narcissus obvallaris*), 20
Tennyson, Alfred, Lord, 27
Teosinthe, 185
termites, 175, 179
tetraploidy in daylilies, 57, 59
thistle, Scotch (*Onopordum acanthium*), 82, 83
Thompson and Morgan, Inc., 45, 73, 164, 165, 222
Throckmorton, Tom, 21
tiger lilies, 41, 89
Tinker Bell (daylily), 59
tissue culture of daffodils, 24–25
toadflax, 155
Trachelospermum jasminoides (Confederate jasmine), 201
Tranquil Lake Nursery, 59, 248
Traub, Hamilton, 57
Treasurer (aster), 162, 163
trilliums, 132
Trommer, Charles, 59–60
Trouvelot, Leopold, 188
trumpet daffodil (*Narcissus pseudonarcissus*), 22
trumpet lily, 96, 97
Tulipa dasystemon, 220
tulips, 26, 27, 93, 132, 135, 142, 171, 211, 218, 219, 220
Tupelo, 207
twin scaling, 24

Unsurpassable (daffodil), 11, 13, 17, 23

Van Mons, Dr., 113
Van Waveren & Sons, M., 20
vegetable garden, 141, 153–54
vegetable names, 180–82; etymology of, 180
vegetable seeds, 185, 186, 187, 188; and gene pool, 184, 185; as "heirlooms," 184, 186
Viburnum carlesii, 99
Viburnum plicatum cv. 'mariesii,' 99
Viburnum x burkwoodii, 99
Viburnum x carkephalum, 99
Victoria amazonica, 167–69
Victoria cruziana, 169
Viette's Farm and Nursery, André, 60, 248
vinca, 16, 142, 176

Index